CREATING STRATEGIC READERS

Techniques for Developing Competency
in Phonemic Awareness, Phonics, Fluency, Vocabulary, and Comprehension

VALERIE ELLERY

Manatee County School District • Bradenton, Florida, USA

INTERNATIONAL
Reading Association
800 BARKSDALE ROAD, PO BOX 8139
NEWARK, DE 19714-8139, USA
www.reading.org

KH

The International Reading Association attempts, through its publications, to provide a forum for a wide spectrum of opinions on reading. This policy permits divergent viewpoints without implying the endorsement of the Association.

Editorial Director   Matthew W. Baker
Managing Editor   Shannon T. Fortner
Permissions Editor   Janet S. Parrack
Acquisitions and Communications Coordinator   Corinne M. Mooney
Associate Editor   Charlene M. Nichols
Production Editor   Amy Messick
Books and Inventory Assistant   Rebecca A. Zell
Assistant Permissions Editor   Tyanna L. Collins
Production Department Manager   Iona Muscella
Supervisor, Electronic Publishing   Anette Schütz
Senior Electronic Publishing Specialist   R. Lynn Harrison
Electronic Publishing Specialist   Lisa M. Kochel
Proofreader   Elizabeth C. Hunt

Project Editor   Charlene M. Nichols

Cover   Design, Linda Steere; Image, Dynamic Graphics

Web addresses in this book were correct as of the publication date but may have become inactive or otherwise modified since that time. If you notice a deactivated or changed Web address, please e-mail books@reading.org with the words "Website Update" in the subject line. In your message, specify the Web link, the book title, and the page number on which the link appears.

Library of Congress Cataloging-in-Publication Data
Ellery, Valerie, 1964–
  Creating strategic readers : techniques for developing competency in
phonemic awareness, phonics, fluency, vocabulary, and comprehension /
Valerie Ellery.
      p. cm.
  Includes bibliographical references and index.
  ISBN 0-87207-561-3
  1. Reading—United States. 2. Language arts—United States. I.
Title.
  LB1050.E42 2005
  372.41—dc22
Fifth Printing, June 2006   2004024963

10/19/06

For Velma, my grandma,
who believed in me and encouraged me to become a teacher.
It was through your love for writing and your inspiring words
that the seed was planted for writing this book.
I will always be grateful to you.

Contents

Acknowledgment

This book is an accumulation of working with students over the years and watching them come to life as readers as I learned to challenge them through strategies and the thought-provoking questions that supported their understanding of what good readers do. I also realized in working with teachers that there are many needs in the educational world for teachers to have resources vitally available to support them in becoming teachers who think and talk strategically. Through many lessons with students, and discussions with teachers and colleagues, the idea of this book was created.

I am so thankful for

- Gregg, my loving and supportive husband, who was always there through endless days and nights, being my cheerleader

- Nick, Derek, Jacey, and Brooke, for being the best kids a mom could ever ask for—thank you for being so patient with me

- Laurie and Nancy, you're the best mom and mother-in-law a daughter could ask for—thank you for the many nights reading and rereading

- Terry Vitiello, my sister-in-law—thank you for your ideas, support, and excellent organizational skills

- Michelle Howard, for the countless hours of encouragement and always being there as my dear friend

- Melinda Lundy and Beth Severson, Literacy Coaches, and Mary Corbin, ESOL and Family Involvement Specialist, for reading, reviewing, and commenting, and your never ending friendships

- Bayside Community Church, for your constant support and encouragement, especially the Bezet family, Cherisse Fonseca, and Ginger Perry

- Sue Travilla, Title I Program Specialist, for the countless days of encouragement and for reading and reviewing throughout the process

- Joanne McFarlin, Curriculum Specialist, for being there to read and comment throughout the early stages of the writing process

- Darlene Sharts, Reading Coach, for your expertise and feedback in the area of phonics

- Jean White, Outside Editing, for your advise and expertise in the beginning process of writing

- Gail Garger, Kim Wilder, Cheryl Bulfin, Amanda Dawsey, Colleen Douthett, Luanne Howe, Joanne Sollazzo, Stacey Vedder, and Merilyn Webb, educators at Witt Elementary who listened and responded with feedback

- Lynn Rabino, for your support and artistic talents

- Matt Baker, IRA Editorial Director, for encouragement and expertise in bringing this book to publication

- Charlene Nichols, IRA Associate Editor, for your patience and encouraging words in the final stages of the editorial process

Introduction

For teachers, the days of stressing the acquisition of reading skills *in isolation* are in the past. To develop *lifelong* readers, it is vital for teachers to also show students how to apply these reading skills strategically to acquire meaning from text. Readers need to know how to apply reading strategies and how these strategies fit into the big picture of reading (Routman, 2003). Independent, strategic readers "simultaneously and seamlessly employ a whole range of strategies and are constantly making refinements and adjustments according to the demands of the text and what they bring to it" (Routman, 2003, p. 129). Strategic readers use basic reading skills naturally and apply strategies independently in order to comprehend what they read. These readers apply their reading skills automatically, concentrating on the strategies rather than the skills.

To understand the distinction between skills and strategies, think about the following baseball metaphor. Authentic practice on the field means having all the necessary tools (e.g., bat, ball, field), rather than just hearing about playing ball. Baseball players practice individual batting skills throughout the week: positioning the feet, holding up the elbows, following through with the swing, and so forth. On game day, in order to be successful batters, players need to focus on the end result: hitting the ball successfully. Thus, the players utilize a different strategy to approach each batting situation, and they continue to problem solve while at bat; for example, they change their swing when they see a curve ball coming. They do all this while smoothly and naturally applying all of the individual batting skills they acquired during practice.

Similarly, students practice specific reading skills: knowing letter sounds, positioning the mouth, recognizing text features, and so forth. Authentic reading practice in the classroom, as on the baseball field, also means having all the necessary tools (e.g., authentic literature, discussions, and literacy centers). To be successful in the world of reading, students need to open up a book and show that they are strategic readers. Students, like the baseball players in the example, also must focus on their end result: reading for meaning. In doing so, students utilize reading strategies while naturally applying all of the skills acquired in authentic practice, and they continue to problem solve while reading.

According to the report by the Commission on Reading, *Becoming a Nation of Readers* (Anderson, Hiebert, Scott, & Wilkinson, 1985), "[R]eading is a process in which information from the text and the knowledge possessed by the reader act together to produce meaning" (p. 8). This interaction between the reader and the text generates critical thinking and problem solving while the reader is engaging in the reading process, allowing readers to be active thinkers rather than passive ones (i.e., to step up to bat rather than just sit on the bench). The job of the classroom teacher is to provide opportunities for this type of reader–text interaction. The teacher does this by supporting the thought process that occurs in the minds of successful readers, as well as by developing in students a repertoire of reading strategies, techniques, and reflective communication that encourage strategic reading. Any teacher can provide the answer when a reader has a problem with a text, but skillful teachers understand that reading is a craft, and they carefully guide students to problem solve on their own using appropriate strategies.

Important skills for teachers include instructional techniques and "teacher talk" that are aligned appropriately to each specific strategy being taught. Teachers need to interact with their students through thoughtful coaching, rather than simple telling and reciting. Accomplished educators guide students' thinking through questioning and interaction; consequently, their students have higher reading achievement than students whose teachers rely on the practice of simply delivering information (Taylor, Pressley, & Pearson, 2000). These adept educators utilize their teacher talk (e.g., "What did you wonder about while reading the text?") to prompt readers to construct, examine, and extend meaning from text. According to Saunders-Smith (2003), "Teacher talk influences two main types of thought processes: inquiry and metacognition. Teacher talk that triggers inquiry processes takes readers into the sources of information before, during, and after reading" (p. 41). The metacognition process requires readers to internalize their thought processes, identify an effective cognitive strategy for acquiring meaning when reading, and monitor their understanding of what is being read to see if the strategy chosen is effective (Deshler, Ellis, & Lenz, 1996). Teacher talk fosters readers' thought processes by scaffolding and challenging readers to continually search for the reasons behind using specific strategies and skills while reading.

Teaching reading as a strategic, decision-making process requires that teachers modify some of their traditional practices such as teaching skills in isolation (Duffy & Roehler, 1986; Pressley et al., 1992; Pressley, Goodchild, Fleet, Zajchowski, & Evan, 1989). In order to move forward successfully, teachers need a plethora of research-based reading strategies at their disposal. Recent U.S. legislation and national studies have put reading at the heart of education. In 2000, the National Reading Panel (NRP) compiled a report (National Institute of Child Health and Human Development [NICHD], 2000) identifying and analyzing five essential components of reading instruction shown to be effective in helping students learn to read: phonemic awareness, phonics, fluency, vocabulary, and comprehension. The NRP selected these areas from their wide range of theories, research studies, instructional programs, curricula, assessments, and educational policies.

Recent mandates have caused educators to reflect on ways to successfully ensure that these five components are being embedded in effective instruction. In 2001, the No Child Left Behind (NCLB) Act redefined the U.S. federal government's role in K–12 education. For example, the Reading First legislation (Part B, Subpart 1 of Title 1 of the NCLB Act), formulated in 2002 and based on the NRP's findings, mandates that schools be held *accountable* for ensuring that all students read by the third grade and that every kindergarten through third-grade reading program contain explicit and systematic instruction in the five components of reading previously mentioned. Therefore, now is the optimal time for educators to concentrate on effective instruction that promotes strategic reading.

Purpose of This Book

The purpose of this book is to assist K–5 teachers in addressing these legislative mandates. This book highlights each of the five components, strategies students can use to gain understanding of each component, instructional techniques and skills, and appropriate teacher talk, all organized within the framework of the four developmental stages of reading.

Educators may utilize this book as a resource to better equip themselves in the craft of teaching reading. This book stresses embedding all five of the components, their strategies, their techniques, and teacher talk into a comprehensive literacy approach. This approach should include scaffolding: modeling for the students, interacting with the students, gradually guiding the students, and allowing ample time for independent application of skills and strategies by the students. This scaffolding, or gradual release of responsibility (Pearson & Gallagher, 1983), should occur repeatedly throughout teaching and learning opportunities. Scaffolding instruction according to the individual needs of readers will help students to become independent, strategic readers.

Organization of This Book

A curriculum, assessment, and instruction framework is presented in chapter 1 of this book. Chapter 1 also discusses the comprehensive literacy classroom and the developmental stages of reading.

Chapters 2–6 focus on the NRP's five components of reading. Each chapter focuses on a specific component, beginning with an overview of that component and identifying strategies that students can use when implementing that component. The strategies do not need to be taught in a specific order; the order should be based on individual students' needs. Each strategy is defined and then followed by instructional techniques that support the application of the strategy. Each technique identifies corresponding developmental reading levels and multiple intelligences. The procedure for each technique should begin with the teacher modeling the entire technique using appropriate literature and then be followed by ample time for students to work toward independent use of the strategy. A list of teacher talk (i.e., statements, questions, and prompts) is provided at the beginning of each of the strategy sections and within each technique; the incorporation of this teacher talk encourages readers to think strategically as they employ the given skills.

Many of the techniques in this book have accompanying reproducibles; these can be found in Appendix A. Appendix B includes recommended reading for more information on the comprehensive literacy classroom and the five essential components highlighted in this book.

The techniques within the strategies are presented in order of the stages of reading (i.e., emergent, early, transitional, and fluent). Although the NRP report did not address some important areas of reading due to time constraints, I felt it was important to include techniques that best support English-language learners (ELLs); applicable techniques are identified in chapters 2–6. However, it is important to note that the Center for the Improvement of Early Reading Achievement (CIERA) recommends that ELL students learn to read in their first language before being taught to read English (U.S. Department of Education, 1988).

With this book as a guide, teachers can become artists with blank canvases, ready to stroke their brush across the page and bring to life their "masterpieces"—strategic readers.

Chapter 1

A Comprehensive Literacy Classroom

The basis for a comprehensive literacy classroom is solid curriculum, assessment, and instruction (CAI). These three essentials are the infrastructure that gives educators a sound foundation upon which to build comprehensive literacy teaching. Literacy involves all aspects of reading, writing, listening, viewing, and speaking. Weaving these strands daily into an uninterrupted block of time is valuable for student achievement.

Curriculum

The first aspect of the CAI literacy classroom is curriculum. Utilizing a standards-based curriculum is the initial step for teachers to be aware of what they want their students to know and be able to do. By aligning lessons with current standards, teachers can express a specific purpose for what they want students to learn and apply. The five components of reading identified by the National Reading Panel's report (NICHD, 2000)—phonemic awareness, phonics, fluency, vocabulary, and comprehension—are embedded within current U.S. state standards, benchmarks, and grade-level expectations. Phonemic awareness is the ability to orally compose a sequence of sounds and manipulate these sounds to form words. Phonics is the ability to recognize the relation between written language (letters) and spoken language (sounds). Fluency is the ability to read orally with speed and accuracy and is the bridge between word recognition and comprehension. Vocabulary is the ability to use words orally and in written communication by applying word meaning effectively. Comprehension is the ability to apply meaning to what is read. It is imperative that teachers and students gain a firm understanding of these five components and their corresponding strategies, which represent what good strategic readers "do."

Applying strategies in a standards-based curriculum involves bringing the students to a metacognitive level within the curriculum. Metacognitive thinking causes students to be conscious of their learning processes and reinforces their learning. They are then able to make conscious choices about what they need to do to learn the standard, and they are able to effectively apply strategies to achieve a level of success as readers and writers. Paris, Cross, and Lipson (1984) describe three types of knowledge that strategic readers possess: declarative knowledge (the thinking strategies themselves), procedural knowledge (how to use the strategies), and conditional knowledge (when to use the strategies). Knowing which strategy to use provides students with the control to comprehend the curriculum. Chapters 2–6 outline the strategies good readers apply independently and at times simultaneously, as needed, to acquire meaning from the text. Strategic readers self-monitor and adjust learning strategies for comprehension (Paris, Wasik, & Turner, 1991).

Literacy is the basis for all other content area learning. If students cannot read and write proficiently, their resulting inability to acquire necessary information in other areas becomes a deficit for learning. Teachers who are serious about their commitment to developing a literacy classroom must put this commitment into practice with a daily schedule that devotes a substantial portion of the day to comprehensive literacy. Integrating the content areas of science, social studies, and even portions of the mathematics curriculum standards is the key to sound and relevant learning. Four important factors that support high-quality literacy learning instruction include maximizing the time students spend on reading, blending reading and writing into every subject area, explicitly instructing students about how to construct meaning from texts, and providing students with many opportunities to discuss what they are reading (Knapp, 1995).

Expectations, procedures, and an environment conducive to learning all need to be determined and in place in order for a literacy classroom to be successful. Brian Cambourne's conditions for learning (1995) is one model to help teachers implement the conditions that should be in place for optimal learning. These conditions are immersion, demonstration, expectation, responsibility, approximations, employment, response, and engagement. Teachers should examine these conditions and approaches in all their literacy endeavors, with their ultimate goal being to ensure effective, quality instruction for superlative learning in all areas. Table 1 defines each condition and shows the links of Cambourne's conditions to a comprehensive literacy classroom. Teachers' ultimate goal should be to provide real and relevant learning opportunities for students to apply the curriculum, make connections, and explore meaning before, during, and after reading strategically.

Assessment

The next component of the CAI literacy classroom is assessment. Teachers should be collectors of artifacts. These artifacts are the evidence that determine which stage each reader has achieved and what action needs to occur to further the students' growth as readers. Teachers can use a variety of formal and informal assessments to know their readers and to inform instruction. According to Traill (1995), the definition for assessment is "the process of observing and accumulating objective evidence of an individual child's progress in learning" (p. 5).

TABLE 1. Conditions for Optimal Learning

Condition	Description	Comprehensive Literacy Classroom
Immersion	To be exposed to an environment rich in spoken and written language	Provide multiple opportunities for reading and writing using a wide variety of materials All literacy approaches
Demonstration	To observe models of proficient, strategic reading and writing	Model explicit, deliberate, and meaningful initial instruction Read-aloud and modeled writing
Expectation	To believe that literacy strategies and skills can and will be acquired	Identify expectations that are reasonable, conveyed to all involved, and posted; procedures listed Informal and formal assessments
Engagement	To want to try authentic reading and writing strategies and techniques; confident with support	Interact in experiences of successful readers and writers Shared literacy
Use	To apply authentic reading and writing throughout daily life	Integrates with other content areas Guided and independent literacy
Approximations	To be free to explore and make attempts at what proficient, strategic readers and writers can do	Promotes risk taking and supports instruction at the learner's need level Guided literacy
Response	To receive feedback on attempts to read and write strategically	Gives specific, timely, and relevant feedback Conferences, small groups, journal responses
Responsibility	To be able to make choices and decisions; engaged rather than observing	Provides opportunities to make choices through centers, logs, and stations Independent literacy

Adapted from Cambourne (1995)

Teachers get to know their readers through a variety of tools such as oral reading records, teacher observations, student conferences, anecdotal notes, developmental checklists, and commercial assessments (e.g., Beaver, 1997). These assessments help teachers determine the students' understanding of the text and what behaviors they are revealing in order to process and obtain meaning from the text. The data from these assessments must then be evaluated, which means "making judgments about the effectiveness of teaching for learning on the basis of credible objective assessment" (Traill, 1995, p. 5). Once the teacher evaluates the assessment, he or she must map out any changes in students' behavior as the students continue to develop as readers, planning instruction accordingly (Fountas & Pinnell, 1999). This allows teachers to differentiate instruction based on the specific needs of the students.

For example, teachers use a screening assessment to determine whether there are any specific deficits in the students' performances. Literacy screening assessments are brief, informal assessments that identify students who are likely to need extra or alternative forms of instruction. If screening results indicate proficiency, then initial instruction continues. If red flags come up from the screening results, further diagnosis is necessary. The teacher then administers a diagnostic assessment to those students who need a more in-depth analysis, in order to determine their strengths and weaknesses. In the classroom, teachers need to select a diagnostic that best assesses the problem area identified through the screening. The results of the diagnostic will then indicate the type of instruction needed for immediate and intense intervention.

Assessment Informs Instruction

Teachers must give periodic, ongoing monitoring assessments for all students to evaluate student progress after instruction to decide whether instruction has been effective and should continue or be changed. This type of assessment can be both formal and informal. The assessment dictates what instruction is appropriate to meet differing student needs. Instruction should be "data-driven"; assessment used to inform classroom practice leads to better application of materials and curriculum goals, making student success possible and pursuable rather than impossible and improbable (Tierney & Readence, 1999).

Developmental Stages or Levels of Reading

Knowing students' reading abilities is essential for teachers. Skillful teachers strategically observe their students' reading and writing behaviors and identify the specific characteristics each student is exhibiting as a literacy learner. As students develop into strategic readers, they gradually move through four stages or levels of reading: emergent, early, transitional, and fluent. Teachers can identify points along this gradual process toward strategic reading through the behaviors the readers demonstrate. Observation of learners at work provides "information needed to design sound instruction" (Clay, 2002, p. 11).

When teachers are able to see their students in light of students' individual reading behaviors, they begin to recognize how they can support their students as readers. For example, if a student has the characteristics of an early reader, the teacher can then decide which strategies, techniques, teacher talk, and resources best support that student's further progress. The teacher uses this interaction to help propel the student into the next stage, that of a transitional reader. Therefore, it is vital that teachers gain a keen insight into these stages. This knowledge will assist educators in deciding what types of assessments and instructional strategies are suitable for their students' specific reading needs.

EMERGENT STAGE. The emergent stage of reading is a time when students begin to make correlations among oral, written, and printed stimuli. These readers enjoy listening to stories, and they understand that print conveys a message. They are acquiring the ability to apply concepts about print to support their development as readers. Their understanding of the direct link of sounds to letters, pictures to words, and speech to sentences clarifies this concept. Through the repetitive use of language and illustrations, these students are able to glean the contextual meaning of written words.

Logographic and environmental information (e.g., stop signs) assists emergent readers in approximating meanings of words. These students benefit from books with short and simple text and with pictures that directly connect to a specific word. The texts should use natural language that has familiar concepts and objects that allow the emergent reader to make connections. In addition to formal curricular instruction, many learner-centered activities are required for nonthreatening experimentation and to focus on the meanings (comprehension) and mechanics (word recognition) of beginning reading.

The Emergent Reader Assessment (see Appendix A) is a rubric scale that helps teachers determine the developmental level of an emergent reader's reading behaviors. Teachers align instruction with the appropriate area of reading that best supports identified behaviors. Teachers observe students and mark and date the indicator box that best reflects students' behavior. Next, teachers analyze the rubric scale to determine areas of strength and weakness for individual students. Then, teachers guide instruction based on the needs of the student. The goal, of course, is to help the student to progress to the next level of reading. When 8 out of 10 boxes are marked "Always," the student is considered a solid emergent reader.

Table 2 (page 10) highlights instructional techniques presented in this book, grouped by the five components of reading. Teachers may use this chart when choosing a component to teach their emergent readers. The techniques are categorized according to when they are best utilized for effective instruction: before, during, or after reading of a particular text.

EARLY STAGE. In the early stage of reading, students have mastered emergent reading behaviors and are becoming more comfortable with the basic concepts about print. They are reading and writing stories at an increasingly higher level of complexity. By using problem-solving skills (e.g., checking and confirming), the early stage reader collects clues about meaning from the letters, words, and illustrations in unfamiliar text. Early stage readers begin to discuss what they are reading with others. These readers are less dependent on rhyme, repetition, and patterns within text. Although repetitive patterns are still present, variations in sentence length and language are common; sentences include core high-frequency words that these students can read automatically. Emergent readers also are beginning to phrase words more fluently. "Their eyes are beginning to control the process of reading, so they do some of their reading without pointing" (Fountas & Pinnell, 1999, p. 5). They are ready for stories and strategies of increasing complexity. The texts selected for early readers should contain simple concepts and story lines that are familiar to students and that relate to real-world experiences.

The Early Reader Assessment (see Appendix A) is a rubric scale that helps teachers determine the developmental level of an early reader's reading behaviors. This tool is used

TABLE 2. Emergent Reader Techniques

	Phonemic Awareness	Phonics	Fluency	Vocabulary	Comprehension
Before Reading	Draw It Mirror/Mirror Rhyming Jar	Blinders High-Frequency 　Words Irregular Words Letter Recognition Predict/Preview/ 　Polish/Produce Star Names	Book Baskets/ 　Browsing Boxes	Charades Picture and 　Word Sorts Read-Alouds	Background 　Knowledge Book 　Introduction Picture Walk
During Reading			Choral Readers Pattern Support Shared Book 　Experience	Read-Alouds	Wordless 　Picture Books
After Reading	Read My Mind Rock, Rhythm, and 　Rhyme Time Sounds We Found	Letter–Sound 　Magnetic 　Connection Onset and Rimes Pattern Stories/ 　Rounding Up 　Rhymes		Museum Walk Read-Alouds Resource 　Buddies Vocabulary Chart Word Hunts	Artistic 　Summary Recording 　Mental Images

to identify areas of strength and weakness for individual students. Teachers mark and date the indicator box that best reflects the student's behavior. The teacher then guides instruction based on the needs of the student. When 8 out of 10 boxes are marked "Always," the student is considered a solid early reader.

Table 3 highlights instructional techniques presented in this book, grouped by the five components of reading. Teachers may use this chart when choosing a component to teach their early readers. The techniques are categorized according to when they are best utilized for effective instruction: before, during, or after reading of a particular text.

TRANSITIONAL STAGE. Students in the transitional stage of reading are able to make sense of longer and more complex books. Transitional stage students easily adapt strategies to support reading for meaning. They use all available clues to find meaning, and these students can efficiently self-correct to maintain the contextual intent. They are beginning to use informational systems (e.g., semantic—meaning, syntactic—structure and grammar, and graphophonics—visual) to self-monitor and to assist in achieving reading independence across the content areas (e.g., math, science, social studies). Transitional

TABLE 3. Early Reader Techniques

	Phonemic Awareness	Phonics	Fluency	Vocabulary	Comprehension

Before Reading	Colored Cubes
	Graphing Phonemes
	Hand Push
	Mirror/Mirror*
	Rhyming Jar*
	Silly Segmenting
		If I Can Spell
		Irregular Words
		Letterboxes
		Look/Say/Cover/
		  Write/Check*
		Stretch It
			Express Yourself
			Eye–Voice Span
			Preview/Pause/
			  Prompt/Praise/
			  Participate
			Selecting "Just
			  Right" Books
				Graphic Cards
				List/Group/Label
				Read-Alouds*
				Semantic Feature
				  Analysis*
				Speaking Out
					Chapter Tours
					Journaling
					PreP
					Skim and Scan
					Text Features

During Reading	Draw a Rhyme
	Fe-Fi
		Chant/
		  Challenge/
		  Chart
		Vowel Patterns
			Beam Reading
			Choral Reader
			Listen to Me
			Neurological
			  Impress Method
			Pattern Support
			Punctuation Police
			Read-Alongs
			Tempo Time
				Cloze Passages	Interpreting Text
					Journaling or
					  Group Chart
					Skim and Scan
					Somebody/
					  Wanted/But/So*

After Reading	Alliteration Activation
	Body Blending
	Egg-Cited About
	  Phonemes
	Hot Seat
	Pair–Share Match
	Rock, Rhythm, and
	  Rhyme Time
	Say It Again
	Syllable Giving
		Brain Tricks
		Chant/Challenge/
		  Chart
		Get Physical
		Letter–Sound
		  Magnetic
		  Connection*
		Making Words
		Onset and Rimes
		Pattern Sort
		Rime Time
		  Detective
			Listen to Me	Alphaboxes
				Four Corners
				Glossary Use
				Journal Circles
				Museum Walk
				Prefixes
				Similar
				  Synonyms*
				Vocabulary Tree
				  Notebook
					Creating a Play
					Drama
					Dramatic
					  Interpretation
					Interpreting Text
					Main Idea Wheel
					Sensory
					  Impressions
					Summary Ball

*Adaptation portion of that particular technique.

readers need relevancy of textual situations to build vocabulary, simple elements (e.g., plot, character, setting, and dialogue), and fluency. They begin to use verbal expressions as they read, and they self-monitor as needed to maintain meaning from the text. Appropriate texts for the transitional reader have more complex language structures (e.g., similes, metaphors) and less emphasis on patterned text.

The Transitional Reader Assessment (see Appendix A) is a rubric scale that helps teachers determine the developmental level of a transitional reader's reading behaviors. Teachers mark and date the indicator box that best reflects the student's behavior. This tool is used to identify areas of strength and weakness for individual students. The teacher then guides instruction based on the needs of the student. When 8 out of 10 boxes are marked "Always," the student is considered a solid transitional reader.

TABLE 4. Transitional Reader Techniques

	Phonemic Awareness	Phonics	Fluency	Vocabulary	Comprehension
Before Reading	Body Blending* Colored Cubes* Silly Segmenting* Think Sounds	Irregular Words* Look/Say/Cover/ Write/Check	Book Clubs Phrase Strips Preview/Pause/ Prompt/Praise/ Participate Totally Tonality	Author Study Contextual Redefinition Knowledge Rating List/Group/Label* What Do You Mean?	Anticipation/ Reaction Guides QARS Think Sheets Two-Column Notes
During Reading		Vowel Patterns Word Detectives	Choral Readers Pausing With Punctuation Readers Theatre Tape/Check/ Chart Time/Tape/ Check/Chart Video Reading	Author Study Cloze Passages	Somebody/ Wanted/But/So Two-Column Notes
After Reading	Alliteration Activation* Pair–Share Match*	Brain Tricks Cool Rules Making Words	Tape/Check/ Chart Time/Tape/ Check/Chart Video Reading Why Reread?	Author Study Book Talks Contextual Redefinition Dictionary Use Prefixes Quick Writes Reflection Connection Semantic Feature Analysis Similar Synonyms Thesaurus Use	Main Idea Wheel Mind Mapping Narrative Pyramid Rewriting a Story Say Something Somebody/ Wanted/But/So Talk Show Two-Column Notes Sifting the Topic From the Details

*Adaptation portion of that particular technique.

Table 4 highlights instructional techniques presented in this book, grouped by the five components of reading. Teachers may use this chart when choosing a component to teach their transitional readers. The techniques are categorized according to when they are best utilized for effective instruction: before, during, or after reading of a particular text.

FLUENT STAGE. Increasingly heavy reliance on the text, with less reliance on illustrations, indicates a reader's progression into the fluent stage of reading. The illustrations are now only of limited support and more often merely assist in extending the text. Fluent readers can comfortably read independently for extended periods. They recognize many words by sight, and reading happens with automaticity. Prosodic features are evident in their reading through use of intonation, expressions, and accents, and they adjust their pacing according to the purpose and difficulty of the text.

Fluent readers have a plethora of strategies for decoding unknown words. These students have become accustomed to challenging vocabulary and become deeply involved with conceptual points of stories. Comprehension occurs at a sophisticated level (i.e., synthesizing and interpreting). The focus in this fluent stage should be a greater immersion into the wide range of reading opportunities. These readers are familiar with complex sentence structures, story concepts, and literary genres.

The Fluent Reader Assessment (see Appendix A) is a rubric scale that helps teachers determine the developmental level of a fluent reader's reading behaviors. Teachers mark and date the indicator box that best reflects the student's behavior. This tool is used to identify areas of strength and weakness for individual students. The teacher then guides instruction based on the needs of the student. When 8 out of 10 boxes are marked "Always," the student is considered a solid fluent reader.

Table 5 highlights instructional techniques presented in this book, grouped by the five components of reading. Teachers may use this chart when choosing a component to teach

TABLE 5. Fluent Reader Techniques

	Phonemic Awareness	Phonics	Fluency	Vocabulary	Comprehension
Before Reading		Irregular Words*	Preview/Pause/ Prompt/Praise/ Participate	Context Complex Clues Genre Study Reflection Connection Vocabulary Clubs	Story Impression Thinking About Questioning SQ3R
During Reading			Interpretation/ Character Analysis Choral Readers Closed-Captioned Television Eye 2 Eye	Genre Study	SQ3R Question Logs: 3Rs Scenario With T-Chart GIST
After Reading		Brain Tricks		Root Words	SQ3R GIST

*Adaptation portion of that particular technique.

their fluent readers. The techniques are categorized according to when they are best utilized for effective instruction: before, during, or after reading of a particular text.

Instruction

Instruction is the final aspect of a CAI literacy classroom. Instruction begins with establishing an environment conducive to learning with a comprehensive literacy block. Within the literacy block, teachers should scaffold instruction using different literacy approaches and provide appropriate modeling in the form of teacher talk. This framework helps teachers align instruction to meet the needs of students' varying learning styles.

Comprehensive Literacy Block

The comprehensive literacy block is a teaching framework for which teachers should use, at a minimum, a 90-minute block of instructional time. Table 6 details the comprehensive literacy block and shows the approaches and the skills each segment of the block teaches (i.e., who is involved, how long it lasts, what type of text is used, and what type of grouping and resources are needed). This table will assist teachers in planning their own comprehensive literacy blocks.

This literacy schedule allows flexibility in the order and sequence of the specific literacy approaches used. For example, the teacher first selects teaching content from the area of language arts (e.g., comprehension, one of the five components of reading, and the strategy of summarizing). Next, the teacher selects a technique within the strategy (e.g., Narrative Pyramid within the strategy of summarizing—see chapter 6) and incorporates specific teacher talk to support the thinking process of the strategy. If this is the first time teaching this technique, the teacher will need to use the approach of modeling the technique, thinking aloud the thought process for the technique. Teachers may prefer to implement a unit of study on a specific concept or strategy using a variety of techniques that support it. Concentrating on this specific strategy for several weeks is powerful for the learner because there is time for modeling, chances for multiple attempts, and practical application.

Comprehensive Literacy Approaches

The literacy approaches presented in this book include reading aloud, modeled writing, shared literacy, guided reading and writing, and independent literacy. These approaches are the basis for a comprehensive literacy block that teachers can utilize to effectively implement the five components of reading within the curriculum.

TABLE 6. Comprehensive Literacy Block

Segment (Approach)	Who	Duration	Difficulty of Text	Grouping	Resources/Application	Content Area
Reading Aloud (Modeling)	Teacher	10–15 minutes	High (Challenge)	Whole class	Picture books, short stories, chapter books, student-generated stories, variety of genres, connections, think-aloud	Language arts, science, social studies, health, mathematics
Modeled Writing (Modeling)	Teacher	10–15 minutes		Whole class	Morning message, language experiences, creative writing, lists, think-aloud	
Shared Literacy (Interacting)	Teacher, Student	30–45 minutes	Moderate–High (Instructional)	Whole class or small groups	Big Books, short stories, excerpts from stories, chapter books, poetry, chants, sentence strips, magazines, newspapers, student-generated writing, minilesson reading/writing workshop	
Guided Reading* (Guiding)	Student, Teacher	40–60 minutes	Moderate–Easy (Instructional/Independent)	Small groups or independent	Same-level groups, literature groups, targeted strategy-/skill-based groups, individual conferences	
Guided Writing* (Guiding)	Student, Teacher				Brainstorming, peer talk, writing folders, conferencing	
Independent Literacy* (Independence)	Student[†]		Easy (Independent)		Journals, literacy response logs, observation notebooks, research projects, literacy centers, silent reading, literature circles, commercial programs	

*These approaches may be occurring simultaneously.
[†]All students participate in a small group 2–4 times per week based on student needs (struggling readers meet more frequently).

READING ALOUD. In this approach, the teacher models reading behaviors of fluent readers by reading aloud to the students and using think-aloud demonstrations. This time in the literacy block familiarizes students with the vocabulary and language being used. Teachers should have a specific purpose for choosing each text that is read aloud; that is, they should know explicitly what area of reading will be highlighted by the text and should combine the text with a strategy for reading. Text selections should be challenging, build background knowledge for the students, and include a variety of genres to appeal to both the students' interests and the topic of study. Reading aloud fosters a sense of community and builds a classroom environment in which reading is important. Examples of texts to read aloud are picture books, short stories, chapter books, students' writing, fiction, and nonfiction. For more about the topic of reading aloud, see Trelease (2001) and Hahn (2002).

MODELED WRITING. In this approach, the teacher demonstrates for the students the reading and writing connection by modeling the writing process of thinking, planning, questioning, drafting, and revising. This block of time exposes students to a variety of writing genres and expands access to writing that would be beyond students' ability. Examples can include morning messages, language experiences, and creative writing drafts, all written by the teacher in front of the students. For more on the subject of modeled writing, see Fletcher and Portalupi (2001) and Calkins (1994).

SHARED LITERACY. This approach has the teacher and student interacting with the text. During this block of time, the initial instruction for a specific skill or strategy takes place. This instruction is explicit, systematic, and integrated intricately with reading and writing. The minilesson is "architectured," according to Calkins (2001, p. 42), by connecting, modeling, trying it out, sharing reflections, and fostering independence.

The first stage of the minilesson shows the students what they will be doing and how learning this specific strategy or skill connects to their previous work. The teacher models one strategy or skill and describes it in a way to allow students to imitate or extend it. The teacher should emphasize the reading–writing reciprocal relationship constantly throughout this block of time. Next in the minilesson, the students try out the skill or strategy with the teacher. Students then discuss their application experience with others, which begins to foster independence.

A systematic schedule of word work is important during this block of time. Using the text (e.g., literature book, poetry, sentence strips) as the basic source for reading and writing, the teacher should support the students in a clear, direct, and orderly way as students strive to become independent, strategic readers. This literacy framework provides a safe, risk-free environment in which students can actively participate, becoming part of a community of readers and writers. Examples to use might be Big Books, short stories, excerpts from stories, chapter books, poetry, chants, sentence strips, magazines, newspaper articles, and student-generated writing. Active participation is encouraged during this approach, through techniques such as Readers Theatre and literature extension activities.

For more on using shared literacy, see Allen (2002); Fisher and Fisher Medvic (2000); McCarrier, Pinnell, and Fountas (1999); Parkes (2000); and Payne and Schulman (1999).

GUIDED READING AND WRITING. This portion of the literacy block is implemented in conjunction with independent reading and writing. Arranging students in small, flexible groups according to each student's specific level and need allows the teacher to guide and support the students' use of effective reading and writing strategies. For guided reading, the teacher selects the text based on the interests and developmental level of the reader and examines the features within the text for specific requirements to correlate with the support the reader needs. The teacher should continuously observe, diagnose, and prescribe strategies within the five areas of reading while in small-group instruction with the students. This time with students allows for reinforcement and practice of the previous strategies and techniques taught within the shared literacy section of the schedule.

At times, there may be a need to form specific skill-based or strategy-based groups for immediate, intense intervention. These small groups with specific needs would meet on at least three occasions per week during this block of time. Some examples of groupings for guided reading are same-level text reading groups, literature study groups, and small-group, targeted-strategy lessons. Guided writing supports students individually or in small conferences, coaching and supporting writing strategies as needed. For more about using guided literacy, see Fountas and Pinnell (2001); Hill (1999); Opitz (1998); Schulman and Payne (2000); and Tyner (2004).

INDEPENDENT LITERACY. Students need time every day to process information at their individual pace and to practice new reading and writing strategies. This real and relevant reading and writing allows students to make connections and explore meaning. Extensive reading time during a planned instructional schedule is valuable to the success of a reading program (Taylor, Frye, & Maruyama, 1990).

In this approach, the students select texts that have appropriate independent reading ranges and use these texts to apply or extend recently demonstrated strategies and techniques. The independent approach applies Cambourne's employment condition (1995) by providing time and opportunity to engage and explore language. Educators who value independent reading and writing know that "exposure to print is efficacious regardless of the level of the child's cognitive and reading abilities. We do not have to wait for 'prerequisite' abilities to be in place before encouraging free reading" (Stanovich, 1992, p. 226). Examples of independent literacy are journals, creative writing folders, literature logs, observation notebooks, letters or messages, literacy centers, "buddy" reading, silent reading, or commercial reading programs. For more about using independent literacy, see Blair-Larsen and Williams (1999) and Rafoth (1999).

Scaffolding

Scaffolding instruction is a concept that focuses on how individuals learn (Collins, Brown, & Newman, 1989; Vygotsky, 1934/1978), providing support in the development of their learning. Pearson and Gallagher (1983) further developed this research with their concept about the gradual release of responsibility (GRR). GRR calls for support to be given by the teacher while the students are learning a new concept, skill, or strategy; that support then slowly diminishes as the students gain responsibility for their own learning. The framework gradually moves from modeling, through sharing and guiding, to a state of self-sufficiency.

Modeling by the teacher occurs with every new learning experience and is imperative before the student can be expected to attempt the unknown. Initially, the teacher models what he or she wants the students to be able to do (e.g., a strategy within one of the five components of reading). Teachers should demonstrate these strategies in a metacognitive manner. For example, if the teacher wants to concentrate on the summarizing strategy, he or she will be the doer and thinker in front of the students. After reading from a selection of text, the teacher begins to think aloud the objective: "I just read a part from this story, and I want to see if I can focus on the key elements of what I am reading, because that is what good readers do. So now I am going to think of a way to show how I can summarize it." The teacher then selects a technique (e.g., Narrative Pyramid) that supports the modeled strategy, and he or she thinks aloud the process of the strategy: First, the teacher demonstrates setting up the pyramid by saying, "I am going to draw some lines in a pyramid format. The top of the pyramid only has one line for one character. I will need to think of a character that was very important in the story and write only that character's name on the first line." This process of thinking aloud demonstrates what happens in the mind of a reader. In effective instruction, this modeling is necessary and is the basis for optimal learning.

Teachers should continue to utilize GRR throughout their instruction of the curriculum. After teacher modeling of each strategy, students need time to interact with the teacher to gain further understanding. When the students begin to try the strategy on their own, the teacher should be there to guide them. The final phase of this scaffolding process is for the student to apply the strategy independently. According to Routman (2002), "When teachers understand and internalize this model, teaching and learning become more effective, efficient, and enjoyable" (p. 43). Comprehensive literacy classrooms are conducive to this maturation of learning because students have the opportunity to become proficient strategic readers and writers in a supportive, risk-free environment. The comprehensive literacy classroom uses this same process of gradual release to implement the approaches previously described for the literacy block: reading aloud, modeled writing, shared literacy, guided reading and writing, and independent literacy.

Figure 1 (page 20) shows the gradual release of responsibility. The "solid-core" instruction is at the center of the target, and instruction gradually moves outside the center for the student to gain independence. Teachers and students can move within the zones as needed throughout the day.

Multiple Intelligences

Research in learning styles indicates that there are multiple individual styles that teachers can identify and use in order to select specific instructional strategies to support students' strengths (Gardner, 1983; Levine, 2002). Gardner's theory of multiple intelligences (1983, 1993) suggests that there are a number of distinct forms of intelligence that each individual possesses to some degree:

- Visual/spatial: The ability to perceive the visual and to think in images and pictures.

- Verbal/linguistic: The ability to communicate in and analyze words and language usage (sounds, meanings, and rhythms).

- Logical/mathematical: The ability to use logic and reason, and to appreciate abstract relationships, including patterns.

- Bodily/kinesthetic: The ability to control body movements and handle objects skillfully (balance and eye–hand coordination).

- Musical/rhythmic: The ability to create, understand, and communicate rhythm, pitch, and timbre through intuitive and analytical means.

- Interpersonal: The ability to recognize, communicate (both verbally and nonverbally) about, and respond to others' moods, motivations, and desires.

- Intrapersonal: The ability to self-reflect and to be aware of inner feelings, values, and thinking processes; recognizing one's own strengths and weaknesses.

- Naturalistic: The ability to distinguish among and classify features of the environment; caring about and interacting with plants, animals, and other objects of nature.

These intelligences blend in various ways along a path of problem solving to create something that is meaningful to the student. Aligning the multiple individual styles that focus on proven research-based practices to instructional techniques ensures success for both educators and learners. Research suggests that the brain is a pattern detector and needs multiple experiences and instructional methods that are congruent in order for the brain to seek and make connections for understanding (Jensen, 1998; Lyons, 2003). For this reason, it is necessary for educators to know their students as readers and writers and to know the strategies, techniques, and teacher talk that are important for the students' success as literacy learners. Building, or scaffolding, upon what the students are able to do and guiding them to new understandings are key to comprehensive literacy.

FIGURE 1. Gradual Release of Responsibility

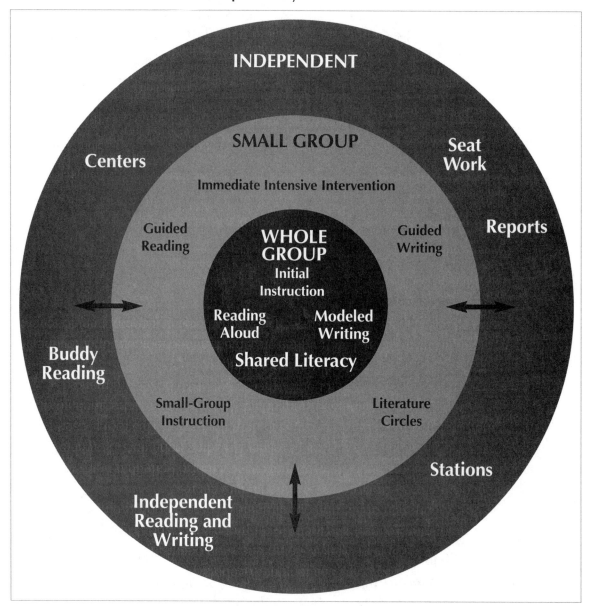

Techniques and Teacher Talk

Instructional techniques are the specific skills and instruction designed to teach a strategy. Chapters 2–6 incorporate a variety of techniques; select the ones that best support the strategy you are teaching and align with the needs of your students.

Incorporated in each technique are suggested examples for teacher talk. Throughout your teaching of the techniques, you should ask questions ("What words or phrases did the author use to help you create an image in your mind?"), make statements ("Try to picture in your mind someone who would remind you of a character in the story"), or say prompts ("I can image what it is like to...") that bring readers to a higher level of thinking. Students who are exposed to higher-order thinking and questioning comprehend more than students who are passively asked lower-order questions (Redfield & Rousseau, 1981). Teacher talk is the link to scaffolding instruction to help students be aware of their use of strategies and to think about the processes that are occurring in order to apply a particular strategy. This is the metacognitive awareness that is imperative for readers to develop in order to become strategic readers.

The Challenge

The CAI cycle continues throughout the learning process. All three components need to be present in a comprehensive, systematic, explicit approach to meet the multiple needs and diverse learning styles within today's classrooms. Figure 2 (page 22) shows the student as the "core" of a comprehensive literacy classroom. It is imperative to keep the student at the center of all decisions on curriculum, assessment, and instruction; the Venn diagram depicts how CAI intersects and allows flexibility for the teacher (e.g., the teacher may assess and then analyze the data to determine the need for immediate, intense intervention in one or more of the five components with specificity in a strategy identified). Curriculum, assessment, and instruction are the infrastructure that, when aligned, create a powerful comprehensive literacy classroom.

I challenge you, the educator, to identify the characteristics of your readers: know your reader. You will be empowered when you know your students' developmental stages (emergent, early, transitional, or fluent). Once you identify these reading stages through appropriate assessments, it is then necessary to align strategies and techniques in all five components of reading instruction at a suitable level for the students as needed. It is my hope that you will be encouraged to have a repertoire of strategies, techniques, and teacher talk to meet the individual needs of the diverse learners within your classroom. You may apply the strategies, techniques, and teacher talk presented in this book in any order according to the needs of your students.

FIGURE 2. The CAI Cycle

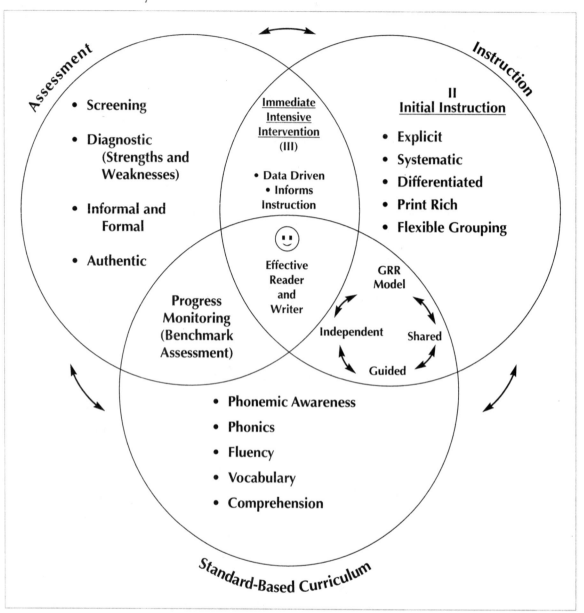

My final challenge is for you to consider reading as an art and yourself as an artist. Look at your students' minds as blank canvases, just waiting and inviting you to give color and meaning to their learning.

Chapter 2

Phonemic Awareness

Phonemic awareness is a vital link to the success of every reader. To support students in becoming proficient readers, it is important to understand what phonemic awareness is, why it is essential, what strategies and techniques to implement, and how to talk to students so they will think strategically. Phonemic awareness is the understanding that speech is composed of a sequence of sounds combined to form words, and it is the main component of phonological awareness. Students need to have a certain level of phonological awareness in order to benefit from formal reading instruction.

According to the International Reading Association (IRA; 1998), phonological awareness encompasses larger units of sound, whereas phonemic awareness stems from this concept but refers to smaller units of sound. These small units of speech correspond to letters of an alphabetic writing system; these letters are called phonemes and can make a difference in a word's meaning. For example, the word *met* has three phonemes, /m/, /e/, /t/. By changing the first phoneme to /j/, we can produce a new word, *jet*, with a completely different meaning.

A student's awareness of phonemes has been shown through extensive research to hold singular predictive power, accounting for as much as 50% of the difference in their reading proficiency at the end of first grade (Juel, 1988; NICHD, 2000; Snow, Burns, & Griffin, 1998; Stanovich, 1986; Wagner, Torgesen, & Rashotte, 1994). With this kind of evolving research, educators are looking more closely at how phonemic awareness affects reading achievement. This relationship between phonemic awareness and learning to read is most likely one of reciprocal causation (Perfetti, Beck, Bell, & Hughes, 1987). The goal is for students to become familiar with the sounds (phonemes) that letters (graphemes) represent and to become familiar with hearing those sounds within words.

Being phonologically aware means knowing ways in which oral language is divided into smaller components and is manipulated (Chard & Dickson, 1999). Phonological awareness develops in a continuum of listening to sounds, word awareness, rhyming, awareness of syllables, and phonemic awareness (being able to isolate, identify, categorize, blend, segment, delete, add, and substitute phonemes). It is important to note that phonemic awareness is included in the larger component of phonological awareness, and that phonological awareness is not the same as phonics. *Phonics* refers to the relationship between phonemes and graphemes (letters, or the written representations of phonemes). Too often, educators interchange phonological awareness, phonemic awareness, and phonics. Table 7 and Figure 3 (pages 24 and 25) help to illustrate the relations among phonological awareness, phonemic awareness, and phonics using a nature metaphor.

TABLE 7. Descriptions of Phonological Awareness, Phonemic Awareness, and Phonics

Terminology	Definition	Metaphor Description
Phonology	The study of the unconscious rules governing speech and sound production.	Sky—Governing the big picture
Phonological Awareness	The awareness of sound structure. The ability to notice, think about, or manipulate the larger unit of sound auditorally and orally.	Clouds—In the sky
Rhyming Awareness	The ability to recognize, isolate, and generate corresponding sounds, especially ending sounds.	Raindrop—Comes out of the cloud (a component of phonological awareness)
Word Awareness	The ability to recognize that spoken language is made up of individual words and that words form sentences.	Raindrop—Comes out of the cloud (a component of phonological awareness)
Syllable Awareness	The ability to identify syllables (i.e., the smallest unit of speech with a vowel sound), distinguish between one and two syllables, and count, blend, and segment syllables in words and sentences.	Raindrop—Comes out of the cloud (a component of phonological awareness)
Phonemic Awareness	The awareness that spoken language consists of a sequence of phonemes (i.e., the smallest unit of sound).	Hail—Also comes out of cloud but contains a combination of particles (onset and rimes, blending, segmenting, manipulating phonemes)
Phonics	The system by which symbols represent sounds in an alphabet writing system. The relationship between spelling patterns and sound patterns.	Ground—Foundation; Rain hits the ground intermittently, helping to make the ground fertile (products of phonological awareness)
Metalinguistic	The ability to think about and reflect upon one's language.	Seed—Planting a seed after making the connection between water and the ground (recognizing the connection among phonological awareness, phonemic awareness, phonics)
Orthography	A method of representing the spoken language with written symbols; spelling.	Roots—Branching off from seed (word families, stages of spelling)
Graphemes	The written symbol used to represent a phoneme.	Stems—The parts you see (letters)
Morphemes	The structure of meaningful language units.	Leaves—Parts of a plant (prefixes, suffixes)
Decode and Write Words	The ability to derive a pronunciation for a printed sequence of letters based on knowledge of spelling and sound correspondence.	Flower—The product of rain and good soil (reading and writing)

FIGURE 3. Illustration of Relationship Among Phonological Awareness, Phonemic Awareness, and Phonics

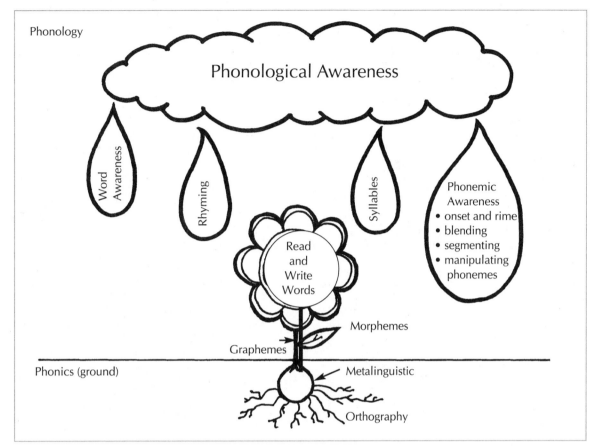

This chapter highlights phonemic awareness in the context of phonological awareness. The strategies and their corresponding techniques detailed in this chapter include the following:

- Rhyming: Rhyming Jar; Rock, Rhythm, and Rhyme Time; Draw a Rhyme; and Pair–Share Match

- Isolating and Identifying Phonemes: Sounds We Found, Mirror/Mirror, Alliteration Activation, Hot Seat, and Think Sounds

- Blending Phonemes: Draw It, Read My Mind, Body Blending, and Syllable Giving

- Segmenting Phonemes: Egg-Cited About Phonemes, Graphing Phonemes, Hand Push, and Silly Segmenting

- Manipulating Phonemes: Colored Cubes, Fe-Fi, and Say It Again

The phonemic awareness matrix in Table 8 (page 26) matches the techniques in this chapter to the developmental levels from chapter 1 (emergent, early, transitional, and fluent). To be effective, the strategies and techniques presented in this chapter should allow ample time for teacher modeling and student application, long before independent application is

TABLE 8. Phonemic Awareness Techniques

	Emergent	Early	Transitional	Fluent

Before Reading	Draw It (B)
	Mirror/Mirror (I)
	Rhyming Jar (R)
		May include all Emergent
		  techniques
		Colored Cubes (M)
		Graphing Phonemes (S)
		Hand Push (S)
		Mirror/Mirror* (I)
		Rhyming Jar* (R)
		Silly Segmenting (S)
			May include all
			  Emergent and Early
			  techniques
			Body Blending* (B)
			Colored Cubes* (M)
			Silly Segmenting* (S)
			Think Sounds (I)
				May include all
				  Emergent, Early,
				  and Transitional
				  techniques

During Reading		Draw a Rhyme (R) Fe-Fi (M)		

After Reading	Read My
	  Mind (B)
	Rock, Rhythm,
	  and Rhyme
	  Time (R)
	Sounds We
	  Found (I)
		Alliteration Activation (I)
		Body Blending (B)
		Egg-Cited About
		  Phonemes (S)
		Hot Seat (I)
		Pair–Share Match (R)
		Rock, Rhythm, and
		  Rhyme Time* (R)
		Say It Again (M)
		Syllable Giving (B)
			Alliteration
			  Activation* (I)
			Pair–Share Match* (R)	

*Adaptation portion of the technique.
Note. The developmental levels are shown across the top of the table horizontally. Down the left side of the matrix are the suggested times when these techniques are most effective—before, during, and after reading. This matrix is a guide and is by no means an exhaustive list. (R) Rhyming; (I) Isolating and identifying phonemes; (B) Blending phonemes; (S) Segmenting phonemes; (M) Manipulating phonemes

expected. Teachers should select and model reading aloud of appropriate literature to apply the techniques in a meaningful manner, which supports authentic learning for strategic reading. By using this process, students are able to see first the whole text (i.e., appropriate literature), then see the parts systematically (i.e., strategies and techniques), and finally, apply the parts back to the whole (i.e., become metacognitively aware of strategies while reading appropriate literature). Utilizing quality literature and promoting language development throughout the techniques will help to enhance students' development of the strategies.

Phonemic Awareness Strategy: Rhyming

Rhyming provides students with an opportunity to begin developing an awareness of sounds, and it is one of the early phases of phonemic awareness. Emergent readers need many opportunities to hear and identify rhymes (end parts that sound alike but do not necessarily look alike) and to repeat the ending sounds by generating words with similar sound groups. Providing students with opportunities to explore the similarities and differences in the sounds of words helps them to have an insight that language has not only meaning and message but also physical form (Adams, 1990).

Appropriate literature that best supports the application of the rhyming strategy has a variety of words in the text that rhyme. *Is Your Mama a Llama?* (Guarino, 1991) and *Down by the Bay* (Raffi, 1990) are two examples of appropriate literature; however, any piece of literature that has rhyming words within the text would be appropriate for use with these techniques.

Teacher Talk: Statements, Questions, and Prompts for Rhyming

Following is a list of suggested teacher talk that encourages readers to think strategically as they employ the rhyming technique. Try using some of these statements, questions, and prompts with your students as you work through the techniques in the following section.

- Does your rhyming word at the end of the sentence make sense? Why or why not?

- How do you know that your words rhyme?

- Why did you move on the word _____? How did you know to move your body on specific words?

- Draw what rhymes with _____. How did you know what to draw?

- How are these two words alike?

- What sounds do you hear at the end of these two words: _____ and _____?

- What part of the word makes the rhyme?

- Do rhymes always have to make sense? Explain your answer.

- Have you ever heard a nonsense rhyme in a story? Give an example.

- Say a word that sounds like _____.

- Which two words rhyme (say three words, such as *cat, bat, fish*)? Why did you pick the two words you did?

Techniques for Rhyming

Rhyming Jar

Purpose: To generate a rhyming word that completes the sentence for meaning.
Level: Emergent (Adaptation for Early)
Multiple Intelligences: Verbal/linguistic, interpersonal
Materials: A jar, rhyming sentences on strips of paper, chart paper

Procedure:

1. Write rhyming sentences on strips of paper, omitting the final rhyming word (e.g., I want a new <u>bed</u>, and I will paint it _____ [red]; Look next to the <u>rake</u>, there is a big _____ [snake]). Place the strips into a jar.

2. Every day, pull a strip from the jar and read it aloud, emphasizing the first rhyming word (e.g., *bed* in the first sentence above) by whispering it. This first word becomes the rhyme of the day. Do not read a rhyming word at the end of the sentence.

3. Have students work in pairs to generate rhyming words to complete the sentence. Suggested teacher talk for this technique might be, "Does your rhyming word at the end of the sentence make sense? Why or why not?"

4. Have students act throughout the day as "detectives," looking for other oral and written words that rhyme with the word of the day. Suggested teacher talk could be, "How do you know that your words rhyme?"

5. Add the discovered rhyming words to a posted class-generated list. Categorize rhyming words according to a unit of study (e.g., animals, color words, sports). The duration of the unit studied will determine the number of sentence strips you will need to create in order to use one each day.

Adaptation: Have students create the rhyming sentence strips to place in the Rhyming Jar.

Rock, Rhythm, and Rhyme Time

Purpose: To move to a rhythm, hear words that rhyme, and generate rhyming words.
Level: Emergent (Adaptation for Early)
ELL Technique: Yes
Multiple Intelligences: Bodily/kinesthetic, musical/rhythmic (adaptation is interpersonal)
Materials: Music of nursery rhymes such as *Rhymin' to the Beat, Volume I* (Hartmann, 1996); tape or CD player; chart paper, paper, and highlighting tape (for Adaptation)

Procedure:

1. Have students stand up, and ask them to prepare to rock with rhythm.
2. Play a prerecorded nursery rhyme, and have students create bodily movements that correlate to the words in the song.
3. Replay the song, this time having the students stand up and sway to the beat, listening for rhyming words that match a word that you or a volunteer calls out. When students hear a word that rhymes with the one you called out, have them do some predetermined gesture to indicate recognition of the rhyme.
4. Using Humpty Dumpty, for example, ask the students to listen for words that rhyme with *ball*. When the students hear the words *wall*, *fall*, and *all*, students should turn around in place (or whatever gesture you have predetermined for them). Suggested

teacher talk might be, "Why did you move on the word _____? How did you know to move your body on specific words?"

Adaptation: The following ideas can change this technique from a concentration on phonemic awareness to one on phonics:

- Have the students generate and post a list of rhyming words they identified in the nursery rhyme.
- Write out the nursery rhymes on a large chart, and have students use highlighting tape to identify the rhyming words.
- Divide the class into teams, and provide each team a sheet of paper with a word from the nursery rhyme written at the top. Give students a certain amount of time (e.g., 40 seconds to 1 minute) to record words that rhyme with the word on top.

Draw a Rhyme

Purpose: To complete sentences by determining a rhyming word that makes sense in a story.

Level: Early

ELL Technique: Yes

Multiple Intelligences: Visual/spatial, verbal/linguistic, bodily/kinesthetic

Materials: Rhyming poems; paper for drawing or white boards; cassette tapes, tape recorder, scissors, felt, and Draw a Rhyme reproducible (see Appendix A; all for Variation)

Procedure:

1. Select a rhyming poem and read it aloud to the students, omitting the ending rhyming words. Suggested teacher talk might be, "Draw what rhymes with _____."
2. On drawing paper or white boards, have students fill in each missing word by drawing their proposed rhyming word. Suggested teacher talk could be, "How do you know what to draw?"
3. After reading aloud the entire poem, have students share their drawings and compare their results with others.

Variation: Tape record some poems for use with this technique, and place them at the listening center. Have students listen to the tapes on their own and draw the rhyming words, or have them precut shapes from felt that represent the desired rhymes. Have students put together the felt pieces to "Build a Rhyme." You can also use the Draw a Rhyme reproducible as a premade activity: Cover up the rhyming words shown along the right side, copy the sheet for each student, and let students draw their pictures directly on the page.

Source: Fitzpatrick (1997)

Pair–Share Match

Purpose: To identify and match rhyming words.

Level: Early (Adaptation for Transitional)

ELL Technique: Yes

Multiple Intelligences: Visual/spatial, bodily/kinesthetic

Materials: Rhyming words, chart paper, Pair–Share Match reproducible (see Appendix A)

Procedure:

1. Select a number of rhyming words from a text recently read in class; the number of words should equal the number of students in your class. Add rhyming words from an additional source, if needed.

2. Copy the Pair–Share Match reproducible, and cut apart the eggs and nests. Write the rhyming words on matching egg and nest pattern cutouts (e.g., write *dog* on an egg, and *fog* on the nest). If you have an odd number of students in your class, then you can serve as the partner for one student, or you can make one group a triad.

3. Distribute to each student either an egg or a nest cutout. Have students "fly" around the room to find the partner who has a word that rhymes with theirs. Suggested teacher talk could be, "How are your words alike?"

4. After all the eggs have found their corresponding nests (rhyming partners), have the newly formed pairs generate other rhyming words to match their words. Suggested teacher talk might be, "What sounds do you hear at the end of each of your words?"

5. As each partner shares his or her match, record the rhyming pairs on chart paper.

6. Reread the text, noting rhymes in the text by whispering them when you encounter them as you are reading. This helps students to identify and hear the rhymes.

Adaptation: Provide blank cutout eggs for students to record their new Pair–Share rhyming words. This phase of the technique combines phonics with phonological awareness.

Source: Adapted from Fredericks (2001)

Phonemic Awareness Strategy: Isolating and Identifying Phonemes

Isolating phonemes is a strategy that allows the students to recognize individual sounds in a word. Attending to these phonemes increases students' awareness that words are made up of individual sounds that connect together to form a word. When students apply this strategy, they are demonstrating their ability to think about and separate individual sounds from one another within a word (e.g., the first sound in *dog* is /d/, the medial sound in *wet* is /e/, and the final sound in *like* is /k/). Students need to explore the articulation of these sounds with techniques that support the correct positioning of their mouths. Positioning of the lips and tongue is vital to articulating sounds correctly.

Identifying phonemes is a strategy in which students focus on separate distinctions of initial, medial, and final sounds in words to recognize their similarities and differences. Students who can use this strategy are able to think about and notice that two or more words may have the same initial sound (e.g., *ball*, *bat*, and *balloon*), medial sound (e.g., *met*, *Greg*, and *tell*), or final sound (e.g., *call*, *pool*, and *doll*). Identifying these sounds is important as students move through the developmental stages of reading, and it provides students with a tool for reading as well as writing.

Appropriate literature that best supports the application of the isolating and identifying phonemes strategy has a variety of words highlighting specific sounds in the text. *Andy: That's My Name* (dePaola, 1973) and *Chicka, Chicka Boom Boom* (Martin & Archambault, 1989) are two examples of appropriate literature; however, any piece of literature that has words with the specific sound you are highlighting would be appropriate for use with these techniques.

Teacher Talk: Statements, Questions, and Prompts for Isolating and Identifying Phonemes

Following is a list of suggested teacher talk that encourages readers to think strategically as they isolate and identify phonemes. Try using some of these statements, questions, and prompts with your students as you work through the techniques in the following section.

- Listen for the sound you hear at the beginning or end of this word.
- How do you position your lips and teeth when you say the _____ sound?
- Think of words that begin with the same sound as _____.
- What other words start the same as the word _____?
- Where do you hear the _____ sound in the word?
- What sound do you hear at the end of the word _____?
- What is the difference between the sound and the letter?
- Try to get your mouth ready to make the _____ sound.
- How do you position your mouth when you start that word?
- With what sound does this word begin?
- How do you make that sound?
- Is the sound _____ in that word closer to the beginning or ending sound?

Techniques for Isolating and Identifying Phonemes

Sounds We Found

Purpose: To isolate and identify beginning and ending sounds.

Level: Emergent

ELL Technique: Yes

Multiple Intelligences: Visual/spatial, verbal/ linguistic, bodily/kinesthetic

Materials: Text, index cards, glue, objects related to text, pictures of objects (these can be hand drawn, from magazines, or clip art), paper bags

Procedure:

1. Read a text, and then show students objects that are mentioned in the text.

2. Glue pictures on index cards. Attach one picture card to each paper bag, and distribute these bags to pairs or teams of students. Suggested teacher talk might be, "Listen for the sounds you hear in the beginning or ending of this word: _____."

3. Have the students search for items around the room that have either the same beginning or ending sound as the picture on their bag, and have them place the found items into the bags.

4. Have students share their findings with the class, and then display the items together with the bags in an area in the room labeled "Sounds We Found." Suggested teacher talk might be, "How do you position your teeth, tongue, and lips when you say the beginning sound for this object?"

5. Reread the text to the students, and hold up objects that relate to sounds in the words.

Mirror/Mirror

Purpose: To identify positioning of the mouth, lips, and teeth with isolated sounds.

Level: Emergent–Early

ELL Technique: Yes

Multiple Intelligences: Visual/spatial, verbal/linguistic, bodily/kinesthetic, interpersonal

Materials: Text, hand-held mirrors

Procedure:

1. Select a word from classroom literature and say it, isolating the beginning sound. With hand-held mirrors, have students practice positioning their lips, teeth, and tongues to say the sound you isolated. Suggested teacher talk might be, "How do you position your mouth when you start the word _____?"

2. Have partners describe to each other what they notice happening to their mouths when they say a certain sound. Suggested teacher talk could be, "How do you position your lips and teeth when you say that sound?"

Alliteration Activation

Purpose: To identify beginning sounds and create additional words that begin with the same sounds.

Level: Early (Adaptation for Transitional)

ELL Technique: Yes

Multiple Intelligences: Visual/spatial, verbal/linguistic

Materials: Text, small objects, bucket or bag, chart paper

Procedure:

1. Select appropriate literature with alliteration.

2. Place a few chosen objects in a bucket or bag. Have students take turns choosing a small object from the bucket or bag, saying the name of the object, and then thinking of an associated word beginning with the same sound as the object. For example, a student could take a pencil out of the bag and say, "pretty pencil." Suggested teacher talk might be, "Think of words that begin with the same sound as _____."

3. Continue to pass the bucket or bag around the room and have students generate alliterations for the objects. Suggested teacher talk could be, "What other words start the same as _____?"

4. List students' responses on chart paper and read or reread a chosen text, noting alliterative words.

Adaptation: Have students introduce themselves by using a verb after their name that has the same beginning sound as their name (e.g., Derek dreams, Jacey jumps, Brooke bounces). Have students create tongue twisters with their names (e.g., Bailey bakes biscuits before breakfast).

Source: Adapted from Love and Reilly (1996)

Hot Seat

Purpose: To identify positioning of isolated sounds.

Level: Early

ELL Technique: Yes

Multiple Intelligences: Visual/spatial, verbal/linguistic, bodily/kinesthetic

Materials: Text; chairs; three cards, each with one letter *B* (beginning sound), *M* (middle sound), and *E* (ending sound); words selected from text; Hula-Hoops (optional)

Procedure:

1. Line up three chairs in the front of the room. Attach one card to each chair, and explain that these are the hot seats. You also can substitute Hula-Hoops in place of the chairs by placing the hoops on the floor and letting students stand inside the circles.
2. Have students line up and take turns sitting in the hot seats.
3. Ask questions about words the class is studying or words from a text you are reading, and have the students demonstrate their responses by sitting in the chair with the card matching their answer. For example, if the word is *cat*, you could ask, "Where do you hear the /t/ in the word *cat*?" The student would move to the last chair labeled *E* and sit in it, representing the ending sound.
4. Reread the text you are studying, and note beginning or ending sounds in words from the text.

Adaptation: Choose a word with more than three sounds. Ask, for example, "Where do you hear the /a/ in *table*?" Once the student is sitting in the middle hot seat, ask, "Is the /a/ closer to the beginning of the word or closer to the end of the word?" Have the student lean toward the chair that represents the answer.

Think Sounds

Phonemic
Awareness:
Isolating and
Identifying
Phonemes

Purpose: To isolate, identify, and match beginning and ending sounds in words.
Level: Transitional
ELL Technique: Yes
Multiple Intelligences: Verbal/linguistic, interpersonal, adaptation is visual/spatial
Materials: Think Sounds reproducible (see Appendix A)

Procedure:

1. Form a small group of students to sit in a circle. Provide these students with a starter word (e.g., *soap*). Suggested teacher talk might be, "What sound does this word end with?"
2. Have the student to the left of you think of a word that begins with the final sound in the word that you choose (e.g., *soap* ends in /p/, so the student could say *pan*). Suggested teacher talk could be, "What sound do you hear at the end of the word _____? Now, try to think of a word that begins with that sound.
3. Have the next student say a word that begins with the ending sound of the last word created (e.g., *pan* ends in /n/, so the student could say *name*). Remind the students to pay attention to the final sound, not the final letter, when creating a new word (e.g., in *name*, /m/ is the final sound, not the letter *e*).

Source: Zgonc (1999)

Phonemic Awareness Strategy: Blending Phonemes

Blending phonemes is a strategy that involves listening to a sequence of separately spoken sounds and then combining the sounds to form a whole word. This synthesis approach gives the students an opportunity to hear individual sounds in words and blend them into a meaningful whole. Techniques should be provided for students to blend by syllable (e.g., /gar/-/den/), onset or initial sound (e.g., the /b/ in *bike*), rime (the vowel and the letters that follow it in a syllable, e.g., the /ike/ in *bike*), and individual phonemes (e.g., /c/-/a/-/t/). According to the NRP report (NICHD, 2000), blending instruction benefits reading acquisition, and it yields even more effect when representing these combined sounds with letters. This combination of connecting phonemes and graphemes helps the students associate phonemic awareness with application to reading and writing.

Appropriate literature that best supports the application of the blending strategy has a variety of words for combining sounds in the text. *Ook the Book* (Rovetch, 2001) and *Hop on Pop* (Dr. Seuss, 1963) are two examples of appropriate literature; however, any piece of literature that has words with the targeted sounds you are using for blending would be appropriate for use with these techniques.

Teacher Talk: Statements, Questions, and Prompts for Blending Phonemes

Following is a list of suggested teacher talk that encourages readers to think strategically as they blend phonemes. Try using some of these statements, questions, and prompts with your students as you work through the techniques in the following section.

- Try to listen to the sounds I say and put them together to make a word.

- What object do you see in your mind when you blend the sounds together?

- How does slowly hearing each individual sound help you when forming a word?

- What word do you form when you blend these sounds together?

- Think about the sounds you hear, and combine them together to form a word.

- What are you doing with the word part sounds in order to form the word?

- What sounds did you blend to form the word?

- How does hearing the onset and then the rime help you to form the word?

Techniques for Blending Phonemes

Draw It

Purpose: To blend phonemes together to form a word, and to draw a picture of the word.
Level: Emergent
ELL Technique: Yes
Multiple Intelligences: Visual/spatial, verbal/linguistic
Materials: Text, paper, pencil or crayons

Procedure:

1. Have students fold a sheet of paper into fourths and listen as you pronounce the names of four objects. The objects you select need to be easy items for the students to draw and should preferably be from the text your class is reading.
2. As you say the name of an object, segment the name either by syllables (/pen/-/cil/), onset and rimes (/r/-/ake/), or phonemes /d/-/e/-/s/-/k/). Suggested teacher talk might be, "Try to listen to the sounds I say and put them together to make a word."
3. Have students blend the sounds you say orally and then draw a picture to represent each word they form. Suggested teacher talk might be, "What object do you see in your mind when you blend the sounds together?"

Source: Blevins (1999)

Read My Mind

Purpose: To hear the onset and rime of a word and blend them together to form the word.
Level: Emergent
ELL Technique: Yes
Multiple Intelligences: Verbal/linguistic, musical/rhythmic
Materials: Text, word list from text with onsets and rimes

Procedure:

1. Say a sentence in a rhythmic or chanting manner, and encourage students to clap their hands as you speak the words. Have them fill in the word at the end of the sentence. For example, "I know a word, it ends with /eek/ and starts with /p/. The word is _____ [*peek*]." Suggested teacher talk might be, "How does hearing the onset and rime help you form the word?"
2. Continue this process using different onsets and rimes (/ot/ + /p/ = *pot*; /elt/ + /m/ = *melt*). Suggested teacher talk could be, "What word do you form when you blend these sounds together?"

Source: Zgonc (1999)

Body Blending

Purpose: To hear the individual units of sound in a word and blend the phonemes together to form the word.

Level: Early (Adaptation for Transitional)

ELL Technique: Yes

Multiple Intelligences: Verbal/linguistic, bodily/kinesthetic, interpersonal

Materials: Text, Hula-Hoops

Procedure:

1. Place one Hula-Hoop on the ground for each phoneme represented in a chosen word (e.g., *met* would have three hoops).
2. Select the proper number of students to each "be a phoneme" in the word, and have each student stand in a hoop.
3. Have one student begin by saying the first sound while simultaneously linking arms with the next student. The next student says the second sound. Suggested teacher talk might be, "Think about the sounds you hear, and combine them to form a word."
4. Continue until all the students standing in the hoops have said their sounds and linked arms to form a word.
5. Have all the linked students take one step forward out of their Hula-Hoops and pronounce the entire word in unison. Suggested teacher talk could be, "How does slowly hearing each individual sound help you when forming a word?"

Adaptation: Have students who physically blended the word search and find "their" word in the text.

Syllable Giving

Purpose: To blend smaller parts of words (syllables) together to form a word.

Level: Early

ELL Technique: Yes

Multiple Intelligences: Verbal/linguistic, bodily/kinesthetic, interpersonal

Materials: Text, wrapped box with a rock inside

Procedure:

1. Circulate the room and select a student. Give that student a box wrapped to look like a present, but that has a rock inside. Say, "I will give you a clue as to what is inside the box." Then, pronounce the name of an object syllable by syllable, placing a long pause on each syllable (e.g., /vi/-/de/-/o/, /car/-/pet/, /dish/-/wash/-/er/, /gui/-/tar/). Suggested teacher talk might be, "What are you doing with the word part sounds in order to form the word?"

2. Shake the box once as you say each syllable. The rock inside will shake to represent the number of individual sounds you hear.
3. When the student correctly blends the syllables together, he or she becomes the next one to present the gift to another student. Suggested teacher talk might be, "What sounds did you blend in order to form the word?"
4. The "gift-giving" student thinks of a word to blend orally by syllables and says the parts of the word for all to hear.

Source: Adapted from Adams et al. (1998)

Phonemic Awareness Strategy: Segmenting Phonemes

Segmenting phonemes is a strategy that incorporates hearing a word and then breaking it into its separate parts. Research shows that phoneme segmentation contributes to students' ability to read and spell words (Ball & Blachman, 1991). There are many techniques that support students in segmenting phonemes. For example, students can segment sentences to words (e.g., "The dog barks" into /the/, /dog/, /barks/); words to syllables (e.g., *garden* into /gar/-/den/); words to onset and rime (e.g., *bike* into /b/-/ike/); and words to individual phonemes (e.g., *cat* into /c/-/a/-/t/). Tangible objects (e.g., buttons, paper clips, or other counters) representing sounds serve as visual support for students, and these objects can then be replaced by letters when segmentation is done in written form (phonics).

Appropriate literature that best supports the strategy of segmenting phonemes has a variety of words that are appropriate for breaking the sounds apart. *The Listening Walk* (Showers, 1991) and *Sounds of a Powwow* (Martin, 1974) are two examples of appropriate literature; however, any piece of literature that has words you are studying for separating sounds would be appropriate for use with these techniques.

Teacher Talk: Statements, Questions, and Prompts for Segmenting Phonemes

Following is a list of suggested teacher talk that encourages readers to think strategically as they segment phonemes. Try using some of these statements, questions, and prompts with your students as you work through the techniques in the following section.

- How many counters did you place inside your egg? Try to shake out each sound you hear in the word _____. (For use with Egg-Cited About Phonemes)
- How many sounds do you hear in the word _____?
- What is the difference between the word _____ and the word _____?
- Which sounds do you hear in the word _____?

- Try to "push" the number of sounds you hear in the word.

- Count the number of parts you hear in the word.

- How does stretching out the word help you?

- What happens when you stretch the word?

- Try to say the word slowly to hear the individual sounds in the word.

- How many syllables do you hear in the word?

Techniques for Segmenting Phonemes

Egg-Cited About Phonemes

Purpose: To hear individual units of sound in words.
Level: Early
ELL Technique: Yes
Multiple Intelligences: Verbal/linguistic, bodily/kinesthetic
Materials: Text, plastic eggs, objects for counters (m&m's, Skittles, paper clips)

Procedure:

1. Select words from a text you are reading in class.
2. Give each student a reclosable plastic egg and some counters.
3. Pronounce a word, and have the students decide how many phonemes are in the word. While saying each phoneme, have students insert the appropriate number of counters into the egg. Suggested teacher talk might be, "How many counters did you place inside your egg? Why?" Have students close the eggs and use them to shake out each individual sound they hear. Suggested teacher talk could be, "Try to shake out how many sounds you hear in the word _____ using your egg."

Graphing Phonemes

Purpose: To identify phonemes and to show the number of phonemes from an object in a picture.
Level: Early
Multiple Intelligences: Visual/spatial, verbal/linguistic, interpersonal
Materials: Text, Graphing Phonemes reproducible (see Appendix A), magazines (for Adaptation)

Procedure:

1. Copy and cut out the picture cards from the Graphing Phonemes reproducible. (You may also choose to select words from a text you are reading in class.) Distribute a set of picture cards to teams of students.

2. Have students take turns saying the name of the object in a picture and determining how many phonemes they hear in that word. Suggested teacher talk might be, "How many sounds do you hear in the word _____?"

3. Have students sort their picture cards by the number of phonemes in each word. Then, have teams depict their findings on the answer key graph and write the total number of phonemes in the space provided. Suggested teacher talk might be, "What is the difference between the word _____ and the word _____?"

Adaptation: Have students select pictures from magazines and sort them by number of phonemes.

Source: Adapted from Blevins (1998)

Hand Push

Phonemic
Awareness:
Segmenting
Phonemes

Purpose: To segment individual units of sounds in a word.
Level: Early
ELL Technique: Yes
Multiple Intelligences: Visual/spatial, verbal/linguistic, bodily/kinesthetic
Materials: Text, overhead projector and objects for counters (beans, chips, paper clip; for Adaptation)

Procedure:

1. Select words from a text you are reading in class. Ask students how many sounds they hear in a particular word. Suggested teacher talk could be, "Which sounds do you hear in the word?"

2. Have the students segment the sounds by using their left palms as a phoneme push mat. As the students pronounce the word, have them use their right-hand fingers to push individual phonemes one at a time onto their "hand mats" to demonstrate segmentation. Suggested teacher talk might be, "Try to push the number of sounds you hear in the word."

Adaptation: Draw boxes on the overhead projector to represent each phoneme in a word, and use the boxes in place of the hand mat. Have students push counters into the individual boxes as they say the sounds in a word.

Silly Segmenting

Phonemic
Awareness:
Segmenting
Phonemes

Purpose: To segment individual units of sounds in a word.
Level: Early (Adaptation for Transitional)
ELL Technique: Yes

Multiple Intelligences: Visual/spatial, verbal/linguistic, bodily/kinesthetic

Materials: Text, clay

Procedure:

1. Give students small balls of clay, and ask them to shape their clay into snakes (long, rolled-up strips of clay).
2. Pronounce a word from a text you are reading, and have students separate their snakes into a corresponding number of segments, with each segment representing a phoneme. Suggested teacher talk might be, "How many sounds do you hear in the word?"
3. Have students point to each section of their snakes and say the sounds separately.
4. Ask students to pick up each individual segment while pronouncing the corresponding phoneme and to place it into the palms of their hands, reforming the word. Suggested teacher talk could be, "What sounds do you hear in the word?"
5. Repeat the process with a new word from the text you are reading.

Adaptation: Instead of breaking the snake apart, have students stretch the clay as they pronounce the individual sounds. The students can place the stretched snake on their desks and repeat the process with a new word and a new ball of clay to compare the lengths of the words.

Phonemic Awareness Strategy: Manipulating Phonemes

In order for students to manipulate sounds strategically, first they will need to be able to blend and segment phonemes. Manipulating phonemes involves adding, deleting, and substituting phonemes in words, and it is the most difficult area of phonological awareness (Love & Reilly, 1996). Students can make new words by adding a phoneme to an existing word (e.g., /p/ + *art* forms the word *part*), removing a phoneme to create another recognizable word (e.g., removing the /c/ from *call* makes the new word *all*), or substituting one phoneme with another to make a new word (e.g., changing the /a/ in *mat* to /e/ forms the new word *met*).

Students should have many opportunities to manipulate phonemes orally as well as in written work, and they should do so progressively, beginning with the initial phoneme, final phoneme, and then the medial phonemes. Instruction that emphasizes phoneme manipulation with letters supports students' ability to acquire phonemic awareness skills better than instruction without letters (NICHD, 2000).

Appropriate literature that best supports the application of the manipulating phonemes strategy has a variety of words in the text suitable for word play. *Jolly Olly* (Plater, 1998) and *Cock-a-Doddle-Moo* (Most, 1996) are two examples of appropriate literature; however, any piece of literature that has phonemes that you can manipulate within words would be appropriate for use with these techniques.

Teacher Talk: Statements, Questions, and Prompts for Manipulating Phonemes

Following is a list of suggested teacher talk that encourages readers to think strategically as they manipulate phonemes. Try using some of these statements, questions, and prompts with your students as you work through the techniques in the following section.

- Why are the cubes different colors? What do they represent? (For use with Colored Cubes)
- How did this technique help you think about the sounds in words?
- What sounds are added or deleted to make the new word?
- How did this activity help you think about the sounds in the words?
- How did you change the word to make a new word?
- What was the original word? What is the new word? How are they different?
- How can you change the word ___ to ___?
- What did you have to do to make the new word?
- What sound do you hear the first time?

Techniques for Manipulating Phonemes

Colored Cubes

Purpose: To represent phonemes with objects and to identify the sound by the object.
Level: Early (Adaptation for Transitional)
ELL Technique: Yes
Multiple Intelligences: Visual/spatial, verbal/linguistic, bodily/kinesthetic
Materials: Text, colored cubes or paper cutouts, index cards (for Adaptation)

Procedure:

1. Give each student two red, two blue, two green, and two yellow square cutouts (or colored block cubes).
2. Pronounce a word (e.g., *at*), and have the students select two different-colored squares to represent the phonemes in the word. Suggested teacher talk could be, "Why are the cubes different colors? What do they represent?"
3. Next, have the students point out which color represents the /a/ sound and which one represents the /t/ sound. Then ask the students to show you the word *cat*. (The students should choose a different-colored square to represent the /c/ sound.)
4. Have students make *sat* by changing the /c/ square to a different color for the /s/ sound. Ask the students to change the vowel from /a/ to /i/ to form a new word, again using

different-colored squares for the sounds. Suggested teacher talk might be, "How did this technique help you think about the sounds in the words?"

Adaptation: To move from phonemic awareness into phonics, substitute letter tiles (i.e., letters on index cards) for the colored squares, or write the letters directly on the squares after manipulating the sounds. To add additional challenges, have the students change the order of the sounds and/or duplicate a sound that already appears elsewhere in the word.

Source: Adapted from Blevins (1999)

Fe-Fi

Purpose: To substitute phonemes to make new words.
Level: Early
Multiple Intelligences: Verbal/linguistic, musical/rhythmic
Materials: Fe-Fi reproducible (see Appendix A; for Adaptation only)

Procedure:

1. Using the song "I've Been Working on the Railroad," substitute the initial sounds of students' first names in the line Fe-Fi-Fiddly-I-O. This line can be found in the chorus that begins with "Someone's in the kitchen with Dinah." Suggested teacher talk could be, "What sounds are added or deleted to make the new words?"

2. Have students come forward in turn, and have the class sing the song with each student's name. For example, if a student named Nick steps forward, the whole class substitutes the /n/ sound for the /f/ sound: Ne-Ni-Niddly-Ni-No. Suggested teacher talk might be, "How did this technique help you think about the sounds in the words?"

Adaptation: Laminate the Fe-Fi reproducible. During transition times in your schedule (changing centers, lining up for lunch), hand the card to a student and ask him or her to start the class singing and creating word plays to the song. You also can put other phonemic awareness songs on cards to use in the same way (see, for example, Yopp, 1992; Yopp & Yopp, 1996).

Source: Yopp (1992)

Say It Again

Purpose: To substitute phonemes to make new words.
Level: Early
Multiple Intelligences: Verbal/linguistic, bodily/kinesthetic
Materials: Words from text, chart

Procedure:

1. Say a word from the text and have the students repeat the word, adding and deleting sounds to begin creating new words. For example, you could say the word *cat* and ask

the students to change the /c/ to /b/ and say it again, forming the new word *bat*. Another example is to have the students say the word *milk* and then say it again without the /l/ sound. It is acceptable if the newly formed word is a nonsense word. Suggested teacher talk might be, "How did you change the word to make a new word?"

2. Record newly created words on a chart so students can see how they manipulated the sounds. Suggested teacher talk could be, "What was the original word? What is the new word? How are they different?"

Assessment

The purpose of assessing phonemic awareness is to determine students' ability to notice, think about, and manipulate sounds. Teachers should evaluate the results of the following assessments to determine the strengths and weaknesses of their individual students. The data from these assessments guides the teacher in creating an appropriate action plan (strategies, techniques, and teacher talk) to meet the diverse needs of the students.

When assessing phonemic awareness, teachers should observe whether students can do the following:

- Follow the beat or rhythm of words
- Recognize and produce a rhyme
- Listen to text and predict words based on rhyme patterns
- Identify the number of syllables in words
- Know letter sounds
- Sort pictures and objects according to sounds in their names
- Identify initial and final sounds in words
- Blend units of sound
- Segment words into units of sound
- Manipulate sounds within words

Following are general criteria from some sample phonemic awareness assessments. This is by no means an exhaustive list; it is only a starting point. Each assessment is designated S for screening, D for diagnostic, and/or PM for progress monitoring.

ASSESSMENT TEST (Adams, Foorman, Lundberg, & Beeler, 1997, pp. 108–131): S, D

Detecting rhymes: Student names a picture, then looks at pictures on the other side of the page and finds one that rhymes with the one he identified.

Counting syllables: Student looks at a picture and counts the number of syllables in the item's name.

Matching initial sounds: Student finds two pictures showing items that begin with the same sound.

Counting phonemes: Student looks at a picture and writes how many sounds she hears in the word.

DYNAMIC INDICATORS OF BASIC EARLY LITERACY SKILLS (DIBELS)
(Good & Kaminski, 2002): S, PM

Identifying letter names: Student looks at some letters and says the names of as many letters as he can.

Segmenting phonemes: Tester says a word; student tells all the sounds in the word.

Fluency with nonsense words: Student looks at a make-believe word and tries to read it as well as possible.

Fluency with oral reading: Student reads aloud for one minute.

FOX IN A BOX (Adams & Treadway, 2000): S, D, PM

Recognizing and generating rhymes: Tester says some words, and student tells whether they rhyme; student says a word that rhymes to finish a poem.

Clapping syllables: Student claps the syllables for words and tells the number of syllables she heard.

Identifying initial and final consonants: Student says only the first sound or last sound in each word.

Blending and segmenting phonemes: Tester says the sounds of a word, one sound at a time, and student puts the sounds together to make the word; or, tester says some words, and student repeats them, one sound at a time.

LINDAMOOD AUDITORY CONCEPTUALIZATION TEST (LAC)
(Lindamood & Lindamood, 1971): D, PM

Comparing number and order of phonemes: Tester says a sound pattern, and student represents each spoken sound with different-colored blocks (same color is used for repeated sounds).

Discriminating phonemes: Tester says a sound pattern, and student shows the sound pattern with colored blocks; student tracks and represents changes that occur in the pattern as single sounds are added, substituted, omitted, shifted, and repeated.

PHONOLOGICAL AWARENESS SKILLS TEST (PAST) (Zgonc, 1999, 2000): PM

Segmenting sentences: Tester reads a sentence; student manipulates a chip for each word he hears in the sentence.

Distinguishing rhymes: Student is asked whether sets of words rhyme.

Producing rhymes: Student produces a word to rhyme with a word she is given.

Blending syllables: Student puts the parts together (/ru/-/ler/) and then pronounces the whole word (*ruler*).

Segmenting syllables: Student says a word, and then manipulates a chip by touching or pushing it forward for each syllable. This process allows students to have a concrete representation of each syllable.

Deleting syllables: Student is asked to first say an entire word (*sunshine*) and then to say it without one of the syllables (say it again without *shine*).

Isolating initial and final phonemes: Student identifies the first or last sound in a word.

Blending phonemes: Tester separates all the sounds in a word (/s/-/i/-/t/), and student says the whole word (*sit*).

Segmenting phonemes: Tester says a word, and student manipulates a chip for each sound she hears in the word.

Deleting initial and final phonemes: Student says a word without the initial or final sound.

Substituting phonemes: Tester says a word, and student replaces the first sound in the word with a sound tester gives.

ROSNER TEST OF AUDITORY ANALYSIS (Rosner, 1975): S, PM

Manipulating phonemes: Student says a word, then repeats it without a particular phoneme.

YOPP SINGER TEST OF PHONEME SEGMENTATION (Yopp, 1995): S, D

Segmenting phonemes: Tester says a word, and student breaks the word apart and says each sound in the word in order.

Phonemic awareness, one of the five areas identified in the NRP report (NICHD, 2000), shows strong relations to success in the acquisition of reading. "Teachers should recognize that acquiring phonemic awareness is a means rather than an end. PA is not acquired for its own sake, but rather for its value in helping learners understand the alphabetic system to read and write" (NICHD, 2000, p. 2-6). The strategies, techniques, and teacher talk presented in this chapter support teachers in maximizing their students' potential in becoming strategic readers. When teachers stroke their brushes (techniques and teacher talk to build phonemic awareness) across their canvases, they are adding another dimension to their masterpieces—strategic readers.

Chapter 3

Phonics

Phonics is a component of reading and writing that involves the reader's ability to synthesize, analyze, contextualize, pattern, spell, and recognize words. Being able to read, pronounce, and write words by associating letters with sounds represents the basis for the alphabetic principle. Coupling this part of the phonics process with the brain's capacity to make connections allows phonics to be a support in the reading process and makes phonics one of the means to a very important end—that is, meaningful reading.

Phonics is part of the graphophonic cueing system that demonstrates the relationship between sounds in speech and letters in print. Proficient strategic readers use the graphophonic cueing system to demonstrate their awareness of graphemes (the visual representations of phonemes), sound–symbol associations, and the structural analysis of a word. This ability to decode unknown words simultaneously using a semantic cueing system (reading for meaning) and a syntactic cueing system (using grammatical structure and word order) supports reading fluently with comprehension and aids in becoming a strategic reader.

Recent research suggests that the most effective phonics instruction is planned, sequential, explicit, and systematic (NICHD, 2000; Stahl, Duffy-Hester, & Stahl, 1998). Therefore, teaching phonics in a comprehensive literacy program allows for specific, focused instruction within the confines of purposeful teaching. "In teaching phonics explicitly and systematically, several instructional approaches have been used. These approaches include synthetic phonics, analytic phonics, embedded phonics, analogy phonics, onset-rime phonics, and phonics through spelling" (NICHD, 2000, p. 2-89). Teachers need to identify the effective strategies within these approaches and "make a conscious effort to examine and reflect upon the strategies they use for teaching phonics in order to select the best type of experiences for the children they teach" (Morrow & Tracey, 1997, p. 651).

This chapter highlights the strategies embedded within phonics approaches and defines the approaches in a strategic manner. The teacher will need to determine which strategy best supports the instructional purpose for the specific lesson. This allows teachers to teach phonics strategies explicitly and systematically while being responsive to the needs and readiness level of each student, using a variety of techniques rather than just one phonics approach. Teachers should determine daily which strategies, techniques, and teacher talk will best correlate with the individual needs of the learners in their classrooms. The strategies and techniques in this chapter include the following:

- Synthesizing: Letter–Sound Magnetic Connection, Get Physical, Letterboxes, and Stretch It

- Analyzing: Star Names, Chant/Challenge/Chart, and Cool Rules

- Contextualizing: Blinders, Predict/Preview/Polish/Produce, and Word Detectives

- Patterning: Pattern Stories/Rounding Up Rhymes, Onset and Rimes, Pattern Sort, Rime Time Detective, and Vowel Patterns

- Spelling: Brain Tricks, If I Can Spell, Making Words, and Look/Say/Cover/Write/Check

- Recognizing: Letter Recognition, High-Frequency Words, and Irregular Words

Table 9 aligns the instructional techniques in this chapter to appropriate developmental levels (emergent, early, transitional, and fluent). Refer to chapter 1 of this book for descriptions of the characteristics of each level. To be effective, the strategies and techniques presented in this chapter should allow ample time for teacher modeling and student application, long before independent application is expected. Teachers should select and model reading aloud of appropriate literature to apply the techniques in a meaningful manner, which supports authentic learning for strategic reading. By using this process, students are able to see first the whole text (i.e., appropriate literature), then see the parts systematically (i.e., strategies and techniques), and finally, apply the parts back to the whole (i.e., become metacognitively aware of strategies while reading appropriate literature). Utilizing quality literature and promoting language development throughout the techniques will help to enhance students' development of the strategies.

Phonics Strategy: Synthesizing

Students apply the strategy of phonetic synthesizing by converting letters (graphemes) into sounds (phonemes) and by then combining those sounds together to create a word. Synthesizing means to combine parts or elements to form a whole. This strategy mirrors the synthetic approach described in the NRP report (NICHD, 2000, p. 2-89). Some educators use the term *synthetic* with the term *explicit* when referring to phonics due to the precise way letters and sounds are associated and then blended together.

Author and researcher Marilyn Adams defines explicit phonics as "the provision of systematic instruction or the relation of letter-sounds to words" (1990, p. 49). This provision is necessary for students who have little prerequisite knowledge about print and phonemic awareness. Implementing the synthesizing strategy systematically enhances the identification and blending of phonemes by providing opportunities to merge sounds in

TABLE 9. Phonics Techniques

	Emergent	Early	Transitional	Fluent
Before Reading	Blinders (C) High-Frequency Words (R) Irregular Words (R) Letter Recognition (R) Predict/Preview/ Polish/ Produce (C) Star Names (A)	May include all Emergent techniques If I Can Spell (Sp) Irregular Words* (R) Letterboxes (Sy) Look/Say/Cover/Write/ Check* (Sp) Star Names* (A) Stretch It (Sy)	May include all Emergent and Early techniques Irregular Words* (R) Look/Say/Cover/Write/ Check (Sp)	May include all Emergent, Early, and Transitional techniques) Irregular Words* (R
During Reading		Chant/Challenge/ Chart (A) Vowel Patterns (P)	Vowel Patterns (P) Word Detectives (C)	
After Reading	Letter–Sound Magnetic Connection (Sy) Onset and Rimes (P) Pattern Stories/ Rounding Up Rhymes (P)	Brain Tricks (Sp) Chant/Challenge/ Chart (A) Get Physical (Sy) Letter–Sound Magnetic Connection* (Sy) Making Words (Sp) Onset and Rimes (P) Pattern Sort (P) Rime Time Detective (P)	Brain Tricks (Sp) Cool Rules (A) Making Words* (Sp)	Brain Tricks (Sp)

*Adaptation portion of the technique.
Note. The developmental levels are shown across the top of the table horizontally. Down the left side of the matrix are the suggested times when these techniques are most effective—before, during, and after reading. This matrix is a guide and is by no means an exhaustive list.
(Sy) Synthesizing; (A) Analyzing; (C) Contextualizing; (P) Patterning; (Sp) Spelling; (R) Recognizing

succession. Incorporating instructional techniques that support these associations enables students to become independent strategic readers.

Appropriate literature that best supports the application of the synthesizing strategy has a variety of words in the text suitable for combining parts of a word to form the whole word. *Annabel* (Cowley, 1996) and *The Baby Uggs Are Hatching* (Prelutsky, 1982) are two examples of appropriate literature; however, any piece of literature that has words that lend themselves to synthesizing would be appropriate for use with these techniques.

Teacher Talk: Statements, Questions, and Prompts for Synthesizing

Following is a list of suggested teacher talk that encourages readers to think strategically as they synthesize. Try using some of these statements, questions, and prompts with your students as you work through the techniques in the following section.

- Look at the letters and think about the sounds that they make to blend the word.
- Visualize the letters coming together with their sounds to form the word.
- How does slowly hearing the sounds help you form a word?
- What word do you see after you record the sounds?
- What word do you form when you blend these letters together?
- How many sounds do you hear in the word _____?
- When you stretch the word, what is happening?

Techniques for Synthesizing

Letter–Sound Magnetic Connection

Purpose: To show that letters have names and that sounds can be associated with letters.
Level: Emergent (Adaptation for Early)
ELL Technique: Yes
Multiple Intelligences: Visual/spatial, bodily/kinesthetic
Materials: Text, magnetic letters, magnetic board

Procedure:

1. Use magnetic letters to practice connecting sounds in chosen words (words should have two to three phonemes). As you say each sound, place the magnetic letters next to each other. Suggested teacher talk might be, "How does slowly hearing the sounds help you form a word?"
2. Pronounce a specific phoneme.
3. Have a student volunteer choose the letter that matches that sound and place it on the magnetic board. Suggested teacher talk could be, "What word do you form when you blend these letters together?"
4. Continue this process until you form a word.
5. Have students position the letters close to one another, then blend and pronounce the sounds a little faster to "read" the word.
6. Reread the text you are studying, noting words from the technique that you modeled.

Adaptation: Use words with four to six phonemes.

Get Physical

Purpose: To express and blend sounds through body movements.
Level: Early
ELL Technique: Yes
Multiple Intelligences: Visual/spatial, verbal/linguistic, bodily/ kinesthetic

Materials: Text, plastic plates, string, erasable markers

Procedure:

1. Choose words from the text you are reading that you want the students to "physically" connect.

2. Attach string to small plastic plates to allow the plates to be worn around students' necks. On the plates, write the letter(s) associated with the individual sounds in a word. Use one letter per plate.

3. Distribute the plates to a number of student volunteers corresponding to the number of sounds in the word you are demonstrating. Instruct the students to put the plates around their necks so that the class can read the letters.

4. Place the students at the front of the room in the correct order for blending the letters. You can ask the students to place themselves in the proper order. Suggested teacher talk might be, "Look at the letters and think about the sounds that they make to blend the words."

5. Have the first student begin to say the sound his letter represents. While still saying his sound, the student links arms with the next and/or previous student. Continue this process until the students are standing, arms linked together, and have said all the sounds in the word. Suggested teacher talk could be, "Visualize the letters coming together with their sounds to form the word."

6. Finally, have all the students together take one step forward and say the entire word in unison.

7. Reread the text you are studying, and note words in the text that students demonstrated.

Letterboxes

Purpose: To hear sounds in words, associate letters to represent the sounds, and blend sounds together to form words.

Level: Early

ELL Technique: Yes

Multiple Intelligences: Visual/spatial, verbal/linguistic, bodily/kinesthetic

Materials: Text, letter sets, Letterboxes reproducible (see Appendix A), straws

Procedure:

1. Give each student his or her own set of letters to manipulate, a Letterboxes reproducible, and a small straw to wave as a wand. An alternative to using individual sets of letters is to use laminated letterboxes and let students use dry-erase markers to write the letters.

2. Choose words that have between two and six phonemes. Call out words for students to listen to, pronouncing the words slowly so that the students can hear the phonemes. Have students write the words in the appropriate letterboxes, depending on how many phonemes each word has. Have the students write the letters in the boxes as they hear

the sounds in the words. Suggested teacher talk could be, "How does slowly hearing the sounds help you to form a word?"

3. Have students wave their wands over a word from left to right as they say its sounds, carefully blending all the sounds together. Tell students that the key is to blend the letter being said with the pronunciations of the subsequent letter(s). Suggested teacher talk might be, "What word do you see after you note the sounds? Read it slowly to hear the sounds in the word you noted."

4. Reread the text you are studying, noting the words you modeled.

Source: Adapted from Cunningham (2000); Murray and Lesniak (1999)

Stretch It

Purpose: To identify that letters have names and that sounds can be associated with letters.
Level: Early
ELL Technique: Yes
Multiple Intelligences: Visual/spatial, verbal/linguistic, bodily/kinesthetic
Materials: Text, laminated squares, elastic strips, stapler, erasable marker, *Shake, Rattle 'N Read* CD (Hartmann, 2000), tape recorder (for optional Adaptation)

Procedure:

1. Staple at least two laminated paper squares each onto a group of elastic strips for a visual representation. Select several words to synthesize from a text you are reading in class.

2. Play "Do the Word Stretch" from the *Shake, Rattle 'N Read* CD. Have students pretend they are holding rubber bands and stretching the words.

3. Using an erasable marker, have students write the letters of a word on the squares. Each square should represent a letter(s) associated with the individual sound in the word. Suggested teacher talk might be, "How many sounds do you hear in the word _____?"

4. Have students stretch the elastic word and then slowly bring the word back together while merging the sounds. Suggested teacher talk might be, "When you stretch the word, what is happening?"

5. Reread the text, using the word the students stretched.

Adaptation: Place several different sizes of the Stretch It elastic strips and an erasable marker at the listening center. Record some words on audiotape, and have students select the appropriate Stretch It strip according to how many sounds they hear in each word on the tape. Then, students write the sounds on the strips. Finally, wipe off students' responses and reuse the strip as you repeat the process.

Phonics Strategy: Analyzing

Analyzing a word requires the students to take an identified word and examine its parts. This strategy encourages students to explore the letter–sound relationship while analyzing the word structure. Students use the analyzing strategy to read a whole word and then "take it apart" in order to investigate how the word works. This strategy aligns with the concepts of the analytic phonics approach. "Analytic programs begin by teaching children some words and then helping children to analyze those words and learn phonics rules and generalizations based on those words" (Cunningham, 2000, p. 184). According to the NRP report, "analytic phonics avoids having children pronounce sounds in isolation to figure out words. Rather, children are taught to analyze letter–sound relationship once the word is identified" (NICHD, 2000, p. 2-99). Students discover implicitly the intricacies of word power when they utilize phonetic analyzing as a strategy.

Appropriate literature that best supports the application of the analyzing strategy has a variety of words in the text suitable for investigating a specific skill. *"Slowly, Slowly, Slowly," Said the Sloth* (Carle, 2002) and *Oh, a-Hunting We Will Go* (Langstaff, 1989) are two examples of appropriate literature; however, any piece of literature that has words in which you can highlight a specific phonetic element you are studying would be appropriate for use with these techniques.

Teacher Talk: Statements, Questions, and Prompts for Analyzing

Following is a list of suggested teacher talk that encourages readers to think strategically as they analyze. Try using some of these statements, questions, and prompts with your students as you work through the techniques in the following section.

- What features of the words are alike?

- What patterns do these words have?

- What sound occurs in all these words?

- What characteristics are similar among these words?

- What rule or generalization do you see in these words?

- How does studying the word help you?

- Try to look at the whole word and then break it into parts as needed.

- What specific skill can you teach us using your name?

- What do you notice about the word?

Star Names

Purpose: To analyze individual names.

Level: Emergent (Adaptation for Early)

ELL Technique: Yes

Multiple Intelligences: Visual/spatial

Materials: Text, name cards for each student, board or chart paper

Procedure:

1. Give each student a card with his or her name written on it.
2. Encourage students to admire their names, analyzing them for a specific aspect (e.g., number of syllables, graphemes, or phonemes; letter formation; letter–sound connections). Suggested teacher talk could be, "What can you teach us from your name?"
3. Write the students' names on a name board or chart and continue analyzing the various concepts within the names. Suggested teacher talk might be, "Tell me something special about your name."

Adaptation: Cut apart the letters on a name card and pass them out to student volunteers. Have these students come to the front of the group, holding up the letters. Have them line up and ask the class to try to read the name in whatever order the letters are in. Ask, "How does the name look?" The student whose name is being analyzed can then help the other students line up properly, or you can write the name on the board for the students to refer to as they are lining up. The class can also put the name into a cheer ("Give me a ___ … what does it spell?").

Sources: Bear, Invernizzi, Templeton, and Johnston (2000); Calkins (2001); Cunningham (2000)

Chant/Challenge/Chart

Purpose: To identify patterns within words.

Level: Early

Multiple Intelligences: Visual/spatial, verbal/linguistic

Materials: Text, highlighting tape, chart paper

Procedure:

1. Display a selected poem, chant, or story that coordinates with a particular theme of study.
2. Use highlighting tape to "capture" several words within the text that illustrate the concept being taught (e.g., words that have the same beginning sounds, words with the same inflectional endings, or words that rhyme).

FIGURE 4. Sample Words We Have Analyzed

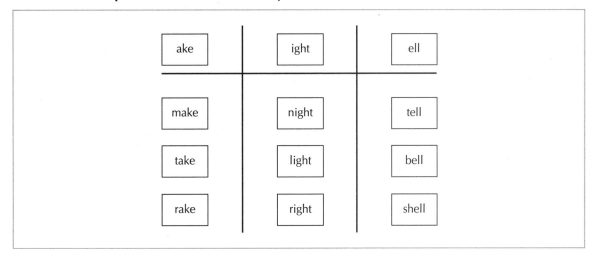

ake	ight	ell
make	night	tell
take	light	bell
rake	right	shell

3. Have students chant the text with a partner, in small groups, or with the whole group.

4. Challenge the students to examine the highlighted words and determine how the words are alike. Suggested teacher talk might be, "What features of the words are alike?"

5. Have students sort the words according to a variety of categories (e.g., beginning sounds, vowel patterns, syllable stress or syllable structure, and roots and stems) and record their findings on a class chart entitled "Words We Have Analyzed." Suggested teacher talk could be, "What pattern do these words have?" See Figure 4 for an example.

6. Have students discuss the characteristics of each of the words they sorted. Suggested teacher talk could be, "What characteristics are similar among these words?"

Cool Rules

Phonics: Analyzing

Purpose: To determine what "rule" or generalization, if any, certain words follow.
Level: Transitional
ELL Technique: Yes
Multiple Intelligences: Visual/spatial
Materials: Texts, notebooks

Procedure:

1. Select words from the text you are reading according to a specific rule or generalization (e.g., i before e except after c or sounded like a as in *neighbor* or *weigh*).

2. Have students analyze all words and determine what rule, if any, the words best represent. Suggested teacher talk might be, "What rule or generalization do you see in these words?"

3. Ask students to search for other words in their text that follow the rule they have identified.
4. Have the students write their findings in their notebooks on a page entitled "Cool Rules."
5. After recording their findings, ask students to work with a partner and share how the rule is shown in each word they chose. Although strategic readers do not necessarily consult rules when reading, knowing the rules can help them to analyze words and to compare an unknown word to known words with similarities. Suggested teacher talk could be, "How does studying the word help you?"

Phonics Strategy: Contextualizing

In contextualizing, students use letter–sound correspondences and integrate this association with context clues to form a word. Context clues are hints within the text that help students decode unknown words. Phonetic contextualizing is a strategy that helps students assume responsibility for applying several cueing systems. Acquiring this strategy empowers students with another way to identify unfamiliar words they encounter as they engage in ongoing reading and writing. Students use whole, meaningful text (semantic cues), an awareness of letter–sound association (graphophonic cues), and their understanding of the English language (syntactic cues) to support contextual reading.

> [Students' understanding of] the context in which a word occurs can help to emphasize or boost the activation of contextually relevant components of the word's meaning, to select alternative interpretations of ambiguous words, and even to create a meaning for the word where there otherwise might be none. (Adams, 1990, p. 175)

The teacher may employ the whole-part-whole approach of teaching "with, through, and about whole written texts," breaking a section of the text into a specific part and then embedding the part "within the context of meaningful reading and writing" (Strickland, 1998, p. 43). This embedded approach, identified in the NRP report (NICHD, 2000, p. 2–89), allows students an opportunity to apply the phonic contextualizing strategy to solve unknown words encountered in text.

Appropriate literature that best supports the application of the contextualizing strategy has a variety of words that are supported by surrounding words. *There Was an Old Lady Who Swallowed a Fly* (Taback, 1997) and *To Market, To Market* (Miranda, 1997) are two examples of appropriate literature; however, any piece of literature that has context surrounding a highlighted word to help students decode the word would be appropriate for use with these techniques.

Teacher Talk: Statements, Questions, and Prompts for Contextualizing

Following is a list of suggested teacher talk that encourages readers to think strategically as they contextualize. Try using some of these statements, questions, and prompts with your students as you work through the techniques in the following section.

- What happens when you read with blinders?

- What will make sense here and match the beginning letter of this covered word?

- How does using your peripheral vision help you?

- After seeing the onset, what word would make sense and visually match the part shown?

- Try to use the letter–sound clues to help you figure out the unknown words.

- What questions did you ask yourself that helped you to figure out the unknown word?

- How do the words around the unknown word help you?

- What words were easy for you to predict? Why?

- How can you predict words?

Techniques for Contextualizing

Blinders

Purpose: To recognize the use of peripheral vision when attempting unknown words.

Level: Emergent

ELL Technique: Yes

Multiple Intelligences: Visual/spatial, bodily/kinesthetic

Materials: Books

Procedure:

1. Have students hold a book on each side of their faces to block their peripheral vision, and have them attempt to walk around the room without bumping into one another. They will find that it is almost impossible to walk around without running into something. Suggested teacher talk could be, "How does using your peripheral vision help you?"

2. Next, have students remove the books and walk around the room again.

3. Discuss with the class how this analogy is similar to reading—that is, students only look at one word at a time to figure out unknown words. Point out that they have "blinders" on when they are only attending to a particular word. Tell them that when they take in all the surrounding words (i.e., use their peripheral vision), they are able to use them to support the strategy of contextualizing. Suggested teacher talk might be, "What happens when you read with blinders?"

Predict/Preview/Polish/Produce

Phonics:
Contextualizing

Purpose: To predict words that would make sense in the text using the surrounding words.
Level: Emergent
ELL Technique: Yes
Multiple Intelligences: Visual/spatial, verbal/linguistic, intrapersonal
Materials: Text, sticky notes or highlighting tape, dry-erase boards (optional), overhead projector (optional)

Procedure:

1. Read a section from the text and omit words by covering them with a sticky note or highlighting tape, saying the word *blank* for each omitted word.

2. Have students turn to a partner and predict what they think are the omitted words. The students also can write their predictions on dry-erase boards, or the teacher may chart some students' predictions on the overhead. Have students discuss with their partners why they chose their predicted words.

3. Preview the first letter of the omitted word by pulling back the sticky note or tape to expose only the first letter. Suggested teacher talk might be, "What would make sense here and match the beginning letter of this covered word?" Have students polish their predictions by checking their previous predictions for the omitted word with the preview you have just given them. Suggested teacher talk could be, "After seeing the onset, what word would best make sense and visually match the part shown?"

4. Reveal the other letters to produce the omitted word.

Word Detectives

Phonics:
Contextualizing

Purpose: To use context clues to figure out unknown words.
Level: Transitional
ELL Technique: Yes
Multiple Intelligences: Visual/spatial, interpersonal, intrapersonal
Materials: Texts, highlighting tape, Word Detectives reproducible badge (see Appendix A)

Procedure:

1. While reading a text selection, have students use highlighting tape to mark words that are unknown to them.

2. After reading, ask students to return to the highlighted words and become "word detectives." Have students use the detective badge to support their strategic word solving. Each point of the star has one instruction. Suggested teacher talk might be, "What questions did you ask yourself that helped you to figure out the unknown word? How do the words around the unknown word help you?"

3. To report their findings, have students meet with the "sheriff" (a designated word-solving helper). The sheriff can give the students feedback and support as needed.

Phonics Strategy: Patterning

Proficient strategic readers use patterning as a strategy to identify unknown words. With this strategy, the reader recognizes parts of the unknown word and compares these with a similar pattern from a known word. Parts can be the beginning letter(s) that precedes the vowel (onset) and the rhyming pattern that follows the onset (rime). "[S]ets of words with matching rimes, such as *bell, tell, sell* are nothing more or less than phonograms or word families" (Adams, 1990, p. 139). In fact, Wylie and Durell (1970) point out that nearly 500 words can be derived from only 37 rimes. Readers can decode and encode these words by dividing them between the onset and rime and then blending these two parts together (e.g., /b/-/ike/ blended together is *bike*). In order to use this patterning strategy, the reader may need to apply his or her prior knowledge of a part of the word (e.g., the /ike/ rime from the word *Mike* can help identify *bike*).

The patterning strategy corresponds with the analogy approach. In this approach, students access parts of the word they already know to figure out unfamiliar words (NICHD, 2000). Students use their prior knowledge to seek the pattern in an unknown word to generate pronunciation to form the new word. According to Cunningham, our brain is a pattern detector, and we should give it every opportunity to investigate and organize patterns (2000). Working with patterns can reinforce letter–sound combinations and students' ability to merge these combinations together to read words accurately. The techniques presented in this section help students acquire the patterning strategy.

Appropriate literature that best supports the application of the patterning strategy has a variety of words that share common patterns. *The Napping House* (Wood, 1984) and *Barn Dance* (Martin & Archambault, 1988) are two examples of appropriate literature; however, any piece of literature that has words for which students can use onset and rime or prior knowledge to decode would be appropriate for use with these techniques.

Teacher Talk: Statements, Questions, and Prompts for Patterning

Following is a list of suggested teacher talk that encourages readers to think strategically as they examine patterns. Try using some of these statements, questions, and prompts with your students as you work through the techniques in the following section.

- How are these words similar or different in their vowel pattern?
- Why did you classify these words together?
- How are these words similar?

- When you hop out a word, what are you doing to the word? (For use with Onset and Rimes technique)
- What pattern do you find in these words?
- If you take the first letter away and add this beginning sound, what new word would you have?
- How do you know that this is a pattern?
- Do you think it might be that word?
- Does this word look like any other words you know?
- What parts are similar?
- Is there another word that you know that has that same "chunk" in it? How does knowing that word help you with this word?
- Try to find words that have this phonogram somewhere in the word.
- What vowel pattern is in the word?
- How does this word fit the pattern in the other words?
- If this is ____ (point and say the word), what word might this be? Why?

Techniques for Patterning

Pattern Stories/Rounding Up Rhymes

Purpose: To identify the rhyme pattern in words.
Level: Emergent
ELL Technique: Yes
Multiple Intelligences: Visual/spatial, verbal/linguistic
Materials: Text, Wikki Sticks or pipe cleaners, index cards, chart or overhead projector, Big Book (optional)

Procedure:
1. Select a rhyme, jingle, or other text with a predictable pattern.
2. Discuss the title, cover, and illustrations in the selected text.
3. Read and discuss the text, and then return to a section from the text that highlights the pattern. Suggested teacher talk could be, "How are these words similar or different with their vowel pattern?"
4. Allow all students to view this section of the text on a chart or overhead projector, or using a Big Book. Read the first part of the selected section again, and have the students identify the rhyming words.
5. "Round up" these words and record them on index cards. Use Wikki sticks or pipe cleaners to create a circle around the words within the text.

6. Continue to read until there are six or seven sets of rhyming words. Write the words on index cards.

7. Pass out the cards, reread the text, and have student volunteers hold up a rhyme card when they hear the corresponding rhyme.

8. Identify the patterns within the words on the cards, and discuss what pattern these word cards have in common. Note any words that have spelling patterns different from the main pattern being discussed. Suggested teacher talk might be, "Why did you classify these word cards together?"

9. Place several of the word cards that have the same spelling pattern together, and have students underline the letters that represent the pattern.

Sources: Adapted from Bear et al. (2000); Cunningham (2000)

Onset and Rimes

Phonics:
Patterning

Purpose: To recognize patterns within words and to form new words with similar patterns. (Note: This technique has four different methods.)

Level: Emergent–Early

ELL Technique: Yes

Multiple Intelligences: Verbal/linguistic, bodily/kinesthetic, interpersonal

Materials (Depending on Method Chosen): Text, markers, Hula-Hoops or large construction paper, Onset and Rimes reproducible (see Appendix A), sentence strips, chart, notebooks, index cards

Whole-Part-Whole Method Procedure:

1. After reading a sentence from a selected text, present students with a word from the text. Read the word to the students, noting the particular rime sound you are studying.

2. Use two different-colored markers (one color for the onset and the other color for the rime) to highlight the word for all the students to see; record the word on a chart.

3. Have students generate other words they can make by changing the onset but keeping the rime. Record their newly formed words underneath the highlighted word. Suggested teacher talk might be, "How are these words similar?"

4. Return to the text, and have a student reread the sentence containing the highlighted word.

5. Ask students to record the original word and the newly generated list of words in a notebook, which will become their "Rime Time" journal of words.

Part-to-Whole Method Procedure:

1. Write some onsets and rimes on index cards, and put them in two stacks at the front of the room. You can use the Onset and Rimes reproducible for a list of rimes to help you get started. Lay out three Hula-Hoops or three large pieces of construction paper on the floor.

2. Have students take turns stepping up to the "Rime Time" area and selecting one onset card and one rime card from the stacks.

3. Ask students to hop into the first Hula-Hoop or onto the paper and pronounce the onset. Then, have students hop into the next Hula-Hoop or piece of paper and say the rime.

4. Finally, have students hop into the third Hula-Hoop or onto the third piece of paper and pronounce the blended word. Continue this process, with several students selecting onsets and rimes to "hop out." Suggested teacher talk could be, "When you hop out the word, what are you doing to the word?

Whole-to-Part Method Procedure:

1. Present students with a list of several sets of words that have the same rime but different onsets.

2. Ask students to examine the words in small groups and discuss how the words are the same and how they are different.

3. Have students write down the words, underlining the onsets and circling the rimes in each set. Then, have students create other words that would match the rime sets and add them to their lists. Suggested teacher talk could be, "What pattern do you find in these words?"

Cloze Procedure:

1. Select a phonogram or rime (e.g., *-ab*), and list several words on index cards that are formed using this phonogram (e.g., *lab, grab, cabin, crab*).

2. Record sentences on sentence strips that use the words in context, omitting the phonogram word from each sentence.

3. Have students read the sentences and determine which word card would complete each sentence.

4. Discuss how changing the onset completely changes the meaning of a word. Suggested teacher talk could be, "If you take the first letter away and add this beginning sound, what new word would you have now?"

Pattern Sort

Purpose: To sort words according to their common patterns.
Level: Early
ELL Technique: Yes
Multiple Intelligences: Visual/spatial, bodily/kinesthetic
Materials: Text; index cards, chart, board, or overhead projector

Procedure:

1. List a variety of words sharing common patterns in a place where all students can see them, such as on index cards, a chart, the board, or the overhead projector. Suggested teacher talk could be, "What vowel pattern do you notice in these words?"

2. Have students sort the words according to their patterns. For an open sort, have students sort the words into groups according to their own judgment, which makes students attend to the connections in the words. Then, students can give a title or label

to the patterns they noted from the words. With a closed sort, you select the categories the students will use. Suggested teacher talk might be, "How do you know that this is a pattern?"

Sources: Bear et al. (2000); Gillet and Kita (1979)

Rime Time Detective

Purpose: To identify rimes or phonograms in words.
Level: Early
Multiple Intelligences: Visual/spatial
Materials: Texts, phonograms/rimes, notebooks

Procedure:

1. Present a phonogram from the text you are reading for students to use for their "detective work" (e.g., -ack).
2. Ask students to search through a variety of texts for words that have the selected phonogram. Suggested teacher talk could be, "What patterns do you find in these words?"
3. Have students record their findings by writing down each word they find, the sentence in which it was found, and the name of the text in which the sentence was found. Each "detective" should save his or her findings in a notebook entitled Word Work, and the detectives should all share their work with one another.

Vowel Patterns

Purpose: To identify and examine vowel patterns, unlocking the alphabetic code, shifting vowel sounds, and reading with accuracy and fluency.
Level: Early–Transitional
Multiple Intelligences: Verbal/linguistic, musical/rhythmic
Materials: Texts, Vowel Patterns reproducible (see Appendix A)

Procedure:

1. Select a vowel pattern to highlight, and choose a text that supports that pattern.
2. Copy the Vowel Patterns reproducible and distribute to each student, or make it into a poster. Sing or say the jingle for the pattern you are using.
   - The closed vowel pattern is a word or syllable that contains only one vowel and is followed by one or more consonants (e.g., *cat*, *went*, *lunch*). The jingle that supports this pattern is, "One lonely vowel squished in the middle says its special sound just a little."

- The open vowel pattern has one vowel at the end of the word that says its letter name to represent the long vowel sound (e.g., *we*, *no*, *fly*). The open vowel pattern jingle is, If one vowel at the end is free, it pops way up and says its name to me.
- The silent *e* pattern demonstrates words or syllables that end in *e*. These words contain one consonant before the final *e* and one vowel before that consonant. The vowel sound says its name to represent the long vowel sound (e.g., *take*, *rope*, and *bike*). The jingle for this pattern is, When the *e* is at the end, the sound is gone; it makes the other vowel in the word say its name long.
- The two-vowel pattern refers to vowel digraphs and vowel diphthongs. Vowel digraphs are known as the "double vowel talkers"; they are syllables containing two adjacent vowels in which the first vowel is long (e.g., *play*, *tree*, *seat*). The vowel digraph jingle is, When two vowels go walking, the first one does the talking and says its name. Vowel diphthongs are syllables that contain two adjacent vowels in which the vowels say neither their long nor their short sounds but instead make a "whine" sound (e.g., *drew*, *book*, *boy*). The jingle for this pattern is, Sometimes when two vowels are together they make a whine sound, like when you fall down and want to be found—ow, aw, oy, and boo-hoo.
- The bossy *r* pattern is a word or syllable containing one vowel followed by the letter *r* (e.g., *star*, *girl*, *water*). The jingle for this pattern is, When the vowel is followed by the letter *r*, the vowel has to let the *r* be the star.
- The *c* + *-le* pattern, which occurs in two-syllable words, has a consonant immediately before an ending *-le* (e.g., *whistle*, *apple*, *purple*). The consonant before the *-le* is included in the syllable break with the *-le*. The *c* + *-le* jingle is, The *-le* grabs the consonant right before it, and it makes a clean syllable break to form the split.

3. Have students list words from the text that follow the vowel pattern. Suggested teacher talk could be, "How do you know that this is a pattern?" "What vowel pattern is within the word?"

Source: Cheyney and Cohen (1998)

Phonics Strategy: Spelling

Spelling as a strategy helps readers transform sounds into letters and letters into written word form. Proficient strategic readers use their phonics knowledge to enable them to read and write words (Cunningham & Allington, 1998). Reading and spelling are interdependent; students need many opportunities to explore sound and letter relationships in real text, manipulate letters to form words, search for patterns within words, and sometimes decode words sequentially. It is through reading that students visually store shapes of words so that, when writing, they can recall how the words looked when they were read. "When students decide that a word doesn't look right, they rewrite the word several different ways using their knowledge of spellings patterns" (Tompkins, 2000a, p. 114). Guiding students through using their visual memory of the word is one technique teachers use, rather than always asking students to sound out words when they are trying to spell a word (Moustafa, 1997).

When students view spelling strategically, they are able to evolve through the developmental stages and "attack" the thinking process that occurs as they gain word power. Gaining word power requires students to process spelling through word studies that enable them to explore; inspect; visualize; chunk; sound out; approximate; and use memory devices, patterns, and their multiple senses (i.e., ears, eyes, and hands). Strategic readers and writers think of spelling as a strategic tool on their quest to gain word power. Keeping the formal procedures and routines of word study as simple and predictable as possible allows students to become inventors, choreographers, and word explorers (Calkins, 2001).

Many studies have noted the various spelling stages and their characteristics (Freeman, 1995; Gentry, 1989; Gentry & Gillet, 1992; Graves, 1982; Pinnell & Fountas, 1998; Tompkins, 2000b; Vacca, Vacca, & Gove, 1995). Following are the stages and some suggested approaches to support the growth of the speller within each stage. Note that researchers and practitioners use multiple names when referring to the same spelling stages.

Prephonetic/Precommunicative/Emergent Stage: Students in this initial stage are not yet connecting letters with the words they are writing to convey a message; they are using scribbles and letter-like forms to represent a message. Their messages may be randomly arranged on the pages (e.g., right to left, top to bottom, left to right, or all over), may be in a nonsense form, and often cannot be read by others. Approaches to support students trying to develop at this stage of spelling are listening to pattern books, identifying words within the text, matching initial and final consonants with sounds, playing with the sounds in words, drawing pictures and then writing about their drawing, dictating stories, and exploring directionality.

Semiphonetic/Early Phonetic/Early Letter Name/Alphabetic Stage: Students demonstrate the early signs of connecting letters and sounds in writing and reading. Their spelling includes single letters to represent words, sounds, and syllables. Students at this stage omit vowels most of the time. Approaches for this stage are using word walls for names, high-frequency words, and easy word patterns; language experiences (i.e., writing personal experiences with teacher support to connect written form with oral language); sorting words according to the initial or final consonant sounds; and changing the onsets of words to form a new word.

Phonetic/Early/Within Word Pattern Stage: Students in this stage spell words the way they hear them and, at times, by patterns they see from other words. Vowels, consonants, and some blends and digraphs may appear in their writing of words, but they may be inconsistent. This stage is important because it represents the beginning use of word segmentation in students' writing. Approaches that support phonetic spellers include using word walls; reading texts with reasonable picture support, appropriate level high-frequency words, and patterned words that can be decoded with ease; exploring long and short vowel sound relationships; using rhyming words; and incorporating phonemic awareness activities.

Structural/Syllables and Affixes/Transitional Stage: Students at this stage demonstrate the use of structural elements (e.g., syllables, inflectional endings, affixes) in their writing. They are consistent in using a vowel in every syllable and are beginning to use the morphemic relationships of words (e.g., happy, happier, happiest, unhappily, happiness, happily). Their spelling is moving from a dependence on phonology (sound) to relying more on visual representations and structures of words. Approaches for this stage are word studies on more complex spelling patterns and structural elements, use of a word wall, reading more complex text with less picture support, practicing solving multisyllabic and irregular technical words, and proofreading.

Conventional/Meaning/Derivational/Advanced/Correct/Fluent Stage: In this last stage, students are spelling the majority of the words correctly in their writing. Students are aware of and use a variety of rules and generalizations of the orthographic (written) system, and know how to use historical roots to derive meaning. Approaches that support this advanced speller are word study on root words and their meanings, examining vowel alterations in derivationally related pairs, and reading complex text with specialized content vocabulary and many multisyllabic words.

Appropriate literature that best supports the application of the spelling strategy has a variety of words in the text suitable for the students' specific stage of spelling. *The Random House Book of Poetry for Children* (Prelutsky, 1983) and *Rat-a-Tat, Pitter-Pat* (Benjamin, 1987) are two examples of appropriate literature; however, any piece of literature that has words that support a particular spelling pattern within the text would be appropriate for use with these techniques.

Teacher Talk: Statements, Questions, and Prompts for Spelling

Following is a list of suggested teacher talk that encourages readers to think strategically as they spell. Try using some of these statements, questions, and prompts with your students as you work through the techniques in the following section.

- What words can you make from these letters?
- What is the secret word that uses all of these letters?
- What are ways you can "think out" how to write the word?
- Try to visualize the word in your mind. Paint the word on the inside of your eyelids.
- Look at the word you wrote. Does the word look right? Why or why not?

- Visualize the word in your mind, and "take a picture" of it.
- How are these words alike?
- How does knowing how to spell _____ help you spell _____?
- How does the word wall help you?
- Check the word wall to see how _____ is spelled to help you spell _____.
- How many syllables are in the word? Does knowing this help you?
- Do you know any other words that sound almost the same?
- Are there any words within words?
- What categories would you sort your words into, based on the patterns you see within the words?
- Try to spell the word _____.
- What patterns do you see in these words?
- Try to change the pronunciation of the word to help you.
- Try to think about other "chunks" that are within the word to help you.
- Name the letters with your inside-your-mind voice.
- Do you remember seeing that word somewhere else? If so, where?

Techniques for Spelling

Brain Tricks

Purpose: To create associations to remember how to spell words. (Note: This technique has three different methods.)

Level: Early–Fluent

Multiple Intelligences: Visual/spatial, verbal/linguistics, bodily/kinesthetic

Materials: Brain Tricks reproducibles (see Appendix A)

Mnemonics Method Procedure:

1. Have students create associations to remember spellings of certain words. For example, to remember how to spell the word *friend*, say "I'll see my friend at the **end** of the week on **Fri**day." Suggested teacher talk might be, "What are some ways you try to 'think out' how to spell a word?"

Making Connections Method Procedure:

1. Copy and distribute the Brain Tricks: Making Connections reproducible. Have students write the words they are studying at the top of the form, in the puzzle pieces.
2. Ask students to take each word and record connections they can make about the word (e.g., rhymes with, starts like, goes with, and means).

3. Continue steps 1 and 2 for all chosen words.

4. Have students share and discuss the connections with a partner.

Visualization Method Procedure:

1. Copy and distribute the Brain Tricks: Visualize reproducible. Have students pretend they are taking a picture of a word. Suggested teacher talk could be, "Try to visualize the word in your mind and 'take a picture' of it."

2. Have students hold up their hands and "click" the word as if they are using a camera to take a picture of the word presented.

3. Ask students to close their eyes and try to see the word, putting a frame around the picture they took.

4. When the students open their eyes, have them write the word in a picture frame on the reproducible.

Source: Pinnell and Fountas (1998)

If I Can Spell

Purpose: To connect words according to their spelling patterns.
Level: Early
ELL Technique: Yes
Multiple Intelligences: Visual/spatial, interpersonal, intrapersonal
Materials: Text, If I Can Spell reproducible (see Appendix A)

Procedure:

1. Copy and distribute the If I Can Spell reproducible. Have students select four words that contain different spelling patterns and record them on the left side of the form. Suggested teacher talk might be, "How are these words alike?"

2. Ask students to search for three other words that have each of the spelling patterns chosen; have students write these to the right of each of the corresponding selected words. The spelling pattern may appear in the initial, medial, or ending parts of the new words recorded.

3. Have students share with a partner how these words connect. Suggested teacher talk could be, "How does knowing how to spell the word _____ help you spell _____?"

Source: Taberski (2000)

Making Words

Purpose: To manipulate letters to discover letter–sound relationships and look for patterns in words.
Level: Early (Adaptation for Transitional)
ELL Technique: Yes

Multiple Intelligences: Visual/spatial, logical/mathematical, intrapersonal

Materials: Words from text, index cards, pocket chart, resealable plastic bags, notebooks, Making Words reproducible (see Appendix A); film canisters, laminated construction paper, adhesive magnetic tape, small strips of paper, cookie sheet, tin can lid (all for Adaptation)

Procedure:

1. Decide on a specific word to "make." Students will use the letters in this word to make smaller words and then will ultimately make the chosen word. (See www.wordless.com for examples of words within words.) When selecting the word, be sure to consider the developmental stages of students with whom you are working.

2. Create a list of some of the words that can be made from the letters in the word.

3. Write all the words on index cards and order them from least amount of letters to most amount of letters. Write each letter on index cards to create a set of letter cards for the students, or copy and distribute the Making Words reproducible. Store cards in resealable plastic bags.

4. Display cards in a pocket chart, or attach magnetic strips to cards and display on cookie sheet.

5. Give students sets of letter cards they can use to spell the particular word. (Students will sometimes make 12 to 15 words from one group of letters.) Suggested teacher talk could be, "What words could you make from these letters?"

6. Determine what two letters can be used to make a word and direct students to use the two letters to make the word. Place these two letters side by side in the pocket chart or on the sheet. Use the newly formed word in a sentence.

7. Let students who incorrectly made the word fix their letters before you move on to the next step.

8. Give the next clue (e.g., change one letter, change both letters around, add a letter). Continue to make new words and move letters on the pocket chart or sheet, as needed.

9. Continue this process, making bigger words, until finally making the one word that uses all the letters presented.

10. In their notebooks, have students record the words they are making in order according to the length of the word and describe what changes they made to make each different word. Suggested teacher talk might be, "What is the secret word that uses all of these letters?"

11. When students make the final word, have them line up the words in the pocket chart in order by number of letters used. Have students use the pocket chart to check their spelling of the words they wrote in their notebook.

Adaptation:

- Set up a Word Work Center. (Note: The idea for this center was contributed by first-grade teacher Wendy Bond.) Laminate colored construction paper and place it on the adhesive side of a piece of magnetic tape. Write the letters needed for the "secret" word on the laminated paper. Cut each letter apart and place it inside an empty film canister. Place a piece of masking tape on the outside of the film canister, and on the masking tape, write down what letters are in the canister and give the canister a number. On the inside of the film canister's lid, write how many words the students can make out of the letters in the canister. The students can then select a word canister and use the letters inside to make words on a metal cookie sheet or tin can lid. Be sure to have students record all the words they make on a sheet of notebook paper.

- Give each student a small rectangular strip of paper. Have them write a specific word on the strip, leaving small spaces between the letters. Instruct the students to either cut or tear the paper between the letters of the word. This instantly will give students their own letter cards to manipulate.

Source: Cunningham and Hall (1994)

Look/Say/Cover/Write/Check

Purpose: To visualize and spell words.

Level: Transitional (Adaptation for Early)

ELL Technique: Yes

Multiple Intelligences: Verbal/linguistic, interpersonal

Materials: Text, words, notebook paper; overhead projector, index cards, folder, or chart; Look/Say/Cover/Write/Check bookmark (see Appendix A); 10 Ways to Help Know My Word reproducible (see Appendix A), salt, sand, flour, string, dough (all for Adaptation)

Procedure:

1. Choose some spelling words, and present the words to students on an overhead projector, a set of cards, a folder, or a chart.

2. Ask students to look at the first word to visualize the overall letter patterns within the word, and to see the shape of the word.

3. Next, have students turn to a partner and say the word. Point out that this is their time to "talk" the word: They can say each of the letters, sounds, patterns they notice, syllables, and so forth. Students can close their eyes and imagine the word in their mind, stretch the word to hear the sounds, and look for patterns.

4. When all the students have looked at the word and pronounced it to a partner, cover the word.

5. Have students write the word on notebook paper, naming each letter as they write it. Show the word again to allow students to check their written word. Suggested teacher talk could be, "Look at the word you wrote; does it look right?"
6. Repeat steps 1 to 5 as needed, focusing on one word at a time. Students can use the Look/Say/Cover/Write/Check bookmark to help them remember the process.

Adaptation: Place salt, sand, or flour on a tray and have students trace the words. Have students use string, play dough, or bread dough to form the words. Use the 10 Ways to Help Know My Word reproducible to spell new words. Suggested teacher talk might be, "Visualize the word in your mind, and paint the word on the inside of your eyelids."

Source: Pinnell and Fountas (1998)

Phonics Strategy: Recognizing

Students who apply the recognizing strategy are able to identify words quickly and automatically. The cognitive process allows for instant recognition of words in written form. Using text that is predictable and easy to memorize supports beginning readers in gaining word recognition abilities (Bear et al., 2000). The speed and accuracy with which a student is able to use this strategy determines the student's fluency and comprehension. "When students recognize words immediately, they find it easier to focus on the meaning of what is being read" (Bishop & Bishop, 1996, p. 53). The techniques in this section focus on supporting students in recognizing letters, sight words (words recognized and pronounced immediately), and high-frequency words (some of the most commonly used words in printed language, which are often irregular).

Appropriate literature that best supports the application of the recognizing strategy has a variety of words in the text suitable for word identification. *The Frog Alphabet Book* (Pallotta, 1990) and *Seven Blind Mice* (Young, 1992) are two examples of appropriate literature; however, any piece of literature that allows students to easily recognize letters, high-frequency words, and sight words within the text would be appropriate for use with these techniques.

Teacher Talk: Statements, Questions, and Prompts for Recognizing

Following is a list of suggested teacher talk that encourages readers to think strategically as they recognize words and letters. Try using some of these statements, questions, and prompts with your students as you work through the techniques in the following section.

- How many times have you used the high-frequency words in your writing this week?

- How does recognizing the words by sight help you when you are reading?

- How would you sort these letters?
- What pictures would you select to represent this letter? Why?
- How does using your five senses help you to recognize words?
- Why do we want to be able to recognize words?
- Does this word have a smaller word inside it to help you remember the word?
- Try to find this letter, word, or phrase around the room.
- How fast can you read this word?

Techniques for Recognizing

Letter Recognition

Phonics: Recognizing

Purpose: To recognize letters by matching, sorting, and creating letters.
Level: Emergent
ELL Technique: Yes
Multiple Intelligences: Visual/spatial, bodily/kinesthetic
Materials: Uppercase and lowercase letters, pictures relating to letters, art supplies

Procedure:

1. Letter Matching: Have students match uppercase letters with corresponding lowercase letters, or letter-to-letter match-up.
2. Letter Sorting: Ask students to classify letters according to various attributes. Suggested teacher talk could be, "How would you sort these letters?"
3. Letter Posters: Instruct students to make posters with pictures pertaining to a specific letter. Suggested teacher talk might be, "What pictures would you use to represent this letter? Why?"
4. Letter Art: Have students make a design with a specific letter, using a variety of materials.

High-Frequency Words

Phonics: Recognizing

Purpose: To recognize high-frequency words in text.
Level: Emergent
ELL Technique: Yes
Multiple Intelligences: Visual/spatial, interpersonal
Materials: Words from text, word walls, highlighters, highlighting tape, Wikki sticks or pipe cleaners, magnetic letters, chalkboard or dry-erase board and markers

Procedure:

1. Word Walls: See under Spelling strategy, this chapter.
2. Highlighting: Have students use highlighters, highlighting tape, Wikki sticks, or any other medium to set the high-frequency word apart from other words in the text they are reading.
3. Make and Break: Have students use magnetic letters to make a word, scramble it up, and remake it.
4. Word Games: Have students use the words to play Bingo and Hangman.
5. Writing and Reading: Give students as much opportunity as possible to use these words in their writing and to recognize them in their reading. This will be valuable in students' learning instant recognition of the words. Suggested teacher talk could be, "How many times have you used your high-frequency words in your writing this week? How does recognizing the words by sight help you when you are reading?"

Irregular Words

Purpose: To recognize words instantly using the five senses.
Level: Emergent (Adaptation for Early–Fluent)
ELL Technique: Yes
Multiple Intelligences: Visual/spatial, bodily/kinesthetic
Materials: Words from text, index cards, word journal or bank, dough, oven, board or overhead projector, tape recorder, fly swatter, graph paper

Procedure:

1. Select appropriate irregular words (i.e., words that are not easily decoded) from classroom literature.
2. Introduce the words by displaying them in sentences.
3. Create a word mask by cutting a section out of the middle of a fly swatter. Place the word mask over the word to make it stand out from the other words in the sentence.
4. Have students use their sense of hearing to process the word into memory by turning to a partner and pronouncing the word aloud. Students may also tape record the new word to replay it in the future. Suggested teacher talk could be, "How does your sense of sight help you to recognize words?"
5. Have students visualize each word by pretending to "take a picture" of the word. The students then "develop" this picture by writing it into their word journal or word bank. (If desired, you can show students an actual object or a picture that corresponds to the word.)
6. Write the word on an index card, and cut the letters apart to allow the students to remake the word.

7. To use the sense of touch to process the word, have students work in teams to roll out dough and use it to form the letters for the word.

8. Bake the words (this uses the students' sense of smell), and then have the teams eat the letters as they spell out each word (this uses the students' sense of taste).

9. Have the students read books and other texts that contain the focus words. Suggested teacher talk might be, "Why do we want to be able to recognize words?"

Adaptation: Have students gradually add words to a word wall. Students can practice and study the displayed words. Students also can go on word searches where students search for words arranged in a grid. In addition, students can create their own word search using graph paper.

Source: Cunningham (2000)

Assessment

The purpose of assessing phonics is to determine students' ability to apply the relationship between sounds and letters to structure words. Educators evaluate the results of these assessments to determine the strengths and weaknesses of each individual student. The data from these assessments guide the teacher in creating an appropriate action plan (strategies, techniques, and teacher talk) to meet the diverse needs of the students.

When assessing phonics ability, teachers observe (at a developmentally appropriate level) whether students can do the following:

- Identify letter knowledge
- Synthesize letter sounds to form words
- Analyze letter sounds to examine word structure
- Utilize context to solve words
- Use prior knowledge to seek patterns in words
- Make connections with words
- Manipulate words
- Spell words
- Recognize sight words
- Recognize high-frequency words

Following are general lists of criteria from some sample phonics assessments. This is by no means an exhaustive list; it is only a starting point. Each assessment is designated S for screening, D for diagnostic, and/or PM for progress monitoring.

DICTATION TEST (Clay, 2002): S, PM

Record the sentence/Hearing and writing sounds in words: Tester reads a sentence, and student writes down the words in the sentence. Tester writes the words when the student is finished. Scores are given for each phoneme used.

EARLY READING DIAGNOSTIC ASSESSMENT (ERDA) (Smith, 2000): S, D

Letter recognition: Tester shows letters from the alphabet, and student says the name of each letter aloud.

Pseudoword decoding: Tester shows a list of nonsense words, and student says them aloud.

Rapid automatized naming (RAN): Tester shows letters, numbers, words, and/or word–number combinations, and student says the items aloud.

ELEMENTARY SPELLING INVENTORY (Bear et al., 2000): S, D

Spelling: Tester says a word, and student writes down all the sounds he or she hears. Tester scores and analyzes student's spelling qualitatively using a feature analysis.

FOX IN A BOX (Adams & Treadway, 2000): S, D, PM

Alphabet recognition: Tester shows an alphabet card, and student names the letters from left to right.

Alphabet writing: Tester says letters, and student writes each letter in uppercase and lowercase forms.

Spelling: Tester reads a list of words, and student writes the words.

Decoding: Student receives a list of words and reads the words from the word list using a window card.

THE NAMES TEST: A QUICK ASSESSMENT OF DECODING ABILITY (Cunningham, 1990): S

Decoding: Student reads aloud a list of names. Tester records and analyzes how the student pronounces each name.

TEXAS PRIMARY READING INVENTORY (TPRI) (Center for Academic and Reading Skills, 1998): S, D, PM

Graphophonic knowledge: Tester shows some upper- and lowercase letters; student names each letter and then says its sound. Student is given some magnetic letters and asked to make words the tester says.

Word reading: Tester shows one word at a time, and student reads each word aloud.

Phonics instruction helps students to apply their knowledge of the alphabetic system. The findings of the NRP report indicate that "it is important to emphasize that systematic phonics instruction should be integrated with other reading instruction to create a balanced reading program" (NICHD, 2000, p. 2-136). The strategies, techniques, and teacher talk presented in this chapter support teachers in maximizing their students' potential in becoming strategic readers and creating a comprehensive literacy classroom. In the craft of teaching reading, teachers use these strategies, techniques, and teacher talk as artistic tools to add dimension to the strategic readers they are helping to create.

Fluency

Fluency represents a level of expertise in combining appropriate phrasing and intonation while reading words automatically. The NRP report defines fluency as "the ability to read a text quickly, accurately, and with proper expression" (NICHD, 2000, p. 3-1). However, fluency is far more complex than attending to word recognition skills. Readers also demonstrate proficiency through fluency skills such as reading accuracy and reading at an appropriate rate. These fluency expectations can serve as outcome measures for reading proficiency as well as for acquisition of reading skills (Torgesen, Rashotte, & Alexander, 2001). The ability to read efficiently brings self-assurance to a reader. Fluent readers are confident readers. When readers are using all their efforts to decode unknown words within the text, they begin to lose the meaning of what they are reading. Their confidence as readers diminishes with every moment that passes as they try to understand the intricate process that their brain is seeking to navigate. "Becoming a fluent reader has as much to do with constructing meaning as it has to do with attending to words on a page" (Forbes & Briggs, 2003, p. 3).

This chapter features strategies students need to develop independence as readers. Having a repertoire of fluency tools readily available allows "the maximum amount of cognitive energy [to] be directed to the all-important task of making sense of the text" (Rasinski, 2003, p. 26). Reading with fluency supports the application of phonemic awareness, phonics, vocabulary, and comprehension. The combination of these other four reading components, fused with fluency, enhances a reader's ability to bring meaning to reading. The National Assessment of Educational Programs (NAEP) addressed fluency in a study (Pinnell et al., 1995) that reported that students who performed poorly on fluency measures also tended to have low comprehension scores. Fluency strategies are essential to comprehension and serve as a proxy for reading proficiency (Fuchs, Fuchs, Hosp, & Jenkins, 2001).

The strategies and techniques in this chapter include the following:

- Phrasing: Eye–Voice Span, Pausing With Punctuation, Phrase Strips, and Eye 2 Eye

- Assisted Reading: Shared Book Experience, Choral Readers, Neurological Impress Method, Read-Alongs, and Preview/Pause/Prompt/Praise/Participate

- Rereading: Pattern Support, Listen to Me, Tape/Check/Chart, Video Reading, and Why Reread?

- Expressing: Express Yourself, Punctuation Police, Readers Theatre, Totally Tonality, and Interpretation/Character Analysis
- Pacing: Commercial Programs, Beam Reading, Tempo Time, Time/Tape/Check/ Chart, and Closed-Captioned Television
- Wide Reading: Book Baskets/Browsing Boxes, Selecting "Just Right" Books, and Book Clubs
- Accuracy: Use the techniques from chapters 2 and 3, especially the recognizing and analyzing techniques from chapter 3, to promote accuracy.

Table 10 aligns the instructional techniques in this chapter with the appropriate developmental levels from chapter 1. To be effective, the strategies and techniques presented in this chapter should allow ample time for teacher modeling and student application, long before independent application is expected. Teachers should select and model reading aloud of appropriate literature to apply the techniques in a meaningful

TABLE 10. Fluency Techniques

	Emergent	Early	Transitional	Fluent
Before Reading	Book Baskets/ Browsing Boxes (WR)	May include all Emergent techniques Express Yourself (E) Eye–Voice Span (Ph) Preview/Pause/Prompt/ Praise/Participate (AR) Selecting "Just Right" Books (WR)	May include all Emergent and Early techniques Book Clubs (WR) Phrase Strips (Ph) Preview/Pause/Prompt/ Praise/Participate (AR) Totally Tonality (E)	May include all Emergent, Early, and Transitional techniques Preview/Pause/Prompt/ Praise/Participate (AR)
During Reading	Choral Readers (AR) Pattern Support (R) Shared Book Experience (AR)	Beam Reading (P) Choral Readers (AR) Listen to Me (R) Neurological Impress Method (AR) Pattern Support* (R) Punctuation Police (E) Read-Alongs (AR) Tempo Time (P)	Choral Readers (AR) Pausing With Punctuation (Ph) Readers Theatre (E) Tape/Check/Chart (R) Time/Tape/Check/Chart (P) Video Reading (R)	Choral Readers (AR) Closed-Captioned Television (P) Eye 2 Eye (Ph) Interpretation/ Character Analysis (E)
After Reading		Listen to Me (R)	Tape/Check/Chart (R) Time/Tape/Check/Chart (P) Video Reading (R) Why Reread? (R)	

*Adaptation portion of the technique.
Note. The developmental levels are shown across the top of the table horizontally. Down the left side of the matrix are the suggested times when these techniques are most effective—before, during, and after reading. This matrix is a guide and is by no means an exhaustive list. (Ph) Phrasing; (AR) Assisted reading; (R) Rereading; (E) Expressing; (P) Pacing; (WR) Wide reading

manner, which supports authentic learning for strategic reading. By using this process, students are able to see first the whole text (i.e., appropriate literature), then see the parts systematically (i.e., strategies and techniques), and finally, apply the parts back to the whole (i.e., become metacognitively aware of strategies while reading appropriate literature). Utilizing quality literature and promoting language development throughout the techniques will help to enhance students' development of the strategies.

Fluency Strategy: Phrasing

Phrasing is the ability to read several words together before pausing, as opposed to word-by-word reading. Good strategic readers phrase words together to derive meaning rather than trying to use the meaning of each word independently. Reading word by word sounds choppy and it can stifle the overall meaning of the passage the student is reading.

When a reader "chunks" the text into syntactically meaningful phrases (e.g., by grammar), the reading rate and comprehension improve. "Studying grammar fosters fluency because grammar alerts the reader to natural phrases in a sentence" (Blevins, 2001, p. 18). The reader needs to have an understanding of noun phrases, verb phrases, and prepositional phrases. This understanding of grammar will support readers as they appropriately chunk text (Blevins, 2001).

The ability to connect important phrases into cohesive chunks is enhanced when the reader "learns that punctuation marks such as commas, semicolons, parentheses, and dashes signal the end of a phrase and requires a pause in reading" (Strickland et al., 2002, p. 135). Good strategic readers use this strategy of phrasing to make a conversational connection in their reading. The goal is to read phrases seamlessly, sounding as if the reader is holding a conversation. This permits the reading to flow, allowing the reader to concentrate on making sense of the reading.

Readers' perceptual spans dictate how much information they can take in about words in a single fixation of their eye movement (NICHD, 2000, p. 3-3). "There are well-known individual differences in eye movement measures as a function of reading skill: Fast readers make shorter fixations, longer saccades, the jump of the eye from one fixation to another, and fewer regressions than slow readers" (Rayner, 1998, p. 392). Readers need many opportunities to practice techniques that support their ability to make shorter fixations in order to strategically phrase appropriately.

Appropriate literature that best supports the application of the phrasing strategy has a variety of meaningful phrases throughout the text. *Fish Is Fish* (Lionni, 1970) and the poem "Furniture Bash" (Silverstein, 1996) are two examples of appropriate literature; however, any piece of literature that chunks words together so that you can derive meaning within the text would be appropriate for use with these techniques.

Teacher Talk: Statements, Questions, and Prompts for Phrasing

Following is a list of suggested teacher talk that encourages readers to think strategically as they employ phrasing skills. Try using some of these statements, questions, and prompts with your students as you work through the techniques in the following section.

- Where are your eyes looking next?
- Try to "push" your eyes forward ahead of your voice.
- Try to "capture" several words at a time with your eyes.
- How many words do you see at a time when you are reading?
- What do you do with your eyes when you read?
- Listen to me read these sentences…which sounded better to you and why?
- How does the punctuation help you when reading?
- How did grouping the words together sound?
- Why does grouping the words together help make sense out of what you are reading?
- What would happen if you paused after each word?
- Does the text make sense when you read just a word by itself? Why?
- What were some of the "chunks" you found?

Techniques for Phrasing

Eye–Voice Span

Purpose: To recognize the value of forward eye movements when reading.
Level: Early
Multiple Intelligences: Visual/spatial, verbal/linguistic
Materials: Texts, overhead projector, passage of text on transparency

Procedure:

1. With the class, begin to read aloud a story or passage placed on an overhead transparency.
2. Just before finishing reading a sentence or paragraph, turn off the overhead projector. Suggested teacher talk could be, "Where are your eyes looking to next?"
3. Have students demonstrate how they can still say the next few words from the passage right after the overhead is turned off.

4. Discuss why this happens (i.e., because of the distance students' eyes were ahead of their voices). Suggested teacher talk might be, "Try to 'push' your eyes forward ahead of your voice."

Source: Blevins (2001)

Pausing With Punctuation

Purpose: To use punctuation to support appropriate pausing for meaning.
Level: Transitional
ELL Technique: Yes
Multiple Intelligences: Visual/spatial, verbal/linguistic, interpersonal
Materials: Texts; sentences on chart paper, overhead projector, or sentence strips

Procedure:
1. Select several sentences from a passage to model how to read using punctuation. First show a sentence on chart paper, an overhead projector, or a sentence strip without punctuation to demonstrate not pausing. Suggested teacher talk could be, "Listen to someone read these sentences…. Which sounded better to you and why?"
2. Ask a volunteer to read aloud these sentences without pausing.
3. Have partners try to determine and mark where punctuation should go to encourage pausing. The pairs should make this determination according to their interpretation of the correct meaning of the text.
4. Have pairs share with the class where they think the punctuation should go.
5. Have students return to the text and compare their versions with where the punctuation marks actually are. Have them practice reading the text accordingly. Suggested teacher talk might be, "How does the punctuation help you when reading?"

Adaptation: Students may practice writing sentences in a variety of ways to demonstrate how punctuation may cause pausing in different parts of the text, which in turn can alter the meaning of the text.

Source: Strickland et al. (2002)

Phrase Strips

Purpose: To read more words together seamlessly before pausing.
Level: Transitional
ELL Technique: Yes
Multiple Intelligences: Visual/spatial, verbal/linguistic, interpersonal

Materials: Texts, sentence strips, Phrase Strips Choices (see Appendix A), pocket chart, pencil or highlighter

Procedure:

1. On sentence strips, list common phrases, and place them in a pocket chart. Use the Phrase Strips Choices to get started.
2. Have students take turns selecting a strip and reading the phrase. Students may need to read the strip aloud several times before it can be read seamlessly. Suggested teacher talk could be, "What would happen if I paused after each word? Does the text make sense when I read just a word by itself? Why or why not?"
3. Then, have students orally put the phrase into a complete sentence.
4. Record the student's sentence on a new sentence strip. If desired, laminate and place the sentence strips in a center to be used in independent practice.
5. Ask students to reread their sentences and to use a pencil to indicate appropriate places for pausing between phrases.
6. Have students share their sentence strips with a partner.

Adaptation: Mark phrase boundaries at each natural break in a text with highlighters or pencil slashes. Have individual students practice reading with the marked text, trying to read fluently to the end of each marked place before pausing. Suggested teacher talk could be, "How did grouping the words together sound?"

Eye 2 Eye

Purpose: To identify eye movements when reading.
Level: Fluent
Multiple Intelligences: Visual/spatial, verbal/linguistic, interpersonal
Materials: Texts, clipboards with sheets for tally marks, pencil

Procedure:

1. Ask students to each sit knee to knee with a partner. Have the first student read aloud 100 words from a passage while the partner observes the reader's eye movements. Suggested teacher talk could be, "Try to 'capture' several words at a time with your eyes."
2. On a clipboard, the observer should record a tally mark for each time the reader's eye "jumps."
3. Have the readers reread the passage two more times, trying to phrase more words together each time (do fewer "jumps" with the eye). The observers should record eye movements all three times.
4. Have observers discuss their observations with their readers. Suggested teacher talk might be, "What do you do with your eyes when you read?"
5. Have the partners switch roles and repeat the activity.

Fluency Strategy: Assisted Reading

Assisted reading is a strategy used to provide the reader with support while building fluency. By listening to good models of fluent reading, students learn how a reader's voice can help text make sense (Kuhn & Stahl, 2003). Many of the techniques used for assisted reading allow the teacher or modeler the opportunity to scaffold students' learning while they are gaining confidence as readers. Peers, parents, and teachers all can provide guidance and feedback on how fluent readers read and how they become aware of and correct their mistakes (Foorman & Mehta, 2002; Shanahan, 2002). Scaffolding while the student is performing is critical to the development of fluency (Rasinski, 1989). This "social reading" benefits the reader because he or she knows there is support when needed and the ability to engage in conversations about the text he or she is reading. "Classroom practices that encourage repeated oral reading with feedback and guidance lead to meaningful improvements in reading expertise for students—for good readers, as well as those who are experiencing difficulties" (NICHD, 2000, p. 3-3).

Appropriate literature that best supports the application of the assisted reading strategy has repetitive patterns, interesting characters, and dialogues. *Over in the Meadow* (Keats, 1992) and "The Gingerbread Man" from *Sing a Song of Popcorn: Every Child's Book of Poems* (Rowena & Bennett, 1988) are two examples of appropriate literature; however, any piece of literature that allows for students to repeat modeled fluent reading, preferably in short phrases, would be appropriate for use with these techniques.

Teacher Talk: Statements, Questions, and Prompts for Assisted Reading

Following is a list of suggested teacher talk that encourages readers to think strategically as they work on assisted reading. Try using some of these statements, questions, and prompts with your students as you work through the techniques in the following section.

- In what way does it help you to hear me read first?
- How does hearing my voice reading help you to read better?
- Listen to _____ read. Try to use the same expression and pace to carry on the story or section.
- How does reading along with the tape help you?
- Try to find one-to-one correspondences between oral words and written words.
- Let me know when you would like to be the lead reader.
- How was it helpful to have _____ beside you when you were reading?
- Respond in your journal to the book we just read.
- Tell your partner something you notice about yourself when you read.

- When you were pausing on a word, what were you thinking?

- Reread this part, using the pointer to guide your way.

- Try to read that again.

- Tell me what you think of my reading.

- How does rereading in your choral reader notebook help you?

- In what way is it easier for you to read a dictated story?

- Try to remember what you said in your story, and match your words to the print.

Techniques for Assisted Reading

Shared Book Experience

Fluency: Assisted Reading

Purpose: To develop fluency while reading in small-group settings, independently, or through choral reading, with assistance as needed.

Level: Emergent

ELL Technique: Yes

Multiple Intelligences: Visual/spatial, verbal/linguistic, interpersonal

Materials: Text, Big Books or overhead projector and text on transparencies, pointer (optional), journal (optional)

Procedure:

1. Display the text so all students can easily view it, perhaps using a Big Book or overhead transparencies. Discuss with students how to preview and make predictions about the text.

2. Read aloud the text, modeling the characteristics of a fluent strategic reader (i.e., pacing, expressing). Suggested teacher talk could be, "Reread this part using the pointer to guide your way."

3. After the reading, engage students in a discussion of the text, allowing them to respond to, and at times retell, what they are reading. Suggested teacher talk could be, "Respond in your journal to the book we just read."

Sources: Allington (2001); Eldredge, Reutzel, and Hollingworth (1996); Holdaway (1979)

Choral Readers

Fluency: Assisted Reading

Purpose: To practice oral reading in a risk-free setting.

Level: Emergent–Fluent

ELL Technique: Yes

Multiple Intelligences: Visual/spatial, verbal/linguistic, musical/rhythmic, interpersonal

Materials: Text; three-ring binders; songs, poems, charts, or excerpts from text

Procedure:

1. Give students a three-ring binder to use as their choral reader notebooks. At the beginning of each week, insert a text selection into the choral reader notebooks. These selections may be songs, poems, chants, or excerpts from texts that correspond with the topic or theme you are studying. You also can use these entries in the choral readers as the springboard for minilessons from all five areas of reading described in this book.

2. Have students listen as you, using all the strategies of a good strategic reader, model the selection.

3. After modeling the reading, echo read the selection with students. Have students reread the modeled segment, attempting to repeat the reading exactly as it was modeled. Choral reading should follow as the students gain confidence with the selection. Suggested teacher talk could be, "How was it helpful to have me beside you when you were reading?"

4. Guide the students in reading the selection together. Students should read aloud at the pace of the modeler, using all the appropriate expressions in order to bring the selection to life.

5. Daily, have students begin their choral reading time by rereading the previous selections together before beginning their assisted reading with the new selection. Suggested teacher talk could be, "How does rereading in your choral reader notebook help you?" These choral reader notebooks may periodically be sent home for the students to show their fluent reading skills to family members.

Adaptation: Have groups of students perform a choral reading of one of their favorite selections to an audience of others in the school. Students can alternate lines with different voice pitch, clapping words while reading, whispering the rhyme, and so forth.

Neurological Impress Method

Purpose: To gain confidence and imitate correct phrasing, pronunciation, and intonation.

Level: Early

ELL Technique: Yes

Multiple Intelligences: Visual/spatial, verbal/linguistic, interpersonal

Materials: Text

Fluency: Assisted Reading

Procedure:

1. Ask a student to sit slightly in front of you so that your mouth is close to the student's ear.

2. Read aloud a passage of text with the student. You should read a little louder and slightly ahead of the student. Suggested teacher talk could be, "How does hearing my voice help you read better?"

3. Track the words by smoothly running your forefinger under the words while reading.

4. Reread the passage several times together before going on to new sections of the text.

5. As the student gains confidence, lower your voice and have the student take the lead as the reader.

6. Gradually release the responsibility of tracking to the student.

7. Continue to speed up, challenging the student to keep the pace. Suggested teacher talk might be, "Listen to me read. Try to use the same expression and pace to carry on the story or section."

Source: Heckelman (1969)

Read-Alongs

Fluency: Assisted Reading

Purpose: To gain confidence by listening to modeled reading and by reading along.
Level: Early
ELL Technique: Yes
Multiple Intelligences: Visual/spatial, verbal/linguistic, interpersonal
Materials: Texts, audio books, tape or CD player

Procedure:

1. Make your own prerecorded book tapes or purchase audio books. Note: Predetermine whether the reading from the tape is too fast or too slow for your students.

2. Have students listen to, and follow along with, the tapes or CDs. Suggested teacher talk could be, "How does reading along with the tape help you?"

3. Encourage students to note one-to-one correspondences between spoken words on the tape and the printed text. Students can practice this technique at a learning center or at home. Suggested teacher talk could be, "Try to find one-to-one correspondences with oral words and written words."

Preview/Pause/Prompt/Praise/Participate

Fluency: Assisted Reading

Purpose: To gain confidence and fluency while reading aloud with guidance.
Level: Early–Transitional
ELL Technique: Yes
Multiple Intelligences: Verbal/linguistic, interpersonal
Materials: Texts

Procedure:

1. Have students work in pairs, with one partner acting as the modeling reader (tutor) and the other as the reader in need (tutee). Have pairs preview a story together by scanning the text.

2. Have the two readers begin reading the text aloud together. When the tutee feels able to continue reading without the support of the tutor, the tutee taps the text or taps the tutor. Suggested teacher talk could be, "Let me know when you would like to begin reading."

3. The tutee continues to read alone until he or she has difficulty with the text. The tutor pauses for three seconds, providing an opportunity for the tutee to self-correct, use word attack strategies, or employ any other effective strategy to independently read through the area of difficulty. The tutor provides prompting if the tutee needs assistance after the three-second pause. If the tutee is then able to decode the word or phrase, he or she may go back to the beginning of the sentence and reread the sentence correctly.

4. The tutor then praises the tutee for rereading with fluency.

5. Then—as an extension of Topping's and Ehly's work—have the partners participate in meaningful dialogue regarding the text they have read. Participating in conversation will help to solidify the meaning of the text that the students are reading. (See chapter 6 for strategies to enhance students' participation in discussions around a text.) Suggested teacher talk might be, "How was it helpful to have _____ beside you when you were reading?"

Source: Topping and Ehly (1998)

Fluency Strategy: Rereading

Rereading is a strategy used to develop rapid, fluent oral reading. This strategy is one of the most frequently recognized approaches to improving fluency (NICHD, 2000; Rashotte & Torgesen, 1985). When students repeat their reading, their amount of word recognition errors decreases, their reading speed increases, and their oral reading expression improves (Samuels, 2002).

An extensive opportunity for practice in pattern recognition is readily available through rereading text passages. When students acquire the rhythm within a predictable pattern book, they benefit from their desire to reread the text.

> Just as a traveler going down a winding road for the second or third time begins to notice specific houses along the way, children on their second and third trip through a text will begin to focus on specific words—committing them to memory. (Morris, 1992, p. 123)

Musicians, athletes, and actors also use this practice strategy to gain fluency; they rehearse the same aspect of their performance repeatedly until they gain independence and confidence. This type of commitment by students to improving the quality of their reading is vital.

Appropriate literature that best supports the application of the rereading strategy has text that is meaningful, is relatively short, possibly contains rhythm, and is enjoyable for the readers. *The Very Hungry Caterpillar* (Carle, 1983) and *Popcorn: Poems* (Stevenson, 1998) are examples of appropriate literature; however, any piece of literature that supports a repetitive, known cumulative sequence (i.e., events build upon one another) and rhythm or rhyme would be appropriate for use with these techniques.

Teacher Talk: Statements, Questions, and Prompts for Rereading

Following is a list of suggested teacher talk that encourages readers to think strategically as they employ rereading skills. Try using some of these statements, questions, and prompts with your students as you work through the techniques in the following section.

- How does knowing the pattern of a text help you?

- What text features are similar?

- What happens each time you read the text?

- Compare your first reading with your second or third reading.

- Try to reread to the point in the text where it stopped making sense to you.

- How does rereading help you make sense of the text?

- Why do readers sometimes need to reread?

- How did reading the text make you feel?

- Let's determine what caused you to need to reread the sentence or passage.

- When you reread the text, try to add expression and pick up your pace just a little.

Techniques for Rereading

Pattern Support

Purpose: To analyze the repetitive features of pattern books and increase fluency.
Level: Emergent (Adaptation for Early)
Multiple Intelligences: Visual/spatial, verbal/linguistic, musical/rhythmic
Materials: Texts, pattern books, materials for class-made pattern books (for Adaptation only)

Procedure:
1. Read a variety of predictable, pattern-oriented books with students. Suggested teacher talk could be, "How does knowing the pattern of the text help you?"
2. Ask students to reread these pattern books to capture the rhythm and to support their oral reading. Suggested teacher talk might be, "What text features are similar?"

Adaptation: You may choose to create your own class-made pattern books. Creating pattern books allows students to experience ownership over the text, giving them a sense of pride when they are rereading. One idea for a pattern book is "My Week." On the bottom half of the pages, write sentences that start with the days of the week and fill in the blanks with the students' schedule information: On Monday, we <u>have Art</u>; On Tuesday, we <u>have Music</u>; On Wednesday, we <u>have P.E.</u>; and so forth. Students may illustrate each page to support the text.

Have students practice with three "listening buddies" in class, and then send the generated pattern books home with a Listen to Me form attached to it (see the Listen to Me technique below). Place these class-made pattern books in a decorated basket or box for each student for further rereading enjoyment.

Listen to Me

Purpose: To interact as a listener and a reader, and to give and receive feedback.
Level: Early
ELL Technique: Yes
Multiple Intelligences: Visual/spatial, verbal/linguistic, interpersonal
Materials: Texts, Reading Bookmark (see Appendix A), Listen to Me form (see Appendix A)

Procedure:

1. Have students select books at their independent level to read aloud to others. They also may use books made in class (see Adaptation for Pattern Support, this page).

2. Have students practice reading aloud to several listening buddies in the classroom. These listening buddies can practice their active listening strategies by leaning in toward the reader, keeping their eyes on the reader, and waiting until the reader is finished before speaking. Students can use the Reading Bookmark as a reminder of the steps students can follow before, during, and after reading.

3. Have students use the Listen to Me form to score and give feedback on the reader's oral reading. Suggested teacher talk could be, "How was your reading according to the Listen to Me form?"

4. After a student has had several practice reads with a book, send the book home with the student to read to three others. Attach a Listen to Me form to the book. The other listeners should sign the form and provide positive feedback on the student's reading.

5. Place the books being used in the student's independent reading basket for him or her to return to during independent reading time. Suggested teacher talk might be, "What happens each time you read the text again?"

Tape/Check/Chart

Purpose: To self-assess using a visible marking process, and to chart progress.
Level: Transitional
Multiple Intelligences: Visual/spatial, verbal/linguistic
Materials: Texts, photocopy of text, three different-colored pens, blank audiotapes and tape player/recorder, stopwatch

Procedure:

1. Have students tape record their own readings and replay the tapes to check for mispronunciations.

2. As students listen to their first readings, ask them to mark any misreads they hear on a photocopy of the text.

3. Ask students to read the text aloud for a second time into the recorder. Have them listen to the second recording, and, with a different color of pen, have them mark the same photocopy of the text to show any mispronunciations of words read the second time. Suggested teacher talk could be, "What happens each time you read the text again?"

4. Have students record a third reading into the tape recorder and mark a third round of misreads on the same photocopy of the text, with a third different-colored pen.

5. Have students tally the different-colored pens' markings. Generally, with each reading, the errors will decrease. Suggested teacher talk might be, "Compare your first reading with your second or third reading. What do you notice?"

Adaptation: Use a stopwatch to time students as they read for one minute and then record the results. Time repeated readings and discuss the results with students.

Source: Allington (2001)

Video Reading

Purpose: To evaluate one's own reading.
Level: Transitional
Multiple Intelligences: Visual/spatial, verbal/linguistic
Materials: Texts, videotapes, video camera, TV/VCR

Procedure:

1. Videotape a student reading aloud a selection from the text.

2. Have the student watch the video and reflect on the reading. Suggested teacher talk could be, "Try to reread to the point in the text where it stopped making sense to you."

3. Ask the student to reread the text, without being videotaped, to practice correcting any errors that occurred on the taped reading. When the student is comfortable with the text, have him do a second reading of the same passage on videotape. Ask the student to share his video readings with family members or caregivers at home.

4. After the student watches his video with family members, have the student read the same passage to them.

Why Reread?

Purpose: To identify the benefits of rereading.
Level: Transitional
Multiple Intelligences: Visual/spatial, interpersonal
Materials: Texts, chart paper

Procedure:

1. On a piece of chart paper in view of all the students, write the question, How can rereading help your reading?

2. In groups, ask students to discuss and record their responses to the question. Suggested teacher talk could be, "How does rereading help you make sense of the text?"

3. Have each group share with the whole group some reasons why rereading is important (e.g., helps readers make sense out of what is being read, helps readers understand better, helps readers notice words that were skipped before, helps readers understand difficult words in context, helps readers read faster). Suggested teacher talk might be, "Why do readers sometimes need to go back and reread?"

4. Add rereading to a class chart of strategies good readers use.

Fluency Strategy: Expressing

Teachers need to incorporate reading with expression into the beginning stages of reading instruction. Thus, students will learn that through expressive reading the text comes to life and has meaning and purpose. Without expression, students' readings will be monotone, laborious, and incomprehensible. Applying this strategy enhances students' understanding that reading is a meaning-making process. "When teachers ask their students to read with expression, they imply that all it takes is putting your mind to it. In truth, if one is not automatic, it is almost impossible to read with expression" (Samuels & Farstup, 1992, pp. 166–183).

When students concentrate on prosodic functions and forms when reading, they can indicate syntax and attitudes and can add appropriate stresses, pitch, and tone where needed to give a conversational sound to their reading. This allows the reader to convey the text's mood and meaning. It is also important that students know the difference between just reading loudly when expressing themselves and actually reading with warm but firm voices (Dowhower, 1994).

Appropriate literature that best supports the application of the expressing strategy has a variety of words and phrases that allow for students to use their voices to bring the text to life. *Hey Little Ant* (Hoose & Hoose, 1998) and *A Reader's Theatre Treasury of Stories* (Braun & Braun, 2000) are examples of appropriate literature; however, any piece of literature that supports the prosodic functions would be appropriate for use with these techniques.

Teacher Talk: Statements, Questions, and Prompts for Expressing

Following is a list of suggested teacher talk that encourages readers to think strategically as they employ expressing skills. Try using some of these statements, questions, and prompts with your students as you work through the techniques in the following section.

- What expression do you think the reader was trying to share in his or her dramatic expression statement?

- How can you make your reading sound more exciting?

- What does a period (or other mark of punctuation) mean?

- What does your voice do when you read a sentence that ends with a question mark?

- Change your voice to sound like the character you are portraying.

- In your mind, do you hear different voices for the different characters?

- Did you use the proper tone to convey the meaning? Why or why not?

- How did the tone of your voice set the mood for your statement?

- What feeling do you think the author wanted the character to have in this part? How do you know what the author wanted?

- Which part did you want to listen to more? Why?

- What message can the volume of your voice send to the audience?

- How does the speed of your voice make your audience feel?

- What are some expressions you could use when reading?

- Did the story sound exciting? Why or why not?

- How would the character say that line?

- What can you change to convince _____ of _____?

- Try to make your reading sound as real as it can be.

- Does your reading sound like you are holding a conversation?

Express Yourself

Purpose: To use voice and body language as a form of expression.
Level: Early
Multiple Intelligences: Visual/spatial, verbal/linguistic, interpersonal
Materials: Texts, index cards, platform, microphone (optional)

Procedure:

1. Use index cards to write your own expression cards and statement cards: Expression cards should each include an emotion that students will be asked to use as they read (e.g., "surprise," "sadness," "wistful," "anger"). Statement cards should each include one simple statement, such as "Don't do that."

2. Have students take turns standing on a platform or stage (this can be a stool, sturdy wooden box, etc.) at the front of the room. If desired, the student "performing" on the stage can use a standing or hand-held microphone.

3. Have the performing student draw one expression card and one statement card.

4. Instruct the the rest of the class—the audience—to say together, "Express yourself!"

5. Have the student think about the card and then read the statement with the specified dramatic expression. For example, if the student draws an expression card that says, "surprise," and a statement card that says, "Don't do that," the student would say to the audience, "Don't do that!" in a very surprised voice. Suggested teacher talk could be, "What expression do you think the reader was trying to share in his or her dramatic expression statement?"

6. Have the audience respond with what kind of expression they think the student performed. Suggested teacher talk might be, "How can you make your reading sound more exciting?"

Punctuation Police

Purpose: To recognize the value of punctuation in oral reading.
Level: Early
ELL Technique: Yes
Multiple Intelligences: Visual/spatial, verbal/linguistic, interpersonal
Materials: Texts, sheriff or police badge, dry-erase board, Punctuation Police tickets (see Appendix A)

Procedure:

1. Choose one student to wear a badge and act as the "punctuation police." Have other students read from a text, while the "police" student follows along with another copy of the same text, listening carefully to the student reading aloud.

2. The student acting as the punctuation police should record on a dry-erase board if or when the reader runs through "punctuation signs" (e.g., fails to pause properly at punctuation marks). The police student should issue a Punctuation Police ticket if the reader makes a punctuation infraction. Suggested teacher talk could be, "What does a period (or other mark of punctuation) mean?"

3. Continue this technique with partners, encouraging students to try to keep a "clean record" for reading. Suggested teacher talk might be, "What does your voice do when you read a sentence that ends with a question mark?"

Readers Theatre

Purpose: To explore language use by orally reading scripts.

Level: Transitional

ELL Technique: Yes

Multiple Intelligences: Visual/spatial, verbal/linguistic, interpersonal

Materials: Texts, scripts, microphones (optional)

Procedure:

1. Begin by providing a dialogue-rich script for the students to use. Scripts can be derived from texts you are studying, may come already prepared, may be selected from a portion of a story, may be student generated, or may be stories you create with dialogue (Strickland et al., 2002). There are numerous websites available where you can download free scripts (e.g., www.readers-theatre.com). Your selections should contain interesting characters, appealing themes, and stimulating plots that enhance language.

2. In one large group or in small groups, have students read the original text and then the newly scripted version to help them compare and contrast the dramatization that they will need to perform the Readers Theatre. Students should have a clear understanding of the types of adjustments needed to transform a text into a play, for example, noting which characters are speaking and how they deliver their lines.

3. Discuss with students their understanding of the text and the importance of the use of language. Suggested teacher talk could be, "You will need to change your voice to sound like the character you are portraying."

4. Have each student select a character and practice reading that character's lines with expression. It is not necessary for students to memorize their parts; they will be holding the script and reading directly from the text when they perform. However, it is the student's responsibility to bring the character to life with prosodic features. This allows the student to participate rather than observe (Young & Vardell, 1993).

5. Allow students many opportunities to rehearse their parts before performing their play.

6. After several rereadings, have students perform a dramatized presentation, expressively reading their parts into a microphone in front of a live audience.

7. Following the performance, give feedback on how well the students portrayed the characters with their expressions. Suggested teacher talk could be, "In your mind, do you hear different voices for the different characters?"

Sources: Hoyt (1992); Shepard (1994); Sloyer (1982)

Totally Tonality

Fluency: Expressing

Purpose: To adjust tone of voice appropriately to correspond with phrases.
Level: Transitional
Multiple Intelligences: Visual/spatial, verbal/linguistic, interpersonal
Materials: Texts, chart, index cards

Procedure:

1. On a chart, write some words describing a variety of tones that readers can use to express an author's purpose (e.g., ironic, serious, sarcastic, humorous). Point out that the tone of voice a reader uses reflects the emotion the character is feeling and the mood of the text.

2. Discuss how tones of voice can completely change the meaning of a text. For example, if a character says, "You are so funny" in a sarcastic tone, then he or she means someone is not funny.

3. On index cards, write some phrases students can read and different tones of voice they can use. Separate the two types of cards, and have students take turns selecting a tone card and a phrase card to practice reading with the selected tone. Suggested teacher talk could be, "Did you use the proper tone to convey the meaning? Why or why not?"

4. After practicing reading with phrases, have students read sections from texts while using a chosen tone voice.

5. Discuss the reason students used a certain tone when reading aloud. Suggested teacher talk might be, "How did the tone of your voice set the mood for your statement?"

Interpretation/Character Analysis

Fluency: Expressing

Purpose: To interpret and portray the traits of character(s) in text.
Level: Fluent
Multiple Intelligences: Visual/spatial, verbal/linguistic, interpersonal
Materials: Texts

Procedure:

1. Ask students to read and reread a section of dialogue from a text, forming their own interpretations of how they should portray the characters' voices. Students should discuss their interpretations of the characters to ensure a correct analysis of the characters in context. This helps to keep meaning from being misconstrued.

2. Have students each perform the part of one of the characters, reading aloud with expression.

3. Discuss with students any new insights they gain from analyzing the characters' voices after the performance. Suggested teacher talk could be, "What feeling do you think the author wanted the character to have in this part? How do you know what the author wanted?"

Sources: Allington (2001); Stayter and Allington (1991)

Fluency Strategy: Pacing

Pacing is a strategy that develops through extensive exposure to reading. This strategy encompasses reading rate, which is the speed at which one reads, as well as reading flow. The simple fact that slow reading requires readers to invest considerably greater amounts of time in reading task than classmates who are reading at a rate appropriate for their grade level should be a major cause for concern for all teachers (Rasinski, 2000). However, reading too fast does not always constitute proficient strategic reading. Pacing permits a reader to be flexible when interacting with the text; the proficient reader is capable of slowing down and speeding up when necessary to construct meaning. Depending on the tasks, readers may need to alter their reading rate and focus on the flow of their reading.

Appropriate literature that best supports the application of the pacing strategy needs to be at the student's independent or instructional reading level. A student's independent reading level is the level at which he or she has an accuracy rate of 95% or better at word recognition; it is considered the "level at which a student can read a text without the teacher's assistance" (Blevins, 2001, p. 23). The instructional level is the level at which a student should be able to read the text with some assistance. (See Table 11 for a formula to figure out students' accuracy rates.) *The Day Jimmy's Boa Ate the Wash* (Noble, 1980) and *This Is the House That Jack Built* (Adams, 1990) are examples of appropriate literature (provided that these books happen to be at your students' independent or instructional reading level); however, any piece of literature that is within a student's independent or instructional levels would be appropriate for use with these techniques.

TABLE 11. Reading Levels and Accuracy Formula

Level	Error Rate
Independent	95–100%
Instructional	90–94%
Frustration	89% and below

To figure accuracy rate: $\frac{\text{\# words read} - \text{\# errors}}{\text{\# words read}}$ = word recognition rate

Teacher Talk: Statements, Questions, and Prompts for Pacing

Following is a list of suggested teacher talk that encourages readers to think strategically as they employ pacing skills. Try using some of these statements, questions, and prompts with your students as you work through the techniques in the following section.

- Try to keep up with the light to increase your rate. (For use with Beam Reading)
- Is it easy or difficult for you to keep up with the pace being modeled, that is, with the tempo? (For use with Tempo Time)
- What is happening as you hear the tempo in the background? (For use with Tempo Time)
- Tell how increasing your rate will help you read.
- How does hearing yourself read and tracking how long it takes you to read help you to pace better?
- Listen to me read these paragraphs. (Read very fast and then at a normal pace.) Which pace is more appropriate?
- How does the speed at which you are reading make a difference for you?
- Do you often have to reread a sentence? Why?
- Does the computer program help you pace yourself as a reader? Why or why not?

Techniques for Pacing

Commercial Programs

Purpose: To develop pacing skills using a computer program as a supplemental resource.
Level: Emergent–Fluent
Multiple Intelligences: Visual/spatial, verbal/linguistic
Materials: Texts, computer, computer-based program

Procedure:

1. Select an appropriate computer program (see list below). The programs listed are supplemental and may be used for immediate, intense intervention in several of the areas of reading noted in chapters 2 through 6.

2. Incorporate one of the following computer-based fluency programs into your comprehensive literacy-based classroom. Suggested teacher talk could be, "Does the computer program help you pace yourself as a reader? Why or why not? How does the speed to which you are reading make a difference for you?"

   - *Great Leaps* (Campbell & Mercer, 1995) is a tutorial program divided into three major areas: (1) phonics, which concentrates on developing and mastering essential sight–sound relationships and/or sound awareness skills; (2) sight phrasing, which supports students in mastering sight words while developing and improving focusing skills; and (3) reading fluency, which provides age-appropriate stories specifically designed to build reading fluency, reading motivation, and proper intonation.

   - *QuickReads* (Hiebert, 2002) is composed of high-interest nonfiction texts at the second- through fifth-grade levels. *QuickReads* develops automaticity by using text that is composed of 98% high-frequency and decodable words. The program combines leveled texts with speech recognition technology. The program provides instant feedback and corrects errors by prompting repeated pronunciation of unknown words.

   - *Read Naturally* (Hasbrouck, Ihnot, & Rogers, 1999) includes guided oral repeated reading and an assessment system for screening and progress monitoring. It also incorporates a phonics component that combines systematic and explicit phonics instruction with fluency skills. The program has books, tapes, and current research-based software to support the reader.

   - *REWARDS* (Reading Excellence Attack and Rate Developing Strategies; Archer, Gleason, & Vachon, 2000) is intended for intermediate to secondary students. It supports students in decoding and reading multisyllabic words in context, increasing reading accuracy and fluency, and improving comprehension. The first 12 lessons support the skills necessary to learn multisyllabic words (blending syllables and pronunciations of affixes and vowel combinations). The last seven lessons focus on helping readers utilize fast and accurate decoding to increase reading rate.

Beam Reading

Fluency: Pacing

Purpose: To pace reading by using a light.
Level: Early
ELL Technique: Yes
Multiple Intelligences: Visual/spatial, verbal/linguistic, interpersonal
Materials: Texts, chart or overhead projector, laser pen or flashlight

Procedure:

1. Display the text on a chart or overhead projector for all students to see. Use a laser pen or flashlight to shine a light on the words as the students read aloud.

2. Move the light along the words at a steady pace. Suggested teacher talk could be, "Try to keep up with the light to increase your reading rate."

3. Encourage students to follow along with the light as they read aloud. The rate at which you shine the light on the words should increase with each rereading of the text selected.

4. Have students practice this technique with partners, taking turns using the light and practicing keeping the pace of the light. Suggested teacher talk might be, "Is it easy or difficult for you to keep up with the pace being modeled?"

Tempo Time

Fluency: Pacing

Purpose: To maintain the reading pace with a predetermined rhythm while reading orally.
Level: Early
Multiple Intelligences: Visual/spatial, verbal/linguistic, musical/rhythmic
Materials: Texts (preferably poetry or pattern books), musical instruments

Procedure:

1. Use maracas or other musical instruments to beat out a tempo. The reader's ability should determine the tempo, and the tempo can increase as the reader improves. Suggested teacher talk could be, "What is happening as you hear the tempo in the background?"

2. Ask students to listen to the tempo that you provide and begin to read, trying to keep up with the tempo time. Suggested teacher talk might be, "Is it easy or difficult for you to keep up with the tempo?"

Time/Tape/Check/Chart

Fluency: Pacing

Purpose: To increase reading rate and evaluate progress.
Level: Transitional
Multiple Intelligences: Visual/spatial, verbal/linguistic
Materials: Texts, photocopies of text, stopwatch, tape recorder, graph paper

Procedure:

1. Have a student read aloud a text while you or a volunteer times the student with a stopwatch, measuring how long it takes the student to read the chosen text. Chart the time on graph paper. Suggested teacher talk could be, "Tell how increasing your rate will help your reading."

2. Have the student record the same reading on a tape recorder and time his or her reading.

3. The student should replay the recording while following along using a photocopied version of the text.

4. Chart the time for the second reading on graph paper. Suggested teacher talk might be, "How does hearing yourself read and tracking how long it takes you to read help you to pace better?"

5. Have the student mark miscues on the photocopy.

6. The student should compare reading times and continue the previous steps as needed.

Adaptation: Have students reflect on and self-assess the reading and the graphed results. Repeat the process two more times. Encourage the students with little signs of progress, which you should note on the graph after each of their repeated readings.

Source: Adapted from Allington (2001)

Closed-Captioned Television

Purpose: To increase reading pace.
Level: Fluent
Multiple Intelligences: Visual/spatial, verbal/linguistic
Materials: Texts, television with closed captioning

Procedure:

1. Choose the closed caption option on the television in the classroom, and have students practice reading the short portions of script on the television screen. Students will have to try to keep up with the pace of the script as it scrolls across the bottom of the screen. Suggested teacher talk could be, "Tell how increasing your rate will help you read. Is it easy or hard for you to keep up with the pace being modeled?"

Source: Koskinen, Wilson, and Jensema (1985)

Fluency Strategy: Wide Reading

Students need to understand that wide reading is imperative in order to build fluency. It is a powerful realization when students discover that the more they read and want to read, the more fluent they become as readers. Research by Nathan and Stanovich (1991) indicates that

> [if students are] to become fluent readers, they need to read a lot. Our job as educators is to see to it that children want to read, that they seek new knowledge via written word and derive satisfaction and joy from the reading process. (p. 79)

Providing the opportunities for students to read and to find enjoyment in their reading is the challenge for today's educators. The wide reading techniques will support students on their journey to becoming fluent readers.

Appropriate literature that best supports the application of the wide reading strategy is high interest, is in a variety of genres, and is at the independent or instructional levels of the students (refer to Table 11, page 97). *Ramona Quimby, Age 8* (Cleary, 1981) and *Buster's Dino Dilemma* (Brown, 1988) are examples of appropriate literature; however, any piece of literature that is within the student's independent or instructional level and that piques the student's interest would be appropriate for use with these techniques.

Teacher Talk: Statements, Questions, and Prompts for Wide Reading

Following is a list of suggested teacher talk that encourages readers to think strategically as they employ wide reading skills. Try using some of these statements, questions, and prompts with your students as you work through the techniques in the following section.

- How do you feel when you are reading a book that is at your level?
- Has your reading rate improved each time you read and reread books from your browsing box?
- How do you know if a book is just right for you?
- What are signs that a book is too easy or too difficult for you?
- Try to pick a book that interests you.
- How does being in a book club help your reading?
- Why is it important to independently read books at your appropriate level?
- How does your reading sound (in your head or aloud) when you are independently reading?

Techniques for Wide Reading

Book Baskets/Browsing Boxes

Purpose: To increase fluency.

Level: Emergent

ELL Technique: Yes

Multiple Intelligences: Visual/spatial, verbal/linguistic

Materials: Baskets and boxes, variety of leveled texts

Procedure:

1. Place multiple levels of books (fiction and nonfiction) and magazines into baskets or boxes. These may be books that were previously read during guided reading time.

2. Have students at different stages of development browse through the book selections to choose one book that is "just right" for them. Students should select books with which they are familiar and that are at their own independent reading level from book baskets. Teachers should discuss with students what books seem to be "just right" for them. Suggested teacher talk could be, "How do you feel when you are reading a book that is at your level?"

3. Have students place their selections into a browsing box (a box or plastic bin that holds each student's collection of independent-level reading books).

4. During independent reading time, have the students read and reread texts from their boxes. Reading these books ensures quality time spent on reading at the appropriate level of each reader. Suggested teacher talk might be, "Has your reading rate improved each time you've read and reread books from your browsing boxes?"

Source: Fountas and Pinnell (1996)

Selecting "Just Right" Books

Purpose: To identify and select books at students' independent reading level.
Level: Early
ELL Technique: Yes
Multiple Intelligences: Visual/spatial, verbal/linguistic
Materials: Variety of leveled texts, three chairs of different sizes, "Goldilocks and the Three Bears," chart paper or blank poster

Procedure:

1. Demonstrate how to choose a "just right" book, and discuss the value of independently reading a book that fits the reader. For example, have students read a page from a text and note each time they have difficulty with a word by raising a finger. If early in the reading students have up five fingers, they should stop reading because the text is not at the independent level.

2. Read aloud the story of "Goldilocks and the Three Bears." Line up three chairs: one too small, one too big, and one just right for the students. Select three books for the demonstration: one too easy, one too hard, and one just right for the students. Suggested teacher talk could be, "How do you know if a book is just right for you?"

3. After modeling how to select a book that is just the right match, have the class generate three posters or charts. The first chart should list what makes a text too easy (e.g., your reading rate is too fast, you know all the words, less energy spent decoding). The

second one should list the traits of a text that is too hard (e.g., your reading rate is too slow, you lose focus as you are reading, it's hard to understand or decode words). The third chart should show what type of book is just right (e.g., your reading rate is just right, you can read most of the words, you can get the meaning from the story).

4. Post the charts in the classroom library area as a reminder for students when selecting their independent reading materials. Suggested teacher talk could be, "What are the signs that the book is too easy or too difficult for you?"

Source: Adapted from Fountas and Pinnell (1999)

Book Clubs

Fluency: Wide Reading

Purpose: To determine a purpose for reading, and to develop fluency.
Level: Transitional
Multiple Intelligences: Visual/spatial, verbal/linguistic, interpersonal
Materials: A variety of texts (four to six copies of the same title)

Procedure:

1. Display a variety of book sets. Each book title should have at least four additional copies on display. Suggested teacher talk could be, "Try to pick a book that interests you for your book club selection."

2. Have students select a book that is at their independent reading level and is interesting to them, and sign them up to be in a book club. Each student will be in a book club with students who are reading the same selection.

3. Have the groups meet and plan how much reading they will do independently before they get together to share and discuss the book. Each week, the clubs should meet to share their ideas, feelings, questions, concerns, and general comments about what they read.

4. Continue the process with new book selections and new clubs being formed. Suggested teacher talk might be, "How does being in a book club help your reading?"

Fluency Strategy: Accuracy

Students who read fluently read with accuracy. The accuracy strategy focuses on being able to identify and apply the graphophonic cueing system (i.e., the relationship between letters and sounds) with ease and precision. In order for students to accurately read, they need to use the phonemic awareness and phonics strategies previously described (see chapters 2 and 3). Gaining independence at their developmental reading level in these two areas of reading will ensure a higher level of automaticity and accuracy as students read.

Research indicates that the brain devotes only a limited amount of attention to any given cognitive task (LaBerge & Samuels, 1974). The more attention a reader devotes to trying to decode an unknown word, the less time and energy he or she has to cognitively gather meaning from the text. Teachers need to assess students' accuracy by using oral reading inventories (e.g., running records, analytical reading inventories, informal reading inventories). (See Table 11, page 97, for a formula to help calculate a student's accuracy rate.) This type of assessment can be used to analyze what the student's specific needs are within the cueing system. It is important to note that this is only one strategy for helping students to read fluently.

McEwan (2002) explains that "students who make no errors but read very slowly have as little likelihood of comprehending what they read as students who read very quickly but guess at and misidentify many words" (p. 54). There must be a balance for the student to read with both fluency and comprehension. Accuracy is a vital link to reading with ease. However, teachers must keep in mind that reading is an art, with many facets that fuse together for a proficient reader to evolve.

The techniques found in chapters 2 and 3 are appropriate for building accuracy, especially the techniques for teaching sight word recognition (i.e., recognizing) and decoding (i.e., analyzing). The techniques for teaching the rereading strategy, found in this chapter, also are appropriate for promoting accuracy.

Assessment

The purpose of fluency assessment is to determine students' ability to combine appropriate phrasing and intonation while reading words automatically. Educators evaluate the results of these assessments to determine the strengths and weaknesses of each individual student. The data from these assessments guide the teacher in creating an appropriate action plan (strategies, techniques, and teacher talk) to meet the diverse needs of the students.

When assessing fluency, teachers should observe whether students can do the following:

- Recognize letters, clusters of letters, and words automatically (quickly and easily)
- Group words into appropriate clause or phrase units
- Read in an appropriately phrased manner
- Read long stretches of text while cross-checking for meaning, grammatical structure, and phonetic application
- Attend to punctuation and syntax
- Emphasize words to enhance expression (intonation and pitch)
- Convey the text's mood and meaning

- Adjust speed and amount of support needed to meet the demands of the text
- Reread to clarify or problem solve
- Read a wide variety of genres

Following are general lists of criteria from some sample phonemic awareness assessments. This is by no means an exhaustive list; it is only a starting point. Each assessment is designated S for screening, D for diagnostic, and/or PM for progress monitoring.

DEVELOPMENTAL READING ASSESSMENT (DRA) (Beaver, 2001): S, D, PM

Accuracy and rate: Student reads aloud, and his oral reading rate is timed using a formula given in the package. Tester records rate and scores phrasing, expression, and rate on a rubric scale.

FOX IN A BOX (Adams & Treadway, 2000): S, D, PM

Reading rate: Student reads for one minute, and tester marks errors.

GRAY ORAL READING TEST–IV (GORT-IV) (Wiederholt & Bryant, 2001): S, D, PM

Accuracy: Student reads aloud a passage while tester records errors.

Rate: Student is timed in seconds while reading aloud.

NAEP'S INTEGRATED READING PERFORMANCE RECORD: ORAL READING FLUENCY SCALE (Pinnell et al., 1995): S, D, PM

Phrasing, syntax, expressiveness, accuracy, and rate: Student reads a narrative text silently, answers three comprehension questions orally, then rereads a portion of the text to the tester.

ONE-MINUTE READING FLUENCY PROBE (Rasinski, 2003): S

Word recognition/accuracy: Student reads aloud for one minute; tester records errors and determines accuracy.

Fluency instruction extends beyond word recognition. The fluent reader recognizes words automatically and can now attend to comprehension. The strategies, techniques, and teacher talk presented in this chapter support teachers in maximizing their students' potential in becoming strategic readers. Fluency is yet another medium by which teachers can create their masterpieces.

Chapter 5

Vocabulary

The NRP report states, "reading vocabulary is crucial to the comprehension process of a skilled reader" (NICHD, 2000, p. 4-3). Vocabulary knowledge influences both comprehension and fluency (Flood, Jensen, Lapp, & Squire, 1991; Robb, 1997). Students need many opportunities for developing a rich vocabulary through listening, speaking, reading, and writing in an integrated manner. Vocabulary instruction should be an integral component in a daily literacy block. Integrating vocabulary instruction provides students with numerous opportunities to manipulate and learn new vocabulary words. Incorporating vocabulary instruction throughout the content areas will encourage students to make connections to new and already known information, discuss meanings of new words, and demonstrate and appropriately apply the new words, providing multiple reexposures to the words. Encouraging students to think strategically when learning new words is essential. In order for words "to be used and committed to long-term memory, they must be reinforced many times in meaningful ways" (Misulis, 1999, p. 1).

This chapter offers vocabulary strategies and techniques that enhance students' understanding of new words and concepts. These strategies include giving both definitional and contextual information about new words, performing cognitive operations when introducing words, and talking about new words constantly (McEwan, 2002). If students do not understand the meaning of the words they read, the reading process merely becomes meaningless decoding (Pinnell & Fountas, 1998). These strategies will help provide students with powerful, in-depth learning as they strive to become successful readers.

The strategies and techniques detailed in this chapter are as follows:

- Associating: Reflection Connection, Semantic Feature Analysis, and Similar Synonyms

- Contextualizing: Cloze Passages, Contextual Redefinition, What Do You Mean? and Context Complex Clues

- Categorizing: Picture and Word Sorts, Word Hunts, Alphaboxes, and List/Group/Label

- Visual Imaging: Charades, Museum Walk, Four Corners, and Graphic Cards

- Analyzing: Vocabulary Tree Notebook, Prefixes, and Root Words

- Word Awareness: Vocabulary Chart, Journal Circles, Speaking Out, Knowledge Rating, and Quick Writes

- Wide Reading: Read-Alouds, Author Study, Book Talks, Genre Study, and Vocabulary Clubs

- Referencing: Resource Buddies, Glossary Use, Dictionary Use, and Thesaurus Use

Table 12 matches the instructional techniques discussed in this chapter to the appropriate developmental levels from chapter 1 (emergent, early, transitional, and fluent). To be effective, the strategies and techniques presented in this chapter should allow ample time for teacher modeling and student application, long before independent application is

TABLE 12. Vocabulary Techniques

	Emergent	Early	Transitional	Fluent
Before Reading	Charades (V) Picture and Word Sorts (Ca) Read-Alouds (WR)	May include all Emergent techniques Graphic Cards (V) List/Group/Label (Ca) Read-Alouds* (WR) Semantic Feature Analysis* (W) Speaking Out (WA)	May include all Emergent and Early techniques Author Study (WR) Contextual Redefinition (Co) Knowledge Rating (WA) List/Group/Label* (Ca) What Do You Mean? (Co)	May include all Emergent, Early, and Transitional techniques Context Complex Clues (Co) Genre Study (WR) Reflection Connection* (W) Vocabulary Clubs (WR)
During Reading	Read-Alouds (WR)	Cloze Passages (Co)	Author Study (WR)	Genre Study (WR)
After Reading	Museum Walk (V) Read-Alouds (WR) Resource Buddies (R) Vocabulary Chart (WA) Word Hunts (Ca)	Alphaboxes (Ca) Four Corners (V) Glossary Use (R) Journal Circles (WA) Museum Walk* (V) Prefixes* (A) Similar Synonyms* (W) Vocabulary Tree Notebook (A)	Author Study (WR) Book Talks (WR) Contextual Redefinition (Co) Dictionary Use (R) Prefixes (A) Quick Writes (WA) Reflection Connection (W) Semantic Feature Analysis (W) Similar Synonyms (W) Thesaurus Use (R)	Root Words (A)

*Adaptation portion of the technique.
Note. The developmental levels are shown across the top of the table horizontally. Down the left side of the matrix are the suggested times when these techniques are most effective—before, during, and after reading. This matrix is a guide and is by no means an exhaustive list. (W) Word associating; (Co) Contextualizing; (Ca) Categorizing; (V) Visual imaging; (A) Analyzing; (WA) Word awareness, (WR) Wide reading; (R) Referencing

expected. Teachers should select and model reading aloud of appropriate literature to apply the techniques in a meaningful manner, which supports authentic learning for strategic reading. By using this process, students are able to see first the whole text (i.e., appropriate literature), then see the parts systematically (i.e., strategies and techniques), and finally, apply the parts back to the whole (i.e., become metacognitively aware of strategies while reading appropriate literature). Utilizing quality literature and promoting language development throughout the techniques will help to enhance students' development of the strategies.

Vocabulary Strategy: Word Associating

The ability to associate words is an important strategy. Proficient readers develop flexibility in using and manipulating words as they apply various techniques to acquire word associations. Understanding how words connect enables the proficient reader to analyze and synthesize information, determining the ways in which words relate to one another.

Word associating allows readers to use alternative words to construct meaning from the text. To link prior experiences with new information, one may construct many kinds of word relationships. When readers use analogies, they draw inferences, and an opportunity for critical thinking occurs. This process of attaching a new concept to an existing one allows the reader to connect and bring meaning to the text.

Appropriate literature that best supports the application of the word associating strategy has key words that provide reinforcement of meaning. *Dogs* (O'Neill, 1999) and *Owen* (Henkes, 1993) are examples of appropriate literature; however, any piece of literature that has words that allow readers to draw inferences and make connections to meaning from the vocabulary would be appropriate for use with these techniques.

Teacher Talk: Statements, Questions, and Prompts for Word Associating

Following is a list of suggested teacher talk that encourages readers to think strategically as they employ word associating skills. Try using some of these statements, questions, and prompts with your students as you work through the techniques in the following section.

- What made you think of that association?
- What features do these words have in common?
- What connects all these examples together?
- How would you connect these two words together?
- Why did you connect these two words?
- What does the similarity tell you about these features?

- How are these words similar and different?

- What connections do these words have?

- What are examples/nonexamples of the word (i.e., synonyms and antonyms)?

Techniques for Word Associating

Reflection Connection

Purpose: To connect words that relate to one another and determine relationships among the words.

Level: Transitional (Adaptation for Fluent)

Multiple Intelligences: Visual/spatial, interpersonal

Materials: Text, index cards, Reflection Connection reproducible (for Adaptation; see Appendix A)

Procedure:

1. Prior to reading a selection, choose and record 10 words or phrases from the selection. The first 5 words or phrases should be from the selected text; the other 5 should be from the text also, but they should relate in some way to the first 5 words (e.g., *sleep/night, dirty/torn*).

2. Create two sets of word or phrase cards, one set for the first 5 words or phrases, and one set for the second 5. Divide students into two groups.

3. Give each student a word or phrase card from the set (if you have more than 10 students, let the students work in pairs or small groups).

4. Have students read their word cards and work together to determine which words or phrases connect and, if so, how the words connect. Suggested teacher talk could be, "What connects all these examples together?"

5. Ask the two main teams to record their predictions to share with the class later. Figure 5 (page 110) shows an example of the process, using the book *Owen* (Henkes, 1993).

6. After reading the text, have teams return to their notes to confirm or modify their connections according to how each word was used in the context of the text. Suggested teacher talk might be, "How would you connect these two words together?"

Adaptation: Select several words from a text you are reading that you would like to focus on with your students. Add words that relate to the focus words and place in groups of 4. Have students use 4 chosen words to complete the following sentence: _____ is to _____ as _____ is to _____ because _____. Students will need to determine how the words connect and record their results on the Reflection Connection reproducible.

Sources: Blachowicz and Fisher (2000); Vacca and Vacca (1996)

FIGURE 5. Sample Reflection Connection

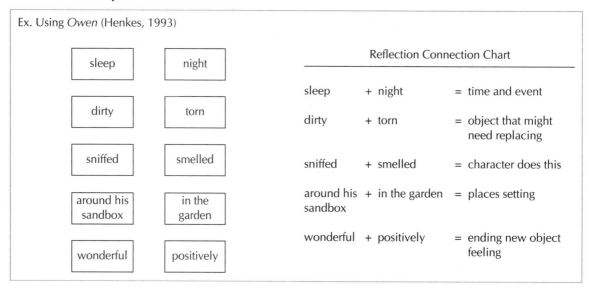

Ex. Using *Owen* (Henkes, 1993)

		Reflection Connection Chart	
sleep	night	sleep + night	= time and event
dirty	torn	dirty + torn	= object that might need replacing
sniffed	smelled	sniffed + smelled	= character does this
around his sandbox	in the garden	around his + in the garden sandbox	= places setting
wonderful	positively	wonderful + positively	= ending new object feeling

Semantic Feature Analysis

Vocabulary:
Word
Associating

Purpose: To explore how sets of key vocabulary words relate to one another and extend content knowledge.

Level: Transitional (Adaptation for Early)

ELL Technique: Yes

Multiple Intelligences: Visual/spatial, verbal/linguistic, interpersonal

Materials: Text, Semantic Feature Analysis matrix (see Appendix A), journals or chart (optional)

Procedure:

1. On the left column of the Semantic Feature Analysis matrix, write 5 to 10 key vocabulary words or phrases that relate to a chosen topic. The general topics or key concepts you choose to work with from the reading may start out concrete (e.g., sea animals, baseball) and gradually become more abstract (e.g., environmental issues, government).

2. Give each student a copy of your matrix with the vocabulary words written in. Have students discuss the properties, features, or characteristics of the topic and list them horizontally across the top row of the matrix. Suggested teacher talk could be, "What features do these words have in common?"

3. Before you read the text, have students collaborate with partners, work in small groups, or work independently to record on the matrix their predictions about the relationships. For each vocabulary word down the left side of the matrix, have students work their way across the matrix horizontally and ask themselves whether the vocabulary word possesses each of the features or properties written across the top. Ask them to write

a plus (+) or minus (–) symbol in each box to indicate the presence or absence of a particular feature. During this process, students may add across the top of the matrix any additional features they discover that assist in the understanding of the concept.

4. Encourage students to explain their findings and to identify terms or features that they still are questioning.

5. After reading the text selection, have students modify any portion of their matrix as needed to reflect what they have learned from the reading. Students may also record a summary of their findings in vocabulary journals, use them to create a "group findings" chart, or discuss them with partners. Suggested teacher talk might be, "How are these words alike or different?"

Adaptation: For early readers, write the properties, features, and characteristics of the topic on the matrix before distributing it to students.

Sources: Baldwin, Ford, and Readence (1981); Johnson and Pearson (1984); Pittelmann, Heimlich, Berglund, and French (1991)

Similar Synonyms

Purpose: To identify words with the same or similar meaning.
Level: Transitional (Adaptation for Early)
ELL Technique: Yes
Multiple Intelligences: Visual/spatial, verbal/linguistic, interpersonal
Materials: Text, sticky notes or correction tape, chart paper, overhead transparency, index cards, pocket chart, highlighting tape (for Adaptation only)

Procedure:
1. Read aloud a selection of text to the students, and then place a sticky note or correction tape over several words within the text.
2. Put students in pairs, and assign one covered word to each pair. Ask the students to generate as many words as they can that have the same or nearly the same meaning as the covered word. Suggested teacher talk could be, "What connections do these words have?"
3. Have students practice reading the sentence by taking turns substituting each of the generated synonyms to complete the sentence.
4. Have partners select one synonym that they believe best represents the original covered word and then write their chosen synonym on top of the sticky note or correction tape.
5. Have the class read the selection together, listen for the chosen similar synonyms, and decide if each chosen word conveys the same meaning as the original word in the context of the selection. Suggested teacher talk might be, "How are these words similar or different?"

Adaptation: With early readers, use highlighting tape so the words are readily visible at all times. Write the selected text on chart paper, an overhead transparency, or on index cards that you place in a pocket chart. Prior to the read-aloud, record synonyms for each of the highlighted words on index cards. Give each student pair a synonym card, and have them decide which highlighted word the card represents. If you are using a pocket chart, the students can place the card in the chart in front of each highlighted word. Read aloud the selection again, and have students stand up when you read their highlighted section. This allows students to make a connection with the printed text and the chosen synonyms.

Vocabulary Strategy: Contextualizing

One of the most effective strategies to increase vocabulary comprehension is to use the context that surrounds an unknown word to discover its meaning. This discovery process transpires through clues contained in the context. The reader can use context in several ways to help convey meaning. For example, sometimes the meaning of a word is explained within the same sentence. At times, synonyms of the unknown word can clarify words within the sentence. A contrast clue may identify meaning. Sometimes, the reader may need to make an inference or continue reading to figure out the relationship between the unknown word and the clues around the unknown word. Strategy instruction is necessary in order to support the reader in explicitly using context within the text to comprehend meaning.

Students need to "realize that it is okay to take a stab at unfamiliar words and figure out an approximate meaning from the context" (Calkins, 2001, p. 168). After students identify the unknown word, they may predict its possible meaning from the context. The context enables students to make an inquisitive stance toward word meaning and to monitor and verify predictions (Tierney & Readence, 1999). Using a variety of contextual analysis techniques allows the student to be active, rather than passive, in the discovery of new words.

Appropriate literature that best supports the application of the contextualizing strategy has strong word choice within the text to support the derived meaning. *The Keeping Quilt* (Polacco, 1988) and *Fly Away Home* (Bunting, 1991) are examples of appropriate literature; however, any piece of literature that uses select word choices to support the meaning within the text would be appropriate for use with these techniques.

Teacher Talk: Statements, Questions, and Prompts for Contextualizing

Following is a list of suggested teacher talk that encourages readers to think strategically as they employ contextualizing skills. Try using some of these statements, questions, and prompts with your students as you work through the techniques in the following section.

- What do you know about the word _____ from this sentence?

- Describe how you used the word in context (definition, cause and effect, opposite).

- How does the context help you understand the meaning of the word?

- Show the context that surrounded the unknown word that helped to reveal its meaning.

- What clues are in the sentence that helped you figure out the word?

- What word do you think best completes the sentence? Why?

- What words within the sentence help support the meaning of _____?

- What is the word being used to signal that an opposite, contrasting thought is occurring?

- Try to think of how you can use this word as a noun or verb.

- What do these two words have in common?

- When you come to a word you don't know, how do you use context clues to determine the meaning of the unknown word?

Techniques for Contextualizing

Cloze Passages

Vocabulary:
Contextualizing

Purpose: To predict an omitted word using surrounding context, and to cross-check with several cueing systems.

Level: Early

Multiple Intelligences: Visual/spatial, verbal/linguistic

Materials: Text; overhead transparency, board, or chart; correction tape or a large sticky note

Procedure:

1. Select a short passage from a text, and display it on an overhead projector, the board, or a chart. Choose several words to omit and place correction tape or a large sticky note over the words. Teachers can choose to delete words randomly or at regular intervals.

2. Guide students in figuring out the missing words by using the "sense" of the surrounding sentences. Suggested teacher talk could be, "What word do you think best completes the sentence? Why?"

3. Have students generate ideas for words that would best complete each of the sentences.

4. Record these ideas either on the sticky note covering each missing word or on chart paper.

5. When students are finished generating their replacement words, slowly peel back the sticky note from the first word to show the word's onset. Allow students to change their

predictions if the words they predicted had a different beginning sound. Then, peel back the sticky note completely, exposing the correct word. This technique provides an opportunity for students to cross-check with several cueing systems: semantic (Does the word chosen to complete the sentence make sense with the rest of the sentence?), syntactic (Does the word chosen sound right for the English language?), and visual (Does the word chosen look right once the sticky note has been removed?).

Variation: Place the sticky note over the word but leave the onset visible, or provide three words from which students can select to best complete the sentence. Have students discuss with a partner what strategies they used to try to figure out the meaning of the unknown word. Suggested teacher talk could be, "What clues are within the sentence that helped you figure out the word?"

Source: Strickland, Ganske, and Monroe (2002)

Contextual Redefinition

Vocabulary: Contextualizing

Purpose: To use background knowledge to examine the meanings of words, and to verify the correct meaning of a word through the context or a dictionary.

Level: Transitional

Multiple Intelligences: Visual/spatial, verbal/linguistic

Materials: Text; overhead transparency, board, or chart; dictionary

Procedure:

1. Select unfamiliar words from a text, and present the words in isolation on an overhead transparency, the board, or a chart. Choose words that are unfamiliar to students but are necessary for their understanding of the text.
2. With partners, have students predict what they think is the meaning of each of the new words. This step allows students to tap into any background knowledge they have, bringing what they know to the meaning of the words.
3. Write and present each word in its appropriate context, using the sentence or sentences directly from the text or developing new sentences that provide contexts for each word. Suggested teacher talk could be, "How does the content help you understand the meaning of the words?"
4. Allow students a chance to change or confirm their predictions, and discuss how seeing the context helped them understand the meanings of the words.
5. Have students verify the word meanings by using a dictionary.
6. Have students discuss how the two steps of contextual redefinition (i.e., seeing the words in isolation and seeing them placed in context) were different. Suggested teacher talk might be, "What words within the sentence help support the meaning of (word)?"

Sources: Readence, Bean, and Baldwin (1998); Tierney and Readence (1999)

What Do You Mean?

Purpose: To demonstrate how students use words in different contexts that change the meaning of the word.

Level: Transitional

ELL Technique: Yes

Multiple Intelligences: Visual/spatial, verbal/linguistic, interpersonal

Materials: Text, What Do You Mean? reproducible (see Appendix A), chart, notebooks

Procedure:

1. Select words with multiple meanings or use the What Do You Mean? reproducible to demonstrate how words can be used in different contexts that change the meaning of the word.
2. Show students a word, and ask them to each tell a partner what they think the word means.
3. Read the word in a sentence from the selected text, and have students discuss with their partners whether their predicted meaning for the word was correct. Suggested teacher talk could be, "How does the context help you understand the meaning of the words?"
4. Give each pair of students one word to use in two different sentences. Have one partner create a sentence using the word as one part of speech (e.g., a noun) while the other partner uses the word as a different part of speech (e.g., a verb) in a different sentence.
5. Have the partners explain their thinking (i.e., sentences) to the class, demonstrating the multiple meanings of the word.
6. List the demonstrated words on a chart, and have students write these words in their notebooks to start a word collection journal. Suggested teacher talk might be, "Try to think of how you can use this word as a noun or as a verb (or other parts of speech, as applicable)."

Context Complex Clues

Purpose: To use context clues to figure out the meaning of an unfamiliar word.

Level: Fluent

Multiple Intelligences: Visual/spatial, verbal/linguistic

Materials: Text, Context Complex Clues reproducible (see Appendix A), notebooks

Procedure:

1. Select a word from a text that may cause the students difficulty in understanding the meaning of the sentence or text passage.
2. Demonstrate a variety of ways students may use the context to figure out the meaning of the unfamiliar word. Copy and distribute the Context Complex Clues reproducible to show students some methods for using context.

3. Read a sentence that uses the word in a different context but that keeps the same meaning for the word (e.g., definition or description clues, linked synonym clues, compare and contrast clues, inferring clues). Suggested teacher talk could be, "What words within the sentence help support the meaning of _____?"

4. Have students write their predictions in their notebooks (you can ask them to start vocabulary logs for this activity) and discuss what clues in the sentence helped to convey the meaning of the word. Suggested teacher talk might be, "Describe how you used the word in context."

Vocabulary Strategy: Categorizing

Categorizing is a strategy that actively engages students and encourages them to organize new concepts and experiences in relation to prior knowledge about the concept. This strategy enlists the use of graphic organizers as visual representations of relationships. Graphic organizers such as concept maps, webs, and Venn diagrams make thinking visible to students (Fogarty, 1997). Categorizing features of vocabulary words enables students to use higher-order thinking and promotes cognitive word awareness in a visible manner. In order to categorize successfully, students need to be able to internalize the patterns under study and begin to make connections (Strickland et al., 2002). Categorizing vocabulary words gives students an opportunity to develop an understanding of the essential attributes, qualities, and characteristics of a word's meaning.

Appropriate literature that best supports the application of the categorizing strategy has a variety of words in the text suitable for sorting according to features and noticeable patterns. *The Great Kapot Tree: A Tale of the Amazon Rain Forest* (Cherry, 1990) and *Chester's Way* (Henkes, 1988) are examples of appropriate literature; however, any piece of literature that has a variety of words that engages the students to think about words' characteristics and commonalities within the text would be appropriate for use with these techniques.

Teacher Talk: Statements, Questions, and Prompts for Categorizing

Following is a list of suggested teacher talk that encourages readers to think strategically as they categorize. Try using some of these statements, questions, and prompts with your students as you work through the techniques in the following section.

- How do you know that word belongs with this group?
- Can you help find words with (*feature*)?
- Tell some things that come to your mind when you think of the word _____?
- What do you know about this word?

- What features do these words have in common?

- What connects all these examples together?

- Check to make sure all the examples given have a commonality.

- What does the similarity tell you about these features?

- Check with a partner to see if you both agree with the categories.

- How does using a word map help you?

- Describe how you categorized your words.

- How does a word map help you develop an understanding of the word or phrase?

- How does the format help you to generate and connect meanings for the focused word(s)?

- How do the words you are studying relate to the story?

- What is the name of the group to which these things belong?

Techniques for Categorizing

Picture and Word Sorts

Vocabulary: Categorizing

Purpose: To determine and sort words by specific features.
Level: Emergent
ELL Technique: Yes
Multiple Intelligences: Visual/spatial, verbal/linguistic, interpersonal, intrapersonal
Materials: Pictures or words from texts, index cards, highlighter

Procedure:
1. Choose 15 to 20 words from a selected text; they should be words that students can identify or read, but not necessarily spell. (For truly emergent readers or poorer readers, you can have students do this activity with pictures.) Write the words on index cards.
2. Have students work in pairs or small groups to discuss the features of each word. Have students put the words into different categories by their similarities or differences. Categories may include colors, action words, or simple nouns. You may determine the categories in advance (a closed sort), or the students may discuss the common features of the words and then determine for themselves how to categorize them (an open sort). Suggested teacher talk might be, "Check with a partner to see if you both agree with the categories."
3. After students place the words within appropriate categories, have a class discussion to allow students to justify their sorting criteria. Suggested teacher talk could be, "What features do these words have in common?"

4. Provide an opportunity for students to edit their sorts if they so desire after the discussion.

5. Review the text, and highlight the words the students used in the sorting activity.

Sources: Henderson (1985); Henderson, Bear, and Templeton (1992); Zutell (1998)

Word Hunts

Purpose: To categorize words by specific features.

Level: Emergent

Multiple Intelligences: Visual/spatial, verbal/linguistic

Materials: Texts, highlighting tape, Wikki sticks or other manipulatives, charts or vocabulary journals

Procedure:

1. Read aloud a story, a poem, content area material, or another text and demonstrate how to locate words from the text that fit into different categories (e.g., sounds, patterns, visual and syllable structures) you have chosen to study. You can use highlighting tape, Wikki sticks, or other manipulatives to set apart these words and show commonalities within certain word features.

2. Have students search for words in their reading and writing that support the specific features being studied. Suggested teacher talk could be, "What does the similarity tell you about these features?"

3. Record the results of these hunts on class charts, or have students write their words in vocabulary journals under the corresponding category headings. These word hunts may be done with partners, in small groups, or individually. Because these are emergent readers, search for a limited number of features. As the students gain confidence, multiple features may be hunted and recorded. Suggested teacher talk could be, "How do you know that word belongs with this group?"

4. Return to the text, and highlight the words the students have charted.

Sources: Bear et al. (2000); Strickland et al. (2002)

Alphaboxes

Purpose: To notice beginning sounds of words in context, and to sort words by beginning letter.

Level: Early

Multiple Intelligences: Visual/spatial, verbal/linguistic, interpersonal

Materials: Text, Alphaboxes reproducible (see Appendix A), highlighter

Procedure:

1. After reading a text selection, have students work in pairs or small groups to discuss and think of words that reflect important points from the text. Suggested teacher talk could be, "How do the words you selected relate to the story?"
2. Ask students to explain how their chosen words relate to the text. Copy and distribute the Alphaboxes reproducible. With the whole group or in pairs, have students decide which words to write in which boxes, according to the words' beginning letters. Suggested teacher talk could be, "Why did you place this word in this box?"
3. Return to the text, and highlight the words the students selected for their alphaboxes.

Adaptation: Have students create sentences using the words in the alphaboxes.

Source: Hoyt (1999)

List/Group/Label

Vocabulary: Categorizing

Purpose: To learn how to categorize words.

Level: Early (adaptation for Transitional)

ELL Technique: Yes

Multiple Intelligences: Visual/spatial, verbal/linguistic, interpersonal, intrapersonal

Materials: Text; chart paper, overhead, or board; highlighter; List/Group/Label reproducible (see Appendix A; for Adaptation)

Procedure:

1. Determine a content-related topic or concept based on what the class is studying and reading.
2. As a class, in small groups, with partners, or individually, have students brainstorm words that relate to the chosen topic or concept.
3. Record these words on chart paper, an overhead projector, or the board in a list form or around an oval containing the central concept.
4. Have students decide how these brainstormed lists can be classified according to their shared relationships and share their reasoning with the whole group. Suggested teacher talk could be, "Describe how you categorized your words." Encourage students to group categories within three types of associations: class (i.e., What is it?—the broad category of things the concept fits into); properties (i.e., What is it like?—the attributes that define the concept); and examples (e.g., illustrations of the concept).
5. Return to the text, and highlight the words students are categorizing.
6. Have students create a label or title that best describes each newly formed category.

Adaptation: Have students use the List/Group/Label reproducible as a visual representation of and a way to form a definition of the studied word. Suggested teacher talk could be, "How does the format help you to connect and generate meaning of the focused words?"

Sources: Johnson and Pearson (1984); Olson and Gee (1991); Schwartz (1988); Schwartz and Raphael (1985)

Vocabulary Strategy: Visual Imaging

Visualizing vocabulary words enables students who are stronger in spatial rather than in verbal intelligence to find or draw pictures that illustrate the definitions of words (Silver, Strong, & Perini, 1998). A student creates an image that represents the definition of the word and calls up this image whenever encountering the word. "The strategy of visualization provides opportunities for students to use their imaginations to facilitate both vocabulary development and comprehension across the curriculum" (Tate, 2003, p. 101).

When students use visual imaging, they think of a word that looks like, or even sounds like, the word they are learning. The more vivid the imagery, the more likely students will be able to connect and mentally recall the vocabulary word to its meaning. Different types of art activate different parts of the brain (Jenson, 2000), and this sensory connection is the bond for visual learners. Linking verbal and visual images increases students' ability to store and retrieve information (Ogle, 2000). "Transforming ideas from reading into artwork, poetry, etc., is an evaluative, interpretive act that reveals the students' level of understanding" (Collins, 1993, p. 3).

Appropriate literature that best supports the application of the visualizing strategy has a variety of words in the text suitable for creating vivid mental images. *Emma* (Kesselman, 1993) and *Charlotte's Web* (White, 1974) are examples of appropriate literature; however, any piece of literature that has a variety of words that encourage students to create images in their minds would be appropriate for use with these techniques.

Teacher Talk: Statements, Questions, and Prompts for Visual Imaging

Following is a list of suggested teacher talk that encourages readers to think strategically as they employ visual imaging skills. Try using some of these statements, questions, and prompts with your students as you work through the techniques in the following section.

- How does your illustration help you remember the new word?
- What do you see when you think of the word _____?
- What is the word _____ like? How does the example remind you of the word?
- What part of the pantomime helped you to know the word?
- Try to look at all the clay forms and create a definition of the word _____.

- Why did you choose that movement to represent the word _____?

- Which word goes with _____? Why does that word go with _____?

- Try to visualize the meaning of the word.

- Tell about an experience you have had that reminded you of this word.

- Try to visualize what the word looks like by using the picture

Techniques for Visual Imaging

Charades

Purpose: To make a mental image of a word to aid in recalling the word.

Level: Emergent

ELL Technique: Yes

Multiple Intelligences: Visual/spatial, bodily/kinesthetic, interpersonal, intrapersonal, verbal/linguistic (Adaptation)

Materials: Text, index cards, symbolic objects

Procedure:

1. Write some chosen vocabulary words or phrases from the text on index cards.

2. Have students take turns selecting a word card and acting out the meaning of the word on the card while holding or moving related or symbolic objects. This technique can include role-playing or pantomiming the meaning of the word or phrase. Suggested teacher talk could be, "What part of the pantomime helped you to know the word?"

3. Have students give suggestions for what the word might be until the correct word is identified.

4. Return to the text, and highlight the words students acted out within the text.

Adaptation: Have teams of students use several of the vocabulary words to create a skit to perform for the entire class. Teams can use pantomime and some verbal interaction while dramatizing the text. Teams also can select a few word cards and take a few minutes to improvise a situation demonstrating each word. This interaction with drama and words helps to develop vocabulary words through dialogue. Suggested teacher talk might be, "Why did you choose that movement to represent the word _____?"

Vocabulary: Visual Imaging

Museum Walk

Purpose: To imprint visual meaning by creating a representation of a word.

Level: Emergent (Adaptation for Early)

Vocabulary: Visual Imaging

ELL Technique: Yes

Multiple Intelligences: Visual/spatial, verbal/linguistic, interpersonal, bodily/kinesthetic

Materials: Text, ball of clay, highlighter, drawing notebook (for Adaptation)

Procedure:

1. Give each student a ball of clay, and introduce a new vocabulary word.

2. Use the new word in a sentence, or state its definition.

3. Have students form a visual image of what the word means to them out of the clay.

4. Display the images around the room, and have the students do a word "museum walk" to view the visual forms of the word. Suggested teacher talk could be, "Try to look at all the clay forms and create a definition of the word _____."

5. Ask students to explain how their forms relate to the meaning of the word. Suggested teacher talk might be, "Why did you choose the way you did to represent the word _____?"

6. Revisit the text, and have students highlight the words they formed.

Adaptation: Assign different words to students working in groups. Have each team create and share a visual image of their word from a large ball of clay. Display the creations around the room, and have the students go on the "word museum walk" as suggested above. Have students carry a drawing notebook with them and draw pictures of the images connected to each word.

Four Corners

Purpose: To visualize the meaning of a word in multiple ways.

Level: Early

Multiple Intelligences: Visual/spatial, verbal/linguistic, bodily/kinesthetic

Materials: Text, unlined paper, pencils or markers, highlighter, magazine pictures (optional), scissors (optional)

Procedure:

1. On a blank sheet of paper, have students draw lines to divide the paper into fourths.

2. In the center of their paper, have students write a key vocabulary word.

3. In the top left corner, have students draw or paste a magazine picture that represents the opposite meaning of the word. Have students mark a big black *X* over the visual image.

4. In the top right corner, have students draw or paste a magazine picture that demonstrates an example of the word. Suggested teacher talk could be, "What is the word _____ like? How does it remind you of that word?"

5. In the bottom left corner of the paper, have students illustrate a personal connection they can make to the word. Suggested teacher talk could be, "Which word goes with _____? Why does that word go with _____?"

6. In the bottom right corner, have students draw—using the letters in the word—a picture that illustrates the meaning of the word.

7. Return to the text, and highlight the words the students studied.

Graphic Cards

Purpose: To recall words by visualizing their meanings.

Level: Early

ELL Technique: Yes

Multiple Intelligences: Visual/spatial, verbal/linguistic, intrapersonal

Materials: Text; computer; graphics computer program; blank, computer-printable cards; highlighter

Procedure:

1. Have students use a computer graphics program to create picture cards for vocabulary words. Suggested teacher talk could be, "Try to visualize what the word looks like by using the picture."

2. The cards should have the word printed at the top and a graphic, chosen by the students, shown under the word. The graphic should be a pictorial representation of the meaning of the word. Suggested teacher talk could be, "How does your illustration help you remember the new word?"

3. Have students print out their cards, creating a set of vocabulary word cards to add to a word bank or collection of words.

4. Return to the text, and highlight the words the students used on their cards.

Adaptation: Have students write the vocabulary word on one side of the card. On the other side of the card, have students draw a pictorial representation of what the word means. The students can review these cards routinely until they form a visual image of the word in their minds.

Vocabulary Strategy: Analyzing

Students use the analyzing strategy to examine the structure of words they are studying. Analyzing the structure, or word parts, is a way to determine the meaning of a word. There are three main word parts: prefixes, suffixes, and roots. Studying the morphemes of words (i.e., the smallest meaningful unit in language) allows students to acquire information about the meaning, pronunciation, and parts of speech of new words from their prefixes, roots, and suffixes (Nagy, Diakidoy, & Anderson, 1991). These word parts help to contribute to the meaning of the word.

According to Nilsen and Nilsen (2003), spending class time on frequently used morphemes is a good teaching practice because it helps students establish structural connections among words. Implementing techniques that support the connections between the structural analysis concepts and the basic definition will help students in understanding the word. Students need to be able to see the relationships in terms of the common roots, and to use this understanding to discern meanings of new words (Anglin, 1993).

Appropriate literature that best supports the application of the analyzing strategy has a variety of words in the text suitable for a specific structural concept. *Much Bigger Than Martin* (Kellogg, 1978) and *If You Take a Mouse to School* (Numeroff, 2002) are examples of appropriate literature; however, any piece of literature that has a variety of words that support structural analysis (e.g., plurals, inflectional endings) would be appropriate for use with these techniques. (See chapter 3 for additional techniques for analyzing word structure.)

Teacher Talk: Statements, Questions, and Prompts for Analyzing

Following is a list of suggested teacher talk that encourages readers to think strategically as they employ analyzing skills. Try using some of these statements, questions, and prompts with your students as you work through the techniques in the following section.

- Look for any parts of a word that help you make sense of it.
- Try to cover up part of the word (e.g., the prefix). What word do you have left?
- Try to take the word apart.
- What words around it tell you something about the word?
- What does the prefix _____ do when added to the start of the word _____?
- What words go together with this word?
- What is the root word of _____?
- Which word has a prefix? Suffix?
- What is the meaning of the prefix or suffix?
- If you know what the root word for _____ means, what do you think _____ means?
- How does knowing the prefix, suffix, or root word of a word help you?
- When thinking of the prefix _____, why did you choose this word?
- How are all these words alike?

Vocabulary Tree Notebook

Purpose: To identify morphemes within a word.

Level: Early

Multiple Intelligences: Visual/spatial

Materials: Text, three-ring binder and/or clasp folders (one per student), Vocabulary Tree reproducible (see Appendix A)

Procedure:

1. Using the Vocabulary Tree reproducible, create a notebook with several vocabulary tree pages for each student. Distribute the notebooks to the students.

2. Have students designate one page in their notebooks for each morpheme (root, stem, or affix) they study. Whenever students encounter a word with that part (e.g., *-ing*), have them write it on the appropriate tree and note where the word was encountered. Suggested teacher talk could be, "Try to take the word apart."

3. Have students share their vocabulary trees with a partner and discuss why the words on a particular tree are related. Suggested teacher talk could be, "How are all these words alike?"

4. Return to the text, and have students locate the words they studied.

Source: Hill (1998)

Prefixes

Purpose: To identify how a prefix affects the meaning of a word.

Level: Transitional (Adaptation for Early)

Multiple Intelligences: Visual/spatial, verbal/linguistic, interpersonal

Materials: Text, chart paper

Procedure:

1. Select from a text several words to study. Help students to examine the words for meaningful parts, focusing on commonly used prefixes. (Table 13, page 126, provides a list to get you started.) Point out to students that a prefix is a group of letters placed at the start of a root word that alters, changes, or specifies the meaning of the root word.

2. Select a prefix, and ask students to think of words that include that prefix. Write students' brainstorming responses on chart paper for all to see. Suggested teacher talk could be, "When thinking of the prefix _____, why did you choose this word?"

TABLE 13. Commonly Used Prefixes

Prefix	Meaning	Examples
auto-	self	automatic, autograph, automobile
bi-	two	biweekly, bicycle, bilingual
de-	reverse action, remove, away	deflate, detach, deodorize
dis-	apart, negative, away	dislike, disagree, disappear
in-	not, free from, out	inactive, invisible
mis-	wrong	misspell, miscount, misfortune
pre-	before	preview, prepay, prepare
re-	back, again	redo, recall, repaint
tri-	three	triangle, tricycle, trilogy
un-	not	undo, untold, unhappy

3. Display the original word chosen with the prefix covered. Have students look at the root word to see if they know it or can think of a related word. Have students put the root word in the context of a sentence, then add the prefix, and finally, discuss how the prefix changes the sentence.
4. Return to the text and have students locate words that have the prefix they are studying. Discuss how the prefix relates to their comprehension of what they are reading.

Adaptation: Repeat steps 1 through 4 focusing on suffixes. (Table 14 provides a list to get you started.) Have students use word sorting techniques (see the techniques from this chapter's categorizing strategy for more ideas) to examine the concept of prefixes and suffixes. Students also can use word walls, word journals, word hunts, and word matching activities to reinforce the analysis of prefixes and suffixes.

Source: Bear et al. (2000)

Table 14. Commonly Used Suffixes

Suffix	Meaning	Examples
-tion	being, act, process (forms noun)	mention, vacation, location
-er	person connected with (forms noun)	runner, teacher, speaker
-less	without (forms adjective)	speechless, breathless, thoughtless
-ing	verb form (forms present participle)	running, singing, swimming
-ness	state of, condition of (forms noun)	likeness, forgiveness, happiness
-s, -es	plural	boys, girls, boxes
-ly	characteristic of (forms adverb)	lovely, happily
-est	comparative (forms adjective)	happiest, funniest, craziest
-ful	full of (forms adjective)	playful, helpful, grateful
-ed	verb form (forms past tense)	played, relaxed, rehearsed

Root Words

Purpose: To understand that a word derives meaning from the root word, also known as the base or stem.

Level: Fluent

Multiple Intelligences: Visual/spatial, verbal/linguistic

Materials: Text, dictionaries, journals, highlighter

Procedure:

1. Have students research the meanings of root words found in the vocabulary for the text or topic they are studying. Tell students that analyzing this foundational part of a word helps them to determine a word's origin and history, which will make the word more memorable. Suggested teacher talk could be, "How does knowing the root word help you?"

2. Have students generate a set of new words by adding affixes (prefixes and suffixes) to the root words. Have them write these new words in a journal. Suggested teacher talk might be, "What is the root word of _____?"

3. Ask the students to use a dictionary to look up the definition for each of the root words from the set of words they generated.

4. Lead students in a discussion on how these words all relate and can be categorized.

5. Have students return to the text and highlight the words they studied.

Vocabulary Strategy: Word Awareness

Students gain a sense of ownership of a word when they can transfer a new vocabulary word to their writing and speaking in a meaningful way (Routman, 1999). Word awareness, also known as word consciousness, is a strategy that brings one's thinking about the usage of a word to an application level. Effective readers acquire up to seven new vocabulary words each day. To enhance vocabulary, students need to have a desire to know words and gain "enjoyment and satisfaction from using them well and from hearing them used well by others" (Graves, 2000, p. 127).

When students know a word, they are able to use that word in speech and writing and to understand the word in text when it appears. Word-conscious students know and use many words, and they are aware of the subtleties of word meaning and the power words can have (Graves, Juel, & Graves, 1998).

Appropriate literature that best supports the application of the word awareness strategy has a variety of words in the text for students to use in their everyday conversations, *Good Driving, Amelia Bedelia* (Parish, 1995) and *The Relatives Came* (Rylant, 1985) are examples of appropriate literature; however, any piece of literature that has a variety of words that engage students to think about them and use them in their own vocabulary would be appropriate for use with these techniques.

Teacher Talk: Statements, Questions, and Prompts for Word Awareness

Following is a list of suggested teacher talk that encourages readers to think strategically as they employ word awareness skills. Try using some of these statements, questions, and prompts with your students as you work through the techniques in the following section.

- What do you know about the word _____?
- How can you find out more about a chosen word?
- How often did you use your chosen word in your journal writing?
- Try to use a new word when you are sharing today.
- Try to rate the word according to how much you know about the word.
- How did being aware of one word today help you to learn about that word?
- How often did you use your word or hear someone else using your word today?
- Do you feel confident to use the word _____ in a conversation or in your writing? Why? Why not?
- How did your word choice affect the other students' understanding of your journal entry?

Techniques for Word Awareness

Vocabulary Chart

Vocabulary: Word Awareness

Purpose: To use new words in everyday language.

Level: Emergent

ELL Technique: Yes

Multiple Intelligences: Visual/spatial, verbal/linguistic, interpersonal, intrapersonal

Materials: Text, chart paper, highlighter

Procedure:

1. Read aloud stories, and record on a vocabulary chart words from the text that are important or interesting for students to know.

2. Refer to the chart during the teaching day, using the words both in conversations and in writing.

3. Have each student choose a word from the list on which to concentrate. Encourage the students to use their chosen words often in their writing and conversations. Suggested teacher talk might be, "How often did you use your chosen word?"

4. Have students sign their names on the vocabulary chart next to the vocabulary word identified for them to use. Place a tally mark beside the student's name each time he or she uses the assigned word in a meaningful way. Suggested teacher talk could be, "How often did you hear someone else use your chosen word?"

5. Return to the text, and have students highlight the words they have been studying.

Source: Routman (1999)

Journal Circles

Purpose: To express an awareness of words in writing.
Level: Early
ELL Technique: Yes
Multiple Intelligences: Visual/spatial, verbal/linguistic, interpersonal
Materials: Text, journals

Procedure:
1. Establish a daily journal writing time, and have students make an effort to use vocabulary words they are currently studying when they write in their journals.

2. When writing time is complete, ask students to join journal circles in which small groups of mixed or similar ability take turns sharing their daily entries and noting the word choices they used in their writing. Journal circle time gives students a chance to "try out" sharing how they used words in context. Suggested teacher talk could be, "Try to use a new word when you are sharing today."

3. After hearing each student orally read his or her journal entry, have the other team members make comments, ask questions, or compliment the reader regarding his or her word choices and overall journal entry. Suggested teacher talk might be, "How did your word choice affect the other students' understanding of your journal entry?"

4. Read a text, and have students point out what words they heard in the text that they have used in their journal entries.

Speaking Out

Purpose: To apply new vocabulary words in everyday conversations.
Level: Early
ELL Technique: Yes
Multiple Intelligences: Visual/spatial, verbal/linguistic, interpersonal, intrapersonal

Materials: Text, notebooks, sticky labels

Procedure:

1. Have students select a word from a text they are reading that they would like to use throughout the week in their conversations.
2. Ask students to keep a daily vocabulary log and during independent writing time have them write how they used their vocabulary word in context for that day.
3. Encourage students to have at least five entries per word before adding a new vocabulary word. Suggested teacher talk could be, "Do you feel confident to use the word ____ in a conversation or in your writing? Why? Why not?"
4. Have students write their word on a sticky label and wear it on their clothes. Each time that a student uses his or her chosen word in conversation, the listener should add a tally mark to the sticky label. This allows other students to support the use of a new vocabulary word through listening. Suggested teacher talk might be, "How did being aware of one word help you learn about that word?"
5. Read a text, and have students highlight the words they chose to study.

Knowledge Rating

Purpose: To identify the level of knowledge of a word.
Level: Transitional
Multiple Intelligences: Visual/spatial, verbal/linguistic, interpersonal, intrapersonal
Materials: Text, notebooks, Knowledge Rating reproducible (see Appendix A)

Procedure:

1. Present students with a list of vocabulary words related to the topic you are studying.
2. Have students analyze their familiarity with the chosen words, and ask them to place a check mark beside their level of word knowledge on a matrix. Suggested teacher talk might be, "Try to rate the word according to how much you know about it."
3. With partners, ask students to discuss what they know about the list of words and select words to focus on during the upcoming reading of the text.
4. Copy the Knowledge Rating reproducible and distribute to each student. Before reading, have the students use the rating matrix to record the selected words and to rate them according to their level of knowledge of each word. Suggested teacher talk could be, "What do you know about the word ____?"
5. After reading, have students reflect on their rating matrix and determine whether their knowledge of certain words changed.
6. Have students place an X in the appropriate column of the matrix to represent any changes. Ask students to keep their rating charts in a personal vocabulary log and review them periodically, making adjustments on words that are becoming more familiar to them.

7. Reread the text, and have students listen for the new words they are studying and think about how they are used in context.

Source: Blachowicz (1986)

Quick Writes

Purpose: To utilize background knowledge to formulate meanings of words.
Level: Transitional
ELL Technique: Yes
Multiple Intelligences: Visual/spatial, verbal/linguistic, interpersonal, intrapersonal
Materials: Text, vocabulary journals

Procedure:

1. Present one new vocabulary word to students prior to reading a text selection.
2. After presenting the vocabulary word, have students write about the word for a few minutes in a vocabulary journal. This writing may include a definition of the word, a synonym or antonym for the word, or a response to a question you present using the word or about the word. Suggested teacher talk might be, "What do you know about the word _____?"
3. In groups, have students share their Quick Write responses and discuss similarities and differences among the responses.
4. Read the text, and emphasize the vocabulary word within the context of the selection.
5. Ask students to revisit their written responses and make any adjustments necessary to correspond with the way the word is used in the context of the text.
6. Have groups discuss their ideas about the word, helping students to put new concepts in their own words (Kohn, 1999). Suggested teacher talk might be, "How did being aware of the word today help you learn about that word?"

Source: Tate (2003)

Vocabulary Strategy: Wide Reading

Wide reading is a strategy that fosters vocabulary development through a variety of opportunities for students to read. Students need at least 20 minutes of daily reading to help increase their vocabulary list by 1,000 words per year (Nagy, Anderson, & Herman, 1987). This daily exposure is a natural way to increase vocabulary. "Children learn new words by reading extensively on their own. The more children read on their own, the more words they encounter and the more word meaning they learn" (Armbruster, Lehr, & Osborn, 2001, p. 35).

Encountering words in reading passages or speaking them in context multiple times is one of the best ways to commit words to long-term memory. Students will benefit from techniques geared toward rehearsing and talking about some of the words and concepts in a book (Calkins, 2001). "Encountering words repeatedly in text builds a fabric of meaning that makes it easier to learn new words" (Fountas & Pinnell, 1996, p. 166).

Appropriate literature that best supports the application of the wide reading strategy appeals to the students' reading levels and interests and fits into a range of genres. *Because of Winn-Dixie* (DiCamillo, 2000) and *Zoobooks: Tigers* (Biel, 2003) are examples of appropriate literature; however, any piece of literature that engages the students, is at the students' independent or instructional reading level, and provides exposure to the type of genre currently under study would be appropriate for use with these techniques.

Teacher Talk: Statements, Questions, and Prompts for Wide Reading

Following is a list of suggested teacher talk that encourages readers to think strategically as they employ wide reading skills. Try using some of these statements, questions, and prompts with your students as you work through the techniques in the following section.

- What are some of the interesting vocabulary words the author uses?

- Why are these words interesting to you?

- How have you used some words from your vocabulary club in your everyday conversation?

- What pattern do you notice the author using for his or her word choice?

- Tell me about some interesting words you are encountering while you are reading.

- How did you select your words for your book talk?

- What kind of words did you notice are common in this specific genre?

- In what genre would you most likely find these words?

- Tell me about some interesting words you heard while listening to the read-aloud.

Techniques for Wide Reading

Read-Alouds

Purpose: To listen to and absorb the vocabulary from a chosen text.
Level: Emergent (Adaptation for Early)
ELL Technique: Yes
Multiple Intelligences: Verbal/linguistic, interpersonal (Adaptation is visual/spatial)

Materials: Text, chart, index cards (for Adaptation)

Procedure:

1. Read aloud a story to the class. (See the ideas in chapter 1 of this book for how to do read-alouds.) Have students listen during the read-aloud and try to absorb the vocabulary from the chosen text. Suggested teacher talk might be, "Tell me about some interesting words you heard while listening to the read-aloud."

2. Instruct students to discuss with a partner interesting words they heard during the read-aloud. Suggested teacher talk could be, "Why are these words interesting to you?"

3. Set the text that you read in an area in the classroom where students can reread it or otherwise revisit the text on their own.

4. Keep a class chart of all the titles read aloud each month. Have students discuss and record their reflections on the texts on this chart and periodically compare previously noted connections with new connections (e.g., text-to-text connections, text-to-self connections).

Adaptation: Write selected words from the story on index cards, and pass them out to the students before the read-aloud. As the students are listening to the story, have them hold up their word cards when they hear the words in the story. After the read-aloud, have the students share how each word was used in the story.

Author Study

Purpose: To imitate authors' words in conversation.
Level: Transitional
Multiple Intelligences: Visual/spatial, verbal/linguistic
Materials: Multiple texts by the same author, sticky tabs, chart paper

Procedure:

1. Have students read several books by a particular author. During this author study, have students look for key words the author uses frequently in his or her writing.

2. List the author's name at the top of a sheet of chart paper, and have students list the words from step 1 in addition to other interesting words the author uses. Suggested teacher talk might be, "What pattern do you notice the author using for his or her word choice?"

3. Encourage students to imitate the author by using the author's words in their everyday conversations. Suggested teacher talk could be, "What are some of the vocabulary words the author uses that are interesting to you?"

4. Create an area in the classroom to display the books and other information about the author you are studying (e.g., an Awesome Author center). Display the author's books with sticky tabs on the pages with the studied words. Encourage students to revisit the author's books.

Book Talks

Vocabulary:
Wide
Reading

Purpose: To identify vocabulary words that support the meaning of a book.
Level: Transitional
ELL Technique: Yes
Multiple Intelligences: Visual/spatial, verbal/linguistic, interpersonal
Materials: Text, student vocabulary logs

Procedure:

1. Encourage students to read a variety of books. Tell students that they will be giving book talks, using the vocabulary from each story to introduce classmates to a particular book. Suggested teacher talk could be, "Tell me about some interesting words you are encountering while you are reading."
2. As they are reading, have students keep vocabulary logs in which they write interesting vocabulary words that help them relate to the meaning of the book.
3. Ask students to share these words when giving their classmates an orientation of the book. Suggested teacher talk might be, "How did you select your words for your book talk?"

Genre Study

Vocabulary:
Wide
Reading

Purpose: To identify similarities and differences among vocabulary words within genres.
Level: Fluent
Multiple Intelligences: Visual/spatial, verbal/linguistic
Materials: Texts in a variety of genres, chart

Procedure:

1. Expose students to several different genres of reading material.
2. During this genre study, keep a chart of specific vocabulary words that correlate with each particular genre (see Table 15 for examples). Suggested teacher talk might be, "What kinds of words did you notice that are common in the specific genre?"
3. Have students frequently discuss the similarities and differences among the vocabulary words within the various genres. Suggested teacher talk could be, "In what genre would you most likely find these words?"

Vocabulary Clubs

Vocabulary:
Wide
Reading

Purpose: To investigate unique and interesting words from texts.
Level: Fluent
ELL Technique: Yes
Multiple Intelligences: Visual/spatial, verbal/linguistic, interpersonal, intrapersonal

TABLE 15. Vocabulary Words for Genre Study

Genre	Description	Vocabulary Words and Phrases
Fantasy	Fiction that contains elements that are not real such as magical powers and animals that talk	Wizard, magical, hero, powers, imagine
Mystery	Story that contains suspense; mysterious	Secret, classified, investigation, discover, clue, evidence, witness, suspense
Folk tale	Story passed on from one generation to another by word of mouth	Once upon a time, This is the story of, Long ago, There once was
Fable	A fictitious story meant to teach a lesson; characters are usually animals	Responsibility, moral, courage, freedom, noble, kindness
Science fiction	Content not pattern, what if, infinite possibilities, imagination	Aliens, encounter, outerspace, scientific, time travel, consequences

Materials: Text, notebooks, highlighters

Procedure:

1. Divide the students into several small groups, and tell students that each group is a vocabulary club.
2. Have these clubs meet each week to share unique and interesting words from the books they are reading. The clubs should discuss the words, what they think they mean, and how they would use them in their everyday conversations. Suggested teacher talk might be, "Tell me about some interesting words you are encountering while you are reading."
3. Ask the clubs to record their words in a "club notebook" for further discussions. Suggested teacher talk could be, "How have you used some words from your vocabulary club in your everyday conversation?"
4. Have students return to the texts and highlight the words they are studying. Have them discuss the way the words are used in context.

Vocabulary Strategy: Referencing

Referencing is a strategy that allows readers to use resources to bring meaning to an unknown word. Students simply select a resource to search for the meaning of the word. However, teachers and students can overrely on this traditional strategy. "Definitions alone can lead to only a relatively superficial level of word knowledge. By itself, looking up words in a dictionary or memorizing definitions does not reliably improve reading comprehension" (Nagy, 2003, p. 5). Instruction for students should focus on how these resources can *aid* in learning meanings of words in the appropriate context. The quality of the definition also is an important factor in being able to use the dictionary as an aid to understanding text (McKeown, 1993; Nist & Olejnik, 1995). Teachers need to work with students in selecting the definition that best supports the meaning of the chosen word. Several techniques are possible, including using a book's glossary, a dictionary, a thesaurus, or a resource buddy.

Appropriate literature that best supports the application of the referencing strategy has a variety of words in the text suitable for sorting according to features and definitions. *My Big Book of Everything* (Priddy, 2001) and *Go Facts: Insects* (Freeman, 2002) are examples of appropriate literature; however, any piece of literature that may have a table of contents, index, or glossary within the text would be appropriate for use with these techniques.

Teacher Talk: Statements, Questions, and Prompts for Referencing

Following is a list of suggested teacher talk that encourages readers to think strategically as they employ referencing skills. Try using some of these statements, questions, and prompts with your students as you work through the techniques in the following section.

- How did the dictionary help you to figure out the word?

- Try to select words to examine and record that are interesting to you.

- What feature helps you to know if a word will be in the glossary?

- Which word means _____? How did you find the meaning for the word?

- How do you use the glossary to help you understand the meaning of a word?

- What feature of the computer could help you with understanding your word better? How does it help you?

- How do you use a thesaurus, glossary, or dictionary?

- Try to tell your buddy what you think the word means. Discuss it together.

- How did your buddy help you understand the unknown word?

Techniques for Referencing

Resource Buddies

Vocabulary: Referencing

Purpose: To work with a partner to analyze unknown words for meaning.
Level: Emergent
ELL Technique: Yes
Multiple Intelligences: Visual/spatial, verbal/linguistic, interpersonal
Materials: Text, journals

Procedure:

1. Assign each of your students an older student from a different classroom to be their resource buddy.
2. Throughout the week, have students keep track of words from their reading for which they need assistance to understand the meaning. Have students write these unknown words in their word journals. Suggested teacher talk might be, "Try to tell your buddy what you think the word means. Discuss it together."
3. Once each week, have students get together with their resource buddies to analyze the unknown words.
4. Have students write in their journals any information the buddy shares about the words. Suggested teacher talk might be, "How did your buddy help you understand the unknown word?"

Glossary Use

Purpose: To utilize a glossary to help identify the definitions of key words.
Level: Early
Multiple Intelligences: Visual/spatial, verbal/linguistic, interpersonal
Materials: Texts with glossaries

Procedure:

1. Work with students to select several words from an informational text and look up their definitions in the book's glossary. Make students aware that nonfiction books often have glossaries of the terms used throughout the text, and that words that appear in the glossary are often boldfaced or italicized in the running text.
2. Have students look for a word in the glossary. Suggested teacher talk could be, "How do you use the glossary to help you understand the meaning of a word?"
3. After reading the definition from the glossary, ask students to retell the definition to a partner and point out where that chosen word is in the text. Suggested teacher talk might be, "What feature helps you to know if a word will be in the glossary?"

Dictionary Use

Purpose: To use a dictionary to determine the meaning of a word.
Level: Transitional
ELL Technique: Yes
Multiple Intelligences: Visual/spatial, verbal/linguistic, interpersonal
Materials: Text, dictionaries, notebooks

Procedure:

1. Review with students how to use a dictionary. Explain that students can use dictionaries to clarify word usage, learn to pronounce words, find out the history of words, investigate parts of speech, and learn the definitions of words.

2. Have students work with partners to examine and identify the various parts of a dictionary (e.g., guide words, parts of speech, definitions, etymologies). Suggested teacher talk might be, "What part of the dictionary did you use to figure out the word?"

3. Ask students to use the dictionaries to examine a word from the text they are reading that is unclear to them. Suggested teacher talk could be, "Try to select words to examine and record that are interesting to you."

4. Have students write their findings in their notebooks or vocabulary logs.

Source: Brozo and Simpson (2002)

Thesaurus Use

Vocabulary: Referencing

Purpose: To use the thesaurus to help determine the meaning of a word.
Level: Transitional
ELL Technique: Yes
Multiple Intelligences: Visual/spatial, verbal/linguistic, interpersonal
Materials: Text, thesaurus, sticky notes

Procedure:

1. Select several words to examine with the students using a thesaurus. Show the students how to use a thesaurus to look up multiple words to represent the word chosen and how, from these choices, one is able to get a better understanding of what the word could mean.

2. With partners, have the students choose a known or unknown word from a text and put a sticky note over the word.

3. Have the students predict other words they could substitute for that word that would still make sense in the passage.

4. Ask students to look up the word in a thesaurus and compare the word they chose to the ones that are under that entry in the thesaurus. Suggested teacher talk might be, "How do you use a thesaurus?" Students can put a check mark by the words that are both on their sticky note and in the thesaurus. They also can add words to their sticky note if desired. (Note: A computer thesaurus is a good resource; it allows students to highlight a chosen word and then find out from the computer some word choices that correspond with the original word. Suggested teacher talk could be, "What feature of the computer could help you with understanding your word better? How does it help you?")

5. As a class, discuss how students can see several words listed together in the thesaurus that all have similar usages in a sentence and can use that list to infer what they think the meaning of a particular word is.

Assessment

The purpose of vocabulary assessment is to determine students' ability to recognize, utilize, and bring meaning to words. Teachers should evaluate the results of these assessments to determine the strengths and weaknesses of their individual students. The data from these assessments guide teachers in creating an appropriate action plan (strategies, techniques, and teacher talk) to meet the diverse needs of the students.

When assessing vocabulary knowledge, teachers should observe whether students can do the following:

- Use surrounding information in a sentence to predict the meaning of an unknown word
- Establish shared meaning relationship between words
- Use word origins or parts of words when appropriate
- Provide a workable definition of a word
- Consult other resources to determine meaning
- Identify characteristics and attributes of words
- Demonstrate the meaning of a word through movement
- Imprint meaning by creating a representation visual of the word
- Apply new words in everyday use
- Identify key vocabulary that determines main idea in a text

Following are general lists of criteria from some sample vocabulary assessments. This is by no means an exhaustive list; it is only a starting point. Each assessment is designated S for screening, D for diagnostic, and/or PM for progress monitoring.

DIAGNOSTIC ASSESSMENT OF READING (DAR) (Roswell & Chall, 1992): D

Word meaning: Student is given a word and asked to orally tell tester what the word means.

EARLY READING DIAGNOSTIC ASSESSMENT (ERDA) (Smith, 2000): D

Pictorial vocabulary task: Student is shown four pictures; he or she selects the best picture to represent the word the tester says.

Oral vocabulary task: Tester gives student a picture and/or a verbal cue; student says the appropriate word.

IOWA TESTS OF BASIC SKILLS: VOCABULARY SUBTEST (ITBS) (Hoover et al., 2001): D

Listening vocabulary: Student listens to tester read the target word and selection choices, and then the student selects the best answer.

Reading vocabulary: Student selects one of four words that best describes a picture; student reads a target word in context and then selects a word or phrase that most closely conveys the same meaning.

PEABODY PICTURE VOCABULARY TEST–III (PPVT-III) (Dunn & Dunn, 1997): S, D

Relational vocabulary: Students answer yes or no to questions about words.

Picture vocabulary: Students indicate which picture best represents a stimulus word.

WOODCOCK READING MASTERY TEST–REVISED (Woodcock, 1987): D, PM

Word comprehension: Tester says a word, and student gives a word that is either opposite or similar in meaning.

Passage comprehension: Student reads a passage and then orally fills in missing words that best complete the passage.

Vocabulary is a key component of effective reading instruction. Both fluency and comprehension are affected by vocabulary knowledge (Flood et al., 1991; Robb, 1997). Vocabulary "is the glue that holds stories, ideas, and content together and that facilitates making comprehension accessible for children" (Rupley, Logan, & Nichols, 1999, p. 5). The NRP report findings indicate that

> vocabulary seems to occupy an important middle ground in learning to read. Oral vocabulary is a key to learning to make the transition from oral to written forms, whereas reading vocabulary is crucial to the comprehension processes of a skilled reader. (NICHD, 2000, p. 4-15)

The strategies, techniques, and teacher talk presented in this chapter support teachers in maximizing their readers' potential in becoming strategic readers. When teachers brush this stroke (techniques and teacher talk in vocabulary) across their canvases, they are adding another dimension to their masterpieces (i.e., strategic readers).

Comprehension

Comprehension is the essence of reading; therefore, teachers should weave comprehension strategies into their everyday teaching across the curriculum. According to the NRP report, "Comprehension strategies are specific procedures that guide students to become aware of how well they are comprehending as they attempt to read and write" (NICHD, 2000, p. 4-5). In fact, teachers need to begin teaching these strategies in kindergarten. "To delay this sort of powerful instruction until children have reached the intermediate grades is to deny them the very experiences that help them develop the most important of reading dispositions" (Pearson & Duke, 2002, p. 248).

Comprehension as a strategic process enables readers to make connections and move beyond literal recall. Teachers need to remember that good comprehension instruction needs to be taught explicitly and strategically. With every technique, it is vital that teachers explain and model directly, guiding students on how the technique builds the corresponding strategy. Teachers need to "make the strategy a part of our unconscious reading process, so that students are able to combine any number of strategies to problem solve before, during, and after they read" (Routman, 2003, p. 129).

The strategies and their corresponding techniques detailed in this chapter are as follows:

- Previewing: Background Knowledge, Book Introduction, Skim and Scan, and Text Features

- Activating and Building Background Knowledge: Prereading Plan (PreP), Anticipation/Reaction Guides, and Think Sheet

- Predicting: Picture Walk, Journaling, Text Features, Story Impression, and Two-Column Note Prediction

- Questioning: Question–Answer Relationships (QARs); Question Logs: 3Rs; Survey, Question, Read, Recite, Review (SQ3R); and Thinking About Questioning

- Visualizing and Sensory Imaging: Recording Mental Images, Wordless Picture Books, Drama, and Sensory Impressions

- Inferring and Drawing Conclusions: Dramatic Interpretation, Interpreting Text, Talk Show, and Scenarios With T-Charts

- Summarizing: Artistic Summary, Journaling or Group Chart, Summary Ball, Narrative Pyramid, Somebody/Wanted/But/So, and GIST (Generating Interactions Between Schema and Text)

- Determining Importance: Chapter Tours, Main Idea Wheel, and Sifting the Topic From the Details
- Synthesizing: Creating a Play, Mind Mapping, Rewriting a Story, Say Something, and Two-Column Notes

Table 16 matches the techniques in this chapter to the developmental levels from chapter 1 (emergent, early, transitional, and fluent). To be effective, the strategies and techniques presented in this chapter should allow ample time for teacher modeling and student application, long before independent application is expected. Teachers should select and model reading aloud of appropriate literature to apply the techniques in a

TABLE 16. Comprehension Techniques

	Emergent	Early	Transitional	Fluent
Before Reading	Background Knowledge (P) Book Introduction (P) Picture Walk (Pr)	May include all Emergent techniques Chapter Tours (D) Journaling (Pr) PreP (A) Skim and Scan (P) Text Features (P, Pr)	May include all Emergent and Early techniques Anticipation/Reaction Guides (A) QARs (Q) Think Sheet (A) Two-Column Notes (Sy)	May include all Emergent, Early, and Transitional techniques SQ3R (Q) Story Impression (Pr) Thinking About Questioning (Q) Two-Column Notes (PR)
During Reading	Wordless Picture Books (V)	Interpreting Text (I) Journaling or Group Chart (S) Skim and Scan (P) Somebody/Wanted/But/ So* (S)	Somebody/Wanted/But/ So (S) Two-Column Notes (Sy)	GIST (S) Question Logs: 3Rs (Q) Scenarios With T-Charts (I) SQ3R (Q)
After Reading	Artistic Summary (S) Recording Mental Images (V)	Creating a Play (Sy) Drama (V) Dramatic Interpretation (I) Interpreting Text (I) Main Idea Wheel* (D) QARs (Q) Sensory Impressions (V) Summary Ball (S)	Main Idea Wheel (D) Mind Mapping (Sy) Narrative Pyramid (S) Rewriting a Story (Sy) Say Something (Sy) Sifting the Topic From the Details (D) Somebody/Wanted/But/ So (S) Talk Show (I) Two-Column Notes (Sy)	GIST (S) SQ3R (Q)

*Adaptation portion of the technique.
Note. The developmental levels are shown across the top of the table horizontally. Down the left side of the matrix are the suggested times when these techniques are most effective—before, during, and after reading. This matrix is a guide and is by no means an exhaustive list.
(P) Previewing; (A) Activating and building background knowledge; (Pr) Predicting; (Q) Questioning; (V) Visualizing and sensory imaging; (I) Inferring and drawing conclusions; (S) Summarizing; (D) Determining importance; (Sy) Synthesizing

meaningful manner, which supports authentic learning for strategic reading. By using this process, students are able to see first the whole text (i.e., appropriate literature), then see the parts systematically (i.e., strategies and techniques), and finally, apply the parts back to the whole (i.e., become metacognitively aware of strategies while reading appropriate literature). Utilizing quality literature and promoting language development throughout the techniques will help to enhance students' development of the strategies.

Comprehension Strategy: Previewing

Previewing motivates students to want to read the text. It enables readers to examine text features, skim to get a sense of what the text is about, and identify the organizational structure. While previewing, readers begin relating to what they already know—their schema—and form several opinions about the text they are reading. Previewing is one of the best strategies for evoking relevant thoughts and memories relating to the text. Previewing allows readers to get their minds ready to read a particular type of text. When they use this strategy, students have a better understanding of what they know about the text, what they would like to learn from the text, and what they anticipate might happen as they read.

Appropriate literature that best supports the application of the previewing strategy should have an interesting title, chapter headings, and/or illustrations. *Fireflies* (Brinckloe, 1986) and *This Is the House That Jack Built* (Adams, 1990) are examples of appropriate literature; however, any piece of literature that has text features that support previewing would be appropriate for use with these techniques.

Teacher Talk: Statements, Questions, and Prompts for Previewing

Following is a list of suggested teacher talk that encourages readers to think strategically as they employ previewing skills. Try using some of these statements, questions, and prompts with your students as you work through the techniques in the following section.

- The title makes me think the book will be about…
- I have read other books by this author. I think this book also will be good because…
- The illustrations help me to…
- Perhaps the pictures will provide clues about…
- What else do you notice from the picture?
- I noticed that the author…

- I noticed that the pictures are helping to tell the story because…
- What is the significance of the title?
- What does the text seem to be about?
- Are you familiar with the topic of the selection?
- What is your purpose for reading this selection?
- How is the text structured?
- What features help you when previewing the book?
- What background information do you know about this text?

Techniques for Previewing

Background Knowledge

Purpose: To use background knowledge to preview a text.
Level: Emergent
ELL Technique: Yes
Multiple Intelligences: Visual/spatial, verbal/linguistic, intrapersonal
Materials: Text

Procedure:

1. Through class discussions, activate students' prior personal experiences that are pertinent to the text you are about to read. Suggested teacher talk could be, "What background information do you know about this text?"

2. Begin to build with students any necessary background knowledge they might need for studying this text (for ideas, see the activating and building background knowledge strategy and its techniques in this chapter). Suggested teacher talk might be, "Ask yourself, 'Am I familiar with the topic of the selection?'"

Book Introduction

Purpose: To preview a story.
Level: Emergent
ELL Technique: Yes
Multiple Intelligences: Visual/spatial, verbal/linguistic, interpersonal
Materials: Text

Procedure:

1. Before reading a chosen book, discuss briefly with the students what the book is about, key concepts in the book, and new vocabulary. Eliciting vocabulary use through discussions with students and then identifying a few of those words directly within the text helps to implant the words in students' minds.

2. Have students preview some of the pictures in the book as a source of information. Suggested teacher talk could be, "Perhaps the pictures will provide clues about…."

3. Encourage students to think aloud, describing their reactions to the illustrations and the text. Suggested teacher talk might be, "What does the text seem to be about?"

Skim and Scan

Purpose: To make first impressions about a text.
Level: Early
Multiple Intelligences: Visual/spatial, verbal/linguistic, intrapersonal
Materials: Text

Procedure:

1. Have students skim the text they are about to read, noting their first impressions. Suggested teacher talk could be, "I noticed that the author…."

2. Encourage student to scan the "lead-ins," subheadings, diagrams, and any other portions of the text that give them a feel for the text they will be reading. Ask students to use these first impressions to begin selecting strategies that they will need to comprehend the text. Teachers may post these strategies in the classroom so the names are more readily accessible to students. Suggested teacher talk might be, "What does the text seem to be about?"

Text Features

Purpose: To use text features to help determine the purpose of a text.
Level: Early
Multiple Intelligences: Visual/spatial, interpersonal
Materials: Text

Procedure:

1. Before reading a chosen book, preview with students the type font, layout, details, genre, table of contents, index, glossary, and other features of the text that might allow students to determine the purpose of the text. Suggested teacher talk could be, "How is the text structured? What features help you when previewing the book?"

Comprehension Strategy: Activating and Building Background Knowledge

Proficient strategic readers bring their prior knowledge to a text to help them discern the meaning of what they are reading. When readers are thinking about what they already know, they are using their schemas to better understand the text. According to Keene and Zimmermann (1997), students connect new information to their own experiences (text to self), to other texts they have experienced (text to text), and to real-world issues (text to world). Strategic readers add or alter their thinking as they encounter new ideas and information from the text. It is critical that teachers not only activate their students' knowledge of topics they are reading about but also be aware of situations in which students have little or no background knowledge so that they can build essential understandings before their students begin reading (Strickland et al., 2002).

Appropriate literature that best supports the application of the activating and building background knowledge strategy needs to have ways for students to connect with the text and use their schemas (i.e., what they already know) or to add to what they need to know about the text selected. *Chrysanthemum* (Henkes, 1991) and *Knots on a Counting Rope* (Martin & Archambault, 1987) are examples of appropriate literature; however, any piece of literature for which students are making connections to build background prior to reading the text would be appropriate for use with these techniques.

Teacher Talk: Statements, Questions, and Prompts for Activating and Building Background Knowledge

Following is a list of suggested teacher talk that encourages readers to think strategically as they activate and build background knowledge. Try using some of these statements, questions, and prompts with your students as you work through the techniques in the following section.

- Read the title or opening paragraph, and name another book similar to this one.
- Make a connection to other texts written by the same author or books that may be related to the same theme.
- What do you know that will help you understand the information in this section?
- Which details from the text connected to your own experiences?
- What other stories did this story remind you of?
- What personal connection did you make with the text?
- How are the events described in this story related to your own experiences? Were they similar? Were they different?
- What does this remind you of?

- What comes to mind when you hear the word ____?
- What do you already know about the text?
- Do you agree or disagree with the statement presented? Why or why not?
- Try to read and confirm whether your answer to the statement is true or false.
- Based on your prior knowledge of the topic, what questions come to mind?
- As a result of our discussion, can you think of any other information that you know about this topic?
- What comes to your mind when you hear the word (or phrase) ____ ?

Techniques for Activating and Building Background Knowledge

Prereading Plan (PreP)

Comprehension: Activating and Building Background Knowledge

Purpose: To develop, add, delete, or modify new insights to text.
Level: Early
ELL Technique: Yes
Multiple Intelligences: Visual/spatial, verbal/linguistic, interpersonal, intrapersonal
Materials: Text, chart paper

Procedure:
1. Identify the central concept in a text selection, and introduce it to the students by saying, "What comes to your mind when you hear the word (or phrase) ____?"
2. Individually, have students write down all of their associations with the topic and what they know about it.
3. Note all students' responses on a chart.
4. Prompt students to reflect on and clarify their background knowledge by asking, "What made you think of ____ ?" For new insights to be developed based on the class discussion, follow up by asking, "As a result of our discussion, can you think of any other information that you know about this topic?"
5. Continue the discussion until the class is finished developing, adding, deleting, or modifying new insights.

Source: Langer (1981)

Anticipation/Reaction Guides

Comprehension: Activating and Building Background Knowledge

Purpose: To read and to confirm predictions about text.
Level: Transitional

Multiple Intelligences: Visual/spatial, verbal/linguistic, intrapersonal
Materials: Text, notebook paper

Procedure:

1. Identify the main topic or concept of a text prior to meeting with students.
2. Create five to eight statements that will challenge or support students' beliefs or that may reflect common misconceptions about the subject, topic, or concept.
3. Record these statements on notebook paper so students can use the paper as a guide during the lesson. Students read each statement and note whether they agree (+) or disagree (x). Suggested teacher talk could be, "Do you agree or disagree with the statement presented? Why or why not? Try to read and confirm whether your answer to the statement is true or false."
4. After students read the text, have them return to the statements and engage in a discussion on how the textual information supported, contradicted, or modified their first opinions.

Source: Herber (1984)

Think Sheet

Purpose: To record background knowledge to guide reading.
Level: Transitional
Multiple Intelligences: Visual/spatial, intrapersonal
Materials: Text, Think Sheet reproducible (see Appendix A)

Procedure:

1. Copy the Think Sheet reproducible and distribute to each student. Choose a text to study, and have students write the text's main topic in the rectangular box on their sheets.
2. On the light bulb side of the sheet, have students list ideas that they have about the main topic based on their prior knowledge.
3. On the question mark side, have students record any questions they have about the main topic. Suggested teacher talk could be, "Based on your prior knowledge of the topic, what questions come to mind?"
4. Ask students to use what they have recorded on their think sheets to guide their reading of the text.
5. Have students read the text. As they locate information related to their original prereading ideas and questions, have students write the information beside their corresponding original statements. Suggested teacher talk could be, "What personal connection did you make from the text?"

Source: Dole and Smith (1987)

Comprehension Strategy: Predicting

Predicting is a strategy that helps readers set expectations for reading, connect early with the text for meaning, and decide what they think will happen. Proficient strategic readers make predictions before reading based on previewing and asking questions. "When readers make predictions about what they'll learn, they activate their schema about the topic and what they know about the type of text they are about to read" (Miller, 2002, p. 145). Predictions can be based on clues in the title, the illustrations, and the details within the text. These organizational structures are the blueprints that show the author's plan for presenting information to the reader (Strickland et al., 2002).

During reading, readers may predict what content will occur in succeeding portions of the text. Readers can describe what they think will be revealed next, based on what they have read so far and based on the personal background knowledge they bring to the text. After reading a portion of the text, readers can confirm whether their predictions were accurate and adjust them as needed.

Appropriate literature that best supports the application of the predicting strategy needs to have interesting titles, illustrations, and other text features that allow students to think on what the text might be about and then to be able to confirm or counter the prediction. *The Year of the Panda* (Schlein, 1990) and *The Doorbell Rang* (Hutchins, 1986) are examples of appropriate literature; however, any piece of literature that encourages students to make predictions based on the text features and language would be appropriate for use with these techniques.

Teacher Talk: Statements, Questions, and Prompts for Predicting

Following is a list of suggested teacher talk that encourages readers to think strategically as they employ prediction skills. Try using some of these statements, questions, and prompts with your students as you work through the techniques in the following section.

- What makes you think _____ is going to happen? Why?

- I wonder if _____; I want to know _____.

- What will happen? I think I know what is going to happen.

- What do you think the text is going to tell you about? What makes you think so? What evidence supports your prediction?

- Try to imagine what is going on in the story.

- What do the characters and the setting look like?

- Check your predictions to see if you were right.

- What information do you expect to read in this selection based on the title?

- What do you predict the author will reveal next, based on the first paragraph or chapter?
- Which details or clues from the selection did you use to make your prediction?
- Which predictions were confirmed by the text?
- Which predictions need to be adjusted or revised?
- Looking at the picture on the cover, what do you imagine this story will be about?
- How do the pictures help you to predict what the story will be about?
- Based on the text features noted, what do you think the story is about?

Techniques for Predicting

Picture Walk

Comprehension: Predicting

Purpose: To use illustrations within a text to make predictions.
Level: Emergent
ELL Technique: Yes
Multiple Intelligences: Visual/spatial, verbal/linguistic
Materials: Text

Procedure:

1. Have students peruse a book, looking at the pictures and describing what they see. Ask students to use the pictures to make predictions. Suggested teacher talk could be, "Looking at the picture on the cover, what do you imagine this story will be about?"

2. Lead students in a discussion about understanding the concepts, key words, or key phrases from the text based on the illustrations. Suggested teacher talk might be, "How do the pictures help you to predict what the story will be about?"

3. While reading the text, have students discuss the predictions they made from the picture walk.

Journaling

Comprehension: Predicting

Purpose: To predict in written form what a text will be about.
Level: Early
ELL Technique: Yes
Multiple Intelligences: Visual/spatial, verbal/linguistic, interpersonal, intrapersonal
Materials: Text, journals

Procedure:

1. Have students keep reading response journals, in which they draw or write what they think a story they are preparing to read will be about and justify why they think it will be that way. Suggested teacher talk could be, "What will happen? I think I know what is going to happen. What do you think the text is going to tell you about _____? What makes you think so? What evidence supports your prediction?"

2. In Journal Circles (see page 129), have students share their journal entries.

3. Read the text, and have students discuss the predictions they recorded in their journals in comparison with the actual events in the text.

Text Features

Comprehension: Predicting

Purpose: To identify features of a text that give clues about the topic or events.
Level: Early
ELL Technique: Yes
Multiple Intelligences: Visual/spatial, verbal/linguistic, interpersonal
Materials: Text

Procedure:

1. Provide minilessons on the text organization in fiction and nonfiction. For example, a Heading Hunt is an activity in which students read the headings in a text and predict what they think the text will be about based on the headings.

2. After identifying various text features, have students work with a partner to make predictions about a particular text. Suggested teacher talk could be, "Based on the text features noted, what do you think the story is about? Which details or clues from the selection did you use to make your prediction?"

3. Throughout the reading of the text, have students stop and use text features to make further predictions as well as to confirm or change their previous predictions.

Story Impression

Comprehension: Predicting

Purpose: To make predictions, and to read and check those predictions.
Level: Fluent
ELL Technique: Yes
Multiple Intelligences: Visual/spatial, verbal/linguistic, interpersonal
Materials: Fiction or other story-oriented text, chart paper

Procedure:

1. Select seven key words that relate to significant information from the text you are studying, and display the chain of words in the order in which they appeared in the text

for all students to see. These words should reflect the following story elements: main characters, setting, problem, events, and solution. Suggested teacher talk could be, "Try to imagine what is going on in the story based on the seven words presented."

2. Have students work in teams to predict a story line using the words presented.

3. After teams have had time to discuss their predictions, have them create a story using all seven words. One student in the class can be the recorder and write the teams' creations on chart paper. Suggested teacher talk could be, "Present to the entire class your story creations. Which details or clues from the selection did you use to make your prediction?"

4. After all the teams have shared their versions of the story, read the story and have students compare and contrast their stories to it.

Source: McGinley and Denner (1987)

Two-Column Note Prediction

Purpose: To record and justify predictions.

Level: Fluent

Multiple Intelligences: Visual/spatial, verbal/linguistic, interpersonal, intrapersonal

Materials: Text, Two-Column Note Prediction Form (see Appendix A)

Procedure:

1. Copy the Two-Column Note Prediction Form and distribute to each student. Have students record their predictions about a text on the left side of the form.

2. On the right side, have students record their thought processes behind these predictions. Suggested teacher talk might be, "What makes you think _____ is going to happen? Why?"

3. Have students share their predictions and then read the text to see whether their predictions were correct. Suggested teacher talk could be, "Which predictions were confirmed by the text?"

Source: Miller (2002)

Comprehension Strategy: Questioning

Questioning is a strategy that helps readers to review content and to relate what they have learned to what they already know. Generating and asking questions also help students to identify issues and ideas in the text, construct meaning, enhance understanding, discover new information, clarify confusion, and solve problems. Asking questions before reading allows readers to set purposes for reading and helps them to determine what they want to learn while reading.

Strategic readers move from general questions to story-specific questions during their interaction with the text, and they integrate information from different segments of text. When the text becomes unclear, strategic readers formulate questions and then continue reading to find details that may later help answer those questions and make sense of the text. Asking and answering questions encourage readers to notice pieces of information within the text that support the main idea. This process of asking and answering questions allows readers to think actively as they read.

Appropriate literature that best supports the application of the questioning strategy needs to capture the mind of the reader and encourage questions before, during, and after reading to comprehend the text. *The Librarian Who Measured the Earth* (Lasky, 1994) and *Charlie Anderson* (Abercrombie, 1990) are examples of appropriate literature; however, any piece of literature that encourages students to ask questions in order to capture the meaning of the text (i.e., to predict what the text will be about, to determine why the author wrote the book, to locate specific answers in text or inferred from the text) would be appropriate for use with these techniques.

Teacher Talk: Statements, Questions, and Prompts for Questioning

Following is a list of suggested teacher talk that encourages readers to think strategically as they employ questioning skills. Try using some of these statements, questions, and prompts with your students as you work through the techniques in the following section.

- What questions did you have while you were reading this text?
- What questions do you have about the story after reading it?
- Where do you find the answers to your questions?
- Can you find the exact words in the book?
- What differences of opinion between (name two characters) did you notice?
- Are the words from the question and the words from the answer in the same sentence, or in two sentences that are right next to each other?
- What kind of question is this?
- Before you start reading, ask three questions that you would like to find out about the text.
- While you are reading, try to find the answers to the questions you asked.
- What questions do you hope this story will answer?
- What information do you hope this text will include?
- How does asking questions help the reader?

- How do readers figure out the answers to their questions?
- How does using a graphic organizer help you to reflect on the questions you have about the text?
- How does forming a question about the text help you comprehend it?
- Try to think of a question that will support comprehension of the text.

Techniques for Questioning

Question–Answer Relationships (QARs)

Purpose: To determine various questioning techniques to aid in comprehension of the text.
Level: Transitional
ELL Technique: Yes
Multiple Intelligences: Visual/spatial, verbal/linguistic, interpersonal, intrapersonal
Materials: Text, QARs reproducible (see Appendix A), notebooks

Procedure:

1. Copy and distribute the QARs reproducible. Introduce the four question–answer relationships: Right There, Think and Search, Author and Me, and On My Own.

2. Explain that these four question–answer relationships can be categorized into the two ways the reader derives the answers:
   - In the Book (text-based)—Suggested teacher talk for these questions could be, "Can you find the exact words in the book?" This type of question requires students to remember exactly what the author said and to return to the text to find where the author said it. "Right There" questions ask readers to respond at the literal level; words from the question and words from the answer will usually be found exactly stated in the text very close to each other. "Think and Search" questions are inferential ones that require readers to derive the answer from more than one sentence, paragraph, or page.
   - In My Head—These questions are not found in the book; they require readers to utilize their background knowledge and understanding of what they are reading to answer the questions. "Author and You" questions are inferential; the words from the book are in the question, but these questions also require input from readers' own prior knowledge to connect with the text and derive an answer. "On My Own" questions require application from readers' background knowledge and at times do not even require reading the text.

3. After discussing the four types of questions, ask groups of students to practice answering the different types of questions, which teachers should produce beforehand. Partners or teams could practice generating their own questions for each other to answer.

4. Have students determine the question–answer relationship of each question and record and justify their answers in their notebooks. Suggested teacher talk might be, "Where do you find answers to your questions?"

5. Have students share their responses and then reread the text to verify their accuracy.

Source: Raphael (1986)

Question Logs: 3Rs

Purpose: To record questions, reactions, and reflections to bring meaning to text.

Comprehension: Questioning

Level: Fluent
Multiple Intelligences: Visual/spatial, verbal/linguistic, intrapersonal
Materials: Text, paper

Procedure:

1. Have students fold paper into three columns to record questions, reactions, and reflections as they read. Have students use the question column to record questions they have as they read the text.

2. As they continue to read the text, have students note their reactions in the second column. Suggested teacher talk could be, "What did you wonder about while you were reading this text?"

3. In the final column, have students note their reflections, connections, or any other thoughts that help bring meaning to the text. Suggested teacher talk could be, "What questions do you have about the story after reading it?"

Survey, Question, Read, Recite, Review (SQ3R)

Purpose: To establish a purpose for reading by asking questions.

Comprehension: Questioning

Level: Fluent
Multiple Intelligences: Visual/spatial, verbal/linguistic, intrapersonal
Materials: Text, SQ3R reproducible (see Appendix A)

Procedure:

1. Copy the SQ3R reproducible and distribute to each student. Have students survey the text material by looking at the title, headings, illustrations, graphics, and key terms. Use the questions in the far left column of the SQ3R sheet to guide students through this survey process.

2. Ask students to think about how each of these items might relate to the text, and have them ask questions about the text to establish a purpose for reading. Encourage students to turn the title, heading, and pictures into questions. Have students write their

questions in the middle column of the SQ3R sheet. Suggested teacher talk might be, "While you are reading, try to find the answers to your questions."

3. Have students read the text to search for answers to their questions, and have them discuss their conclusions about the various elements they surveyed and write notes in the far right column of the SQ3R sheet.

4. Have students recite or write answers to the questions, looking away from the text to recall what was read. Students may need to reread the text for any remaining unanswered questions.

5. Have students review the information learned by applying it in another context. Examples may be creating a graphic organizer that depicts the main idea, role-playing parts of the text, drawing a flow chart, summarizing, and participating in group discussions.

Sources: Martin (1985); Robinson (1961)

Thinking About Questioning

Purpose: To ask questions to aid in comprehension.
Level: Fluent
ELL Technique: Yes
Multiple Intelligences: Visual/spatial, verbal/linguistic, interpersonal, intrapersonal
Materials: Text, chart paper

Procedure:

1. Divide a piece of chart paper into three columns with three separate headings: What do we know about asking questions? How does asking questions help the reader? and How do readers figure out the answers to their questions?

2. Discuss with students some possible answers to the questions, and allow time for students to think about the questions.

3. Write students' answers on the chart in the appropriate column.

4. Continue to ask these questions with the students before, during, and after reading various texts, and record their ongoing input on the chart.

Source: Miller (2002)

Comprehension Strategy: Visualizing and Sensory Imaging

Visualizing is a strategy that enables readers to make words on the page of a text real and concrete (Keene & Zimmermann, 1997). This strategy helps readers engage with the text, strengthens their relationship to the text, and stimulates imaginative thinking, which aids in comprehension. The reader visualizes by creating a picture in his or her mind based on descriptive details within the text to assist understanding. Before and after reading, sensory language helps readers form appropriate mental images in their heads about what is happening in the text.

Visualizing provides a springboard for memory recall and retention and makes reading an active process by stimulating the mental interchange of new ideas and experiences. "Visualizing personalizes reading, keeps us engaged, and often prevents us from abandoning a book" (Harvey & Goudvis, 2000, p. 97). Creating sensory images equips readers to draw conclusions, bring to mind details, and create interpretations of the text. Forming these images during reading seems to increase the amount readers understand and recall (Irwin, 1990).

Using drama is another way to explore a story and its content in a visual way. A research study on drama by McMaster (1998) found that vocabularies presented in a drama content provided students with the opportunity to acquire the meanings visually. "Drama for language learning not only provides a whole learning experience but brings language learning to life" (Robbie, Ruggierello, & Warren, 2001, p. 2). Using drama appeals to all the senses and encourages the use of sensory imaging as a strategy for acquiring meaning of text.

Appropriate literature that best supports the application of the visualizing strategy needs to have words and phrases that provoke thinking and are full of images for the mind. *The Seashore Book* (Zolotow, 1994) and *Greyling* (Yolen, 1991) are examples of appropriate literature; however, any piece of literature that encourages students to make visual images based on the language used in the text would be appropriate for use with these techniques.

Teacher Talk: Statements, Questions, and Prompts for Visualizing and Sensory Imaging

Following is a list of suggested teacher talk that encourages readers to think strategically as they employ visualizing skills. Try using some of these statements, questions, and prompts with your students as you work through the techniques in the following section.

- Try to imagine the setting.

- What pictures came to your mind as you read this page?

- As you listen to this story, create a picture in your mind of what you think is happening.

- What sensory details did the author use to help you create a picture of the story in your mind?

- What images did you see in your mind as you read?

- What sounds did you hear as you read?

- What words or phrases did the author use to help you create an image in your mind?

- Did you create a movie in your mind? If so, describe it.

- Try to picture in your mind someone who would remind you of a character in the story.

- In my mind's eye, I imagine _____.

- In my head, I can see _____.

- How did you visualize the beginning of the text in your head?

- I have a picture of _____.

- I imagine _____.

- I can imagine what it is like to _____.

Techniques for Visualizing and Sensory Imaging

Recording Mental Images

Purpose: To listen to a story and draw visual images of it.

Level: Emergent

ELL Technique: Yes

Multiple Intelligences: Visual/spatial, verbal/linguistic, interpersonal

Materials: Text, paper, markers or crayons

Procedure:

1. Have students fold a sheet of paper into fourths and use it to draw the mental images they see as they listen to you do a read-aloud. Do not show the pictures in the text as you read. Suggested teacher talk could be, "In my mind's eye, I can imagine _____."

2. Stop reading periodically to allow time for students to sketch their images. Suggested teacher talk could be, "Try to picture in your mind someone who would remind you of a character in the story."

3. Ask students to discuss how their mental images changed as new information was read from the text.

4. Reread the text, having students reflect on the sketches and how they helped to bring meaning to the text.

Source: Miller (2002)

Wordless Picture Books

Comprehension: Visualizing and Sensory Imaging

Purpose: To create illustrations that support the meaning of a text.

Level: Emergent

ELL Technique: Yes

Multiple Intelligences: Visual/spatial, verbal/linguistic, interpersonal

Materials: Text, drawing paper

Procedure:

1. As you read a story with students, discuss how to create mental pictures of it. Suggested teacher talk could be, "What picture comes to mind as I read the text, or as you read the text?"

2. After reading a text, have students create their own pictures of the parts of the text that were not illustrated. Ask students to draw the "missing parts" that they created in their minds and to share their drawings with a small group. Suggested teacher talk could be, "Try to imagine what the setting looks like." Compile students' drawings to create a picture book.

3. Reread the original text, reflecting on the illustrations the students drew to capture the mental images.

Source: Harvey and Goudvis (2000)

Drama

Comprehension: Visualizing and Sensory Imaging

Purpose: To bring story images to life.

Level: Early

ELL Technique: Yes

Multiple Intelligences: Visual/spatial, verbal/linguistic, interpersonal

Materials: Text, props

Procedure:

1. Have students read a text with no pictures, and then ask them to use appropriate props to act out images that were in their minds as they read the selection. Suggested teacher talk might be, "Did you create a movie in your mind? If so, describe it."

2. Ask several students to read the same unillustrated text. Suggested teacher talk could be, "How did you visualize the beginning of the text?"

3. Have students come to the front of the room, perform, and try to create the images in the minds of the other students (the audience) who did not read the text.

4. Ask the audience to discuss what they saw and to summarize what they think the text would be about based on the dramas performed.

Sensory Impressions

Purpose: To utilize senses to attend to story details.

Level: Early

ELL Technique: Yes

Multiple Intelligences: Visual/spatial, verbal/linguistic, interpersonal

Materials: Text, Sensory Impressions reproducible (see Appendix A)

Procedure:

1. Have students read a text selection that is rich in sensory details. Suggested teacher talk could be, "What sensory details did the author use to help you create a picture of the story in your mind?"

2. Copy the Sensory Impressions reproducible and distribute to each student. Ask students to stop throughout their reading to write or draw their responses to the specific sensory questions written on each finger of the hand. Suggested teacher talk might be, "What sounds did you hear as you read?"

3. Ask students to work in groups to compare their answers and discuss any differences in their responses.

Comprehension Strategy: Inferring and Drawing Conclusions

Inferring is a strategy that permits readers to merge their background knowledge with text clues to come to a conclusion about an underlying theme or idea. Drawing conclusions helps readers gather more information and ideas and understand the writer's point of view. Readers gather and question details from the text in order to draw these conclusions. They arrive at a decision or opinion by reasoning from known facts or evidence that seem to require that a specific conclusion be reached. Such readers use implicit information to make a logical guess or read between the lines.

Strategic readers create unique understandings of the text, make predictions and inferences, and confirm or deny those predictions based on textual information. These readers test their developing comprehension of the text along with extending their comprehension beyond literal understandings of the printed page (Keene & Zimmermann, 1997). "Inferencing is the bedrock of comprehension…it is about reading faces, reading body language, reading expressions, and reading tone, as well as reading text" (Harvey & Goudvis, 2000, p. 105).

Appropriate literature that best supports the application of the inferring and drawing conclusions strategy needs to have pictures or language that help to elicit inferences. *Stellaluna* (Cannon, 1993) and *How Many Days to America?* (Bunting, 1988) are examples of appropriate literature; however, any piece of literature that encourages the students to discuss, restate, relate, and manipulate the language to reflect their thinking would be appropriate for use with these techniques.

Teacher Talk: Statements, Questions, and Prompts for Inferring and Drawing Conclusions

Following is a list of suggested teacher talk that encourages readers to think strategically as they employ inferring skills. Try using some of these statements, questions, and prompts with your students as you work through the techniques in the following section.

- I wonder…
- What evidence does the author provide to support _____?
- What does the author want you to realize?
- What facts can you derive based on the following clues?
- What clues did the author give that led to your conclusion?
- What is the main conclusion from _____?
- What details or evidence supports your conclusion?
- What reasoning helped you draw your conclusion?
- What is the story beneath the story?
- What would happen if _____?
- Why do you think that would happen?
- Predict what _____ will do.
- Try to read between the lines.
- How do you know that?
- How do you think the character feels?
- This statement means _____.
- How do you combine the clues in the paragraph with what you already know to draw a conclusion?

Techniques for Inferring and Drawing Conclusions

Dramatic Interpretation

Purpose: To form and share unique interpretations of text through drama.
Level: Early
ELL Technique: Yes

Multiple Intelligences: Visual/spatial, verbal/linguistic, interpersonal
Materials: Text, preferably poetry

Procedure:

1. Select a poem of which students have at least some background knowledge; however, the content should be challenging enough to make students think through the poem carefully to understand it. Read the poem to students.

2. Have students work with a partner to reread the poem and decide on a way to interpret it through acting. Suggested teacher talk could be, "This statement means _____."

3. Ask students to use the clues from the text to make their interpretations. Suggested teacher talk might be, "What did the poem say that caused you to think that way?"

4. Have the pairs perform their interpretations.

5. After the performances, reread the poem and have students reflect on how their performances helped them to comprehend it.

Source: Miller (2002)

Interpreting Text

Purpose: To read between the lines to construct meaning.
Level: Early
Multiple Intelligences: Visual/spatial, verbal/linguistic, interpersonal
Materials: Texts, copies of text excerpt, overhead projector (optional), transparency of text excerpt (optional)

Procedure:

1. Enlarge a section of a text that supports inferring and display it with an overhead projector, or make and distribute copies so that all students can see the text and follow along.

2. Read aloud the passage, pausing at key sections to ask, "So what's *really* going on?"

3. Discuss with students what you and they think is really going on. If desired, you can have students read a section silently and then stop to talk in pairs about how every part of the text takes on a deeper layer when readers make their own interpretations. Suggested teacher talk could be, "Why do you think that would happen? What is the story beneath the story?"

Source: Calkins (2001)

Talk Show

Purpose: To reflect on and discuss the content of a book.
Level: Transitional

ELL Technique: Yes
Multiple Intelligences: Visual/spatial, verbal/linguistic, interpersonal
Materials: Text, microphone (toy or real), T-chart

Procedure:

1. Choose a group of three students to pretend that they are on a talk show: One student should host the show, one should pretend to be the author of a book the students have read, and one should pretend to be the reader of the book. Give the students a real or toy microphone to hold when they speak.

2. Have the host open the show by giving an introduction about the book they will be discussing on the show. Have students begin with their discussion of the book. The author should make statements that imply information, and the reader should make inferences from those statements. For example, if the author states, "The main character discovered real joy," then readers might infer that the main character was unhappy or upset about something but an event occurs which results in his or her happiness. Suggested teacher talk could be directed to the reader from the host: "What evidence does the author provide? What does the author want you to realize?"

3. Have the host begin to summarize the discussion with statements like, "So, what I hear you saying is _____."

4. Make notes during the talk show on a T-chart (i.e., a chart with a large T separating the author's statements from the readers' inferences) to discuss later with the "audience" (i.e., the other students in the classroom).

5. Reread the text, and have students reflect on the show and on how it supported their comprehension of the text.

Scenarios With T-Charts

Purpose: To make inferences about a scenario based on evidence.
Level: Fluent
Multiple Intelligences: Visual/spatial, verbal/linguistic, interpersonal
Materials: Text, paper

Comprehension: Inferring and Drawing Conclusions

Procedure:

1. Use scenarios from the text from which students can practice inferring. Have students listen to these scenarios or read them to each other and decide what inferences they can draw based on the evidence in the scenarios.

2. Have partners take turns stating their inferences and then noting what evidence from the scenario helped to lead them to their inferences about the section of the text. Suggested teacher talk could be, "What clues did the author give that led to your conclusion?"

3. Have the pairs create T-charts on paper. Students should write their inferences on the left side and write the evidence, or the "why" behind their thinking, on the right side of the chart. Suggested teacher talk might be, "What reasoning helped you draw your conclusion?"

4. Reread the text, having students note any changes directly on the T-chart as they listen to you read. Suggested teacher talk could be, "How did inferring support you in comprehending the text?"

Comprehension Strategy: Summarizing

Summarizing is a strategy that helps the reader identify and organize the essential information found within a text. Strategic readers summarize during reading by putting together information and focusing on the key elements of what they are reading. These key elements are brief and related to important ideas, events, details, structural clues, or other information that supports the reader in bringing meaning to the text. Students continually organize these key elements throughout their reading of a text while filtering out less significant details. Research by Pearson and Duke (2002) suggests instruction on summarizing to improve students' overall comprehension of text content.

In order to make generalizations about a story rather than simply retell the specifics, strategic readers select important information after reading and bring together these ideas in their own words. A summary is an objective retelling; it does not make obvious judgments. Summarizing is a succinct reduction of passages into a simple compilation of facts.

Appropriate literature that best supports the application of the summarizing strategy needs to have identifiable story elements (characters, setting, events, problem, solution). *Shiloh* (Naylor, 1992) and *The View From Saturday* (Konigsburg, 1997) are examples of appropriate literature; however, any piece of literature that encourages students to summarize the story elements would be appropriate for use with these techniques.

Teacher Talk: Statements, Questions, and Prompts for Summarizing

Following is a list of suggested teacher talk that encourages readers to think strategically as they employ summarizing skills. Try using some of these statements, questions, and prompts with your students as you work through the techniques in the following section.

- What words from a story jump out at you to help make an artistic representation?

- What was the focus of the reading selection?

- Think of all the parts in the story and put them together as if you were going to tell another person about the story.

- How could you say this using only a few sentences?
- What clues are within the text features?
- What does the author say?
- Which details are most and least significant?
- How can you use key ideas to condense the information in this story?
- Which words helped you describe the gist of the story?
- What do you think is the main idea of this story? Of this paragraph?
- What clues are within the text?
- What visual clues can you identify?

Techniques for Summarizing

Artistic Summary

Purpose: To artistically and orally summarize a piece of literature.
Level: Emergent
ELL Technique: Yes
Multiple Intelligences: Visual/spatial, verbal/linguistic, interpersonal
Materials: Text, art supplies

Procedure:
1. Read a story, and have students depict their story summaries through art projects such as creating a collage, timeline, mobile, poster, diorama, or cartoon strip. Suggested teacher talk might be, "Which words 'jump out' at you to help you make your artistic representation?"
2. Have students present their artistic interpretations, along with an oral presentation, to the class. You also can place the artwork on a display in the classroom along with a written summary of the text. Suggested teacher talk could be, "Which words helped you describe the gist of the story?"
3. Reread the text, and have students reflect on their understanding of the literature based on their artistic representations.

Journaling or Group Chart

Purpose: To identify and record summaries for discussion.
Level: Early
ELL Technique: Yes

Multiple Intelligences: Visual/spatial, verbal/linguistic, interpersonal
Materials: Text, chart paper or journals, Story Map reproducible (for Adaptation;
     see Appendix A)

Procedure:

1. As a story is being read (individually or as a read-aloud), have students stop to discuss and record important issues, themes, and ideas. Have students keep journals to use for this purpose, or take notes from group discussions on chart paper. Suggested teacher talk could be, "What was the focus of the reading selection? Which details are most and least significant?"

Adaptation: Copy the Story Map reproducible and distribute to each student. Ask students to complete the map while the story is being read and identify the characters (who they are and what the author tells about them), the setting (where and when the story takes place), the problems and events (what problems the characters faced, whether those problems changed throughout the story), and the solution (the conclusion, or how things worked out).

Summary Ball

Purpose: To create a group summary.
Level: Early
ELL Technique: Yes
Multiple Intelligences: Visual/spatial, verbal/linguistic, interpersonal
Materials: Text, beach ball, chart paper, permanent marker

Procedure:

1. After reading a narrative, write the questions Who, What, Where, When, Why, and How on an inflated beach ball, using a permanent marker.
2. Have students toss around the ball in a small group. Ask each student who catches the ball to look to see which word is closest to his or her right thumb and to answer that question with regard to the text just read.
3. If more than one student gets the same question, the first student can answer the question, and subsequent students can elaborate on what the first student said about that topic. Suggested teacher talk could be, "How could you say this using only a few sentences?"
4. Record the students' responses on chart paper in list format, to provide a group story summary.
5. Have students reread the text and reflect on the summary created. Suggested teacher talk might be, "How did creating a group summary support your understanding of the story we read?"

Source: Adapted from Cunningham and Allington (1998)

Narrative Pyramid

Purpose: To organize events in a story.

Level: Transitional

Multiple Intelligences: Visual/spatial, verbal/linguistic

Materials: Text

Procedure:

1. Choose a story the students have read, and tell the students they will be constructing an eight-line narrative pyramid of words. Suggested teacher talk could be, "Think of all the parts in the story and put them together as if you were telling another person the story."

2. Have the students construct their pyramids as follows:
   - The top line should contain the character's name in a single word.
   - For the second line, have students choose two words to describe that character.
   - On the third line, have students use three words to portray the setting.
   - On the fourth line, ask students to explain the problem using four descriptive words.
   - Lines five, six, and seven should present three different events that occurred, each line using five, six, and seven words, respectively.
   - For the eighth line, have students select eight words to express the solution to the problem.

3. Have students use their pyramids as a reference to summarize the text. Suggested teacher talk might be, "Using your pyramid, what was the text about?"

Source: Waldo (1991)

Somebody/Wanted/But/So

Purpose: To construct a graphic organizer to outline the story elements.

Level: Transitional (Adaptation for Early)

ELL Technique: Yes

Multiple Intelligences: Visual/spatial, verbal/linguistic, interpersonal

Materials: Text, paper, Hula-Hoops (for Adaptation)

Procedure:

1. Have students fold a sheet of paper into fourths and write the following headings on the four sections: Somebody, Wanted, But, and So.

2. Using a story that the students have read, have students complete their individual charts by writing a statement under each section: Somebody (identify the character), Wanted (describe the character's goal or motivation), But (describe a conflict that impedes the character), and So (describe the resolution of the conflict). Suggested teacher talk could be, "How can you use key ideas to condense the information in this story?"

Adaptation: Place four Hula-Hoops on the classroom floor, and tell students that each hoop represents one of the four headings (Somebody, Wanted, But, So). After reading a story, have students stand inside the hoops and summarize each corresponding aspect as they walk through the hoops. Suggested teacher talk might be, "Which details are the most and least significant?"

Source: Schmidt and Buckley (1990)

GIST (Generating Interactions Between Schema and Text)

Purpose: To formulate a summary based on condensing and building on previous summaries.

Level: Fluent

ELL Technique: Yes

Multiple Intelligences: Visual/spatial, verbal/linguistic, interpersonal

Materials: Text

Procedure:

1. Have students read several passages from a text and write a short passage containing 20 words that are most critical to understanding the content. Have students work in groups to generate summary statements, using these words. Suggested teacher talk could be, "Which details are most and least significant?"

2. Ask students to read three to five more paragraphs from the text and incorporate their former summary into a new summary account, still using 20 words or fewer. Continue this process, using the summary statements to create a final summary of the text read. Suggested teacher talk could be, "What was the focus of the reading selection?"

Source: Moore, Moore, and Cunningham (1998)

Comprehension Strategy: Determining Importance

Determining Importance is a strategy that requires the reader to distinguish between what is important and what is merely interesting. "When great readers are reading this stuff that has so many ideas in it, they have to listen to that mental voice tell them which words, which sentences or paragraphs, and which ideas are important" (Keene & Zimmermann, 1997, p. 86).

Readers are required to identify the topic and supporting details and to identify or invent their own main idea or summary statement by combining ideas across sentences. Sometimes, however, the reader needs to understand and remember more information than can be summed up in a brief statement. Finding the essence of the text is the key to determining what is important. The reader needs to make decisions as to what parts of a text deserve the most attention, remembering that not all the information presented is of equal value. Determining importance is critical when reading texts that emphasize learning of information, as in nonfiction. "When kids read and understand nonfiction, they build background for the topic and acquire new knowledge. The ability to identify essential ideas and salient information is a prerequisite to developing insight" (Harvey & Goudvis, 2000, p. 119). Strategic readers are able to look for text features that signal cues and for ideas that help to distinguish the important from the unimportant within the text and between fiction and nonfiction text.

Appropriate literature that best supports the application of the determining importance strategy needs to have strong essential information made evident through text features, ideas, and themes within the text. *The Titanic: Lost—And Found* (Donnelly, 1988) and *Henry and Mudge* (Rylant, 1996) are examples of appropriate literature; however, any piece of literature that encourages students to identify key ideas or themes that are relevant to the text would be appropriate for use with these techniques.

Teacher Talk: Statements, Questions, and Prompts for Determining Importance

Following is a list of suggested teacher talk that encourages readers to think strategically as they determine importance. Try using some of these statements, questions, and prompts with your students as you work through the techniques in the following section.

- What is essential?
- How did you know these details were more important than other details?
- What does the author offer as a theme or opinion?
- What is the author's message?
- Look carefully at the first and last line of each paragraph.
- Tell me about some of the important ideas that struck you.
- Which facts are important or essential to the text?
- Notice that the cue words are followed by important information.
- Use the margin to make notes.
- Highlight only necessary words and phrases.
- Show in the text what you read that was the most important idea.
- Locate and record only necessary words and phrases that support the conventions you can find in the text.

Chapter Tours

Purpose: To preview text and identify key nonfiction features.
Level: Early
ELL Technique: Yes
Multiple Intelligences: Visual/spatial, verbal/linguistic, interpersonal
Materials: Text, a hat marked "Tour Guide"

Procedure:

1. Have students take a "tour" of a nonfiction text they will be reading. Ask them to preview the text and identify features such as photographs, labels, and key words that will help them determine what is important. Suggested teacher talk could be, "Look carefully at the first and last line of each paragraph."

2. Have students take turns putting on the tour guide hat and leading a small group through a tour of the text students will be reading. Encourage students to make comments like a real tour guide, such as, "Now, on your left you will notice…." Suggested teacher talk could be, "Can you tell me about some of the important ideas that struck you?"

3. Read the text, and have students reflect on how the tour guide activity supported their comprehension.

Source: Wood, Lapp, and Flood (1992)

Main Idea Wheel

Purpose: To identify the main idea of a text.
Level: Transitional (Adaptation for Early)
ELL Technique: Yes
Multiple Intelligences: Visual/spatial, verbal/linguistic, interpersonal
Materials: Text, Main Idea Wheel (see Appendix A)

Procedure:

1. Copy the Main Idea Wheel and distribute to each student. Have students identify and record the important concept from a text in the center part of the wheel. Suggested teacher talk could be, "What is essential?"

2. On the spokes of the wheel, have students record important details that support the main concept. Suggested teacher talk might be, "How did you know it was important?"

3. Have students share their wheels with the class, and lead a discussion about what various students placed on their spokes as being important.

4. Reread the text, and have students reflect on the ideas and statements they wrote on their spokes and on how these ideas supported their process of making meaning from the text.

Adaptation: Have students draw pictures of important details from the text on the wheel.

Source: Adapted from Irwin and Baker (1989)

Sifting the Topic From the Details

Comprehension:
Determining
Importance

Purpose: To identify, organize, and reflect on supporting details.
Level: Transitional
ELL Technique: Yes
Multiple Intelligences: Visual/spatial, verbal/linguistic, interpersonal
Materials: Text, paper

Procedure:

1. Have students fold a sheet of paper into three sections lengthwise, creating three columns.

2. In the first column, have students write the topic of a chosen text.

3. Ask students to write the details that support the topic in the second column. Suggested teacher talk could be, "What is essential? How did you know these details were important?"

4. Have students write their personal responses (thoughts, feelings, and questions) to the information in third column.

5. Reread the text, and have students reflect on the responses they wrote.

Source: Harvey and Goudvis (2000)

Comprehension Strategy: Synthesizing

Synthesizing is the merging of new information with prior background knowledge to create an original idea. Strategic readers stop periodically while reading to digest what they have read and what it means before continuing. This process personalizes reading by allowing readers to form opinions and "[combine] separate pieces of knowledge to come up with knowledge that is new, at least new to the person doing the thinking" (Irwin, 1990, p. 102). This process allows readers to make judgments that promote higher-order "elaborative" thinking. The teacher who abandons the "one right answer" approach will elicit these divergent responses (Irwin, 1990).

Synthesizing usually occurs in conjunction with analysis. Readers sift through a plethora of information, pulling out key ideas and putting these ideas together to have an overall sense of what they are reading. This process draws together the results of developing thoughts into a conclusion to interpret or evaluate. The synthesizing strategy "combines elements into a pattern not clearly there before" (Tate, 2003, p. 6). The ability to synthesize when reading requires that readers integrate all of the comprehension strategies described previously in this chapter—which itself, actually, is synthesizing.

Appropriate literature (whether fiction or nonfiction) that best supports the application of the synthesizing strategy needs to have strong text elements and patterns. *A Color of His Own* (Lionni, 1976) and *The Kissing Hand* (Penn, 1993) are examples of appropriate literature; however, any piece of literature that encourages the students to extend literal retellings and add background knowledge would be appropriate for use with these techniques.

Teacher Talk: Statements, Questions, and Prompts for Synthesizing

Following is a list of suggested teacher talk that encourages readers to think strategically as they employ synthesizing skills. Try using some of these statements, questions, and prompts with your students as you work through the techniques in the following section.

- What new ideas or information do you have?

- What parts of this text can you use to create a new idea?

- What is the gist of the story?

- How could you test your theory?

- Try to propose an alternative to the situation.

- How has your thinking changed since reading that part of the text?

- How else could you _____?

- Try to verbalize what is happening within the text.

- What did you think about first? Now what are you thinking?

- How would you re-create _____?

- What do you understand now that you did not understand before?

- I didn't understand it when the author said _____, but now I understand that _____.

- Try to write down what you are thinking and continue to think as you add new thoughts to your previous ones.

Techniques for Synthesizing

Creating a Play

Purpose: To interpret students' understandings of text through drama.

Level: Early

ELL Technique: Yes

Multiple Intelligences: Visual/spatial, verbal/linguistic, interpersonal

Materials: Text, props that correspond with text

Procedure:

1. Read a story, and tell students they will be acting it out. Suggested teacher talk could be, "How would you re-create _____?"
2. Give students time to discuss, plan, and practice their interpretations of the text in small groups. Students can use whatever props they need to re-create the story that they read.
3. After students perform their interpretations for the class, have students discuss how their understanding of the text has changed, if at all. Suggested teacher talk could be, "I did not understand it when the author said _____, but now I understand that _____."

Mind Mapping

Purpose: To make connections to words or concepts from a text with artwork.

Level: Transitional

Multiple Intelligences: Visual/spatial, verbal/linguistic, intrapersonal

Materials: Text, paper, markers or crayons

Procedure:

1. Read a text, and have students create a map of it. Have them start by writing a central word or concept (or drawing a picture) in the center of a sheet of paper. Suggested teacher talk could be, "What words helped to identify the main idea?"
2. Have students draw or write five to seven main ideas that relate to that central word or drawing; these ideas should radiate out from the center. (Students may find it useful to turn their paper on the side in a landscape format for mapping.) By personalizing the map with their own symbols and designs, students will construct visual and meaningful relationships between their ideas and the text.
3. Reread the text, and have students reflect on their maps to better comprehend the text. Suggested teacher talk might be, "How has your thinking changed after drawing the map?"

Source: Buzan (1993)

Rewriting a Story

Purpose: To organize thoughts from a specific point of view.

Level: Transitional

Multiple Intelligences: Visual/spatial, verbal/linguistic, interpersonal, intrapersonal

Materials: Text

Procedure:

1. After reading a text, have students rewrite a passage from the story in first person from any character's point of view. Suggested teacher talk could be, "What new ideas or information do you have after looking at the text from a different perspective?"

2. In teams, invite students to share any new perspectives they have gained about the character from their rewriting activity. Suggested teacher talk could be, "What made you think that way?"

Say Something

Purpose: To monitor thinking about text while reading.

Level: Transitional

ELL Technique: Yes

Multiple Intelligences: Visual/spatial, verbal/linguistic, interpersonal, intrapersonal

Materials: Text

Procedure:

1. Put students in pairs, and assign each pair a text to read (both partners read the same text).

2. Instruct students to determine in advance the intervals at which they will stop in their reading (e.g., after a paragraph, a half page, a whole page) to say something about the text. (The more unfamiliar or complex the text, the smaller the amounts of reading that will need to be done at a time.) Suggested teacher talk could be, "Try to verbalize what is happening in the text."

3. Have the partners read to the designated place in the text and stop to take turns making one statement about what they have just read. Students can state their reflections, a question, a fact, a connection, an inference, and so forth.

4. Have students continue reading the texts, stopping at designated intervals to make statements to each other.

Source: Harste, Short, and Burke (1989)

Two-Column Notes

Purpose: To synthesize factual information.

Level: Transitional

Multiple Intelligences: Visual/spatial, verbal/linguistic, interpersonal

Materials: Expository text, Two-Column Notes reproducible (see Appendix A)

Procedure:

1. Copy and distribute the Two-Column Notes reproducible. Have students read passages from an expository text.

2. Have students stop as they read to record any factual information they learn on the left side of the form under Book Thinking. Suggested teacher talk could be, "What new ideas or information do you have now?"

3. On the right side of the form under Process Thinking, have students record new interpretations, questions, or statements they had while reflecting on and processing information from the text and which helped them acquire deeper meaning from the text. Suggested teacher talk might be, "Try to propose an alternative to the situation."

Source: Adapted from Harvey and Goudvis (2000)

Assessment

The purpose of comprehension assessment is to determine students' ability to derive meaning from text. Teachers should evaluate the results of these assessments to determine the strengths and weaknesses of their individual students. The data from these assessments guide the teacher in creating an appropriate action plan (strategies, techniques, and teacher talk) to meet the diverse needs of the students.

When assessing comprehension, teachers should observe whether students can do the following:

- Make predictions

- Establish a purpose for reading and monitor reading by asking questions

- Create mental images of what they are reading

- Make connections (text to self, text to text, and text to world)

- Merge background knowledge and text clues to point toward a conclusion about an underlying theme (inference)

- Retell all the details of a text

- Identify and organize the essential information found in a text

- Identify features of fiction and nonfiction text

- Relate important ideas to each other

- Self-monitor comprehension and apply an appropriate strategy for making meaning

Following are general lists of criteria from some sample comprehension assessments. This is by no means an exhaustive list; it is only a starting point. Each assessment is designated S for screening, D for diagnostic, and/or PM for progress monitoring.

DEVELOPMENTAL READING ASSESSMENT (DRA) K–3 (Beaver, 1997): S, D, PM

Oral comprehension: Student starts at the beginning and tells what happened in a story. Tester scores student responses using a retelling rubric.

DEVELOPMENTAL READING ASSESSMENT (DRA) 4–8 (Beaver & Carter, 2003): S, D, PM

Written comprehension: Student writes a summary and then answers literal, interpretive, and reflective questions.

DIAGNOSTIC ASSESSMENT OF READING (DAR) (Roswell & Chall, 1992): D

Silent reading comprehension: Student reads a selection independently and answers four questions at the end; student gives an oral summary of what he or she has read.

EARLY READING DIAGNOSTIC ASSESSMENT (ERDA) (Smith 2000): D

Reading comprehension: Student reads sentences or passages and answers questions about them.

FOX IN A BOX (Adams & Treadway 2000): S, D, PM

Oral comprehension: Student is asked questions about a story he or she has read: What do you think ___ will do next? Did that really happen? Tell me everything you remember from the story.

Comprehension is a key component of effective reading instruction. Effective comprehension instruction actively engages students in text and motivates them to use strategies and techniques. The NRP report indicates that "a variety of reading comprehension strategies leads to increased learning of strategies to specific transfer of learning, to increased memory and understanding of new passages" (NICHD, 2000, p. 4-52). Such effective comprehension requires explicit and purposeful teaching. "Instruction in comprehension strategies is carried out by a classroom teacher who demonstrates, models, or guides the reader on their acquisition and use. When these procedures have been acquired, the reader becomes independent of the teacher" (NICHD, 2000, p. 4-40).

The strategies, techniques, and teacher talk presented in this chapter and throughout the book support teachers in maximizing their readers' potential in becoming strategic readers.

Appendix A

Teacher Materials

Chapter 5

Chapter 6

EMERGENT READER ASSESSMENT

Student Name _____

Directions: Place a check mark and date in the indicator box that best reflects the student's behavior.

Observable Behaviors	Indicators			
	Never	Rarely	Often	Always
(PA) Recognizes and continues repetitive pattern				
(PA) Isolates and identifies phonemes in words				
(PA) Blends phonemes to form a word				
(PA/P) Identifies letter names and sounds				
(P) Distinguishes print/pictures and letters/words				
(P) Matches voice to print one-to-one correspondence				
(P) Recognizes some high-frequency words (10–12 words)				
(F) Follows an assisted reader as an echo				
(C) Makes meaningful predictions based on illustrations				
(C) Understands that print conveys a message				

Additional behaviors (noted at teacher's discretion [e.g., concepts about print]):

Areas of Reading

(PA) Phonemic Awareness   (P) Phonics   (F) Fluency
(V) Vocabulary   (C) Comprehension

EARLY READER ASSESSMENT

Student Name _____

Directions: Place a check mark and date in the indicator box that best reflects the student's behavior.

Indicators

Observable Behaviors	Never	Rarely	Often	Always
(PA) Segments and manipulates phonemes				
(PA/P) Uses letter–sound correspondence				
(P/F) Recognizes basic pronunciation marks				
(F) Reads word by word				
(P/V) Recognizes some sight words				
(V) Expresses an awareness of word meaning				
(P/C) Begins to self-monitor reading behaviors, uses cueing systems				
(C) Uses text and illustrations to predict, check, and confirm meaning				
(C) Participates in book discussions, makes text-to-self connections				
(C) Recognizes and retells story elements				

Additional behaviors (noted at teacher's discretion [e.g., concepts about print]):

Areas of Reading

(PA) Phonemic Awareness   (P) Phonics   (F) Fluency
(V) Vocabulary   (C) Comprehension

TRANSITIONAL READER ASSESSMENT

Student Name _____

Directions: Place a check mark and date in the indicator box that best reflects the student's behavior.

Indicators

Observable Behaviors	Never	Rarely	Often	Always
(P) Demonstrates a variety of decoding strategies independently				
(P/C) Relies heavily on text and less on pictures				
(F) Reads with fluent phrasing				
(F) Begins to pace reading				
(P/V) Recognizes many sight words				
(V) Demonstrates an increased vocabulary through word relationships				
(C) Participates in discussion about literary elements (main idea, story elements, compare/contrast)				
(C) Retells beginning, middle, and end of story				
(C) Summarizes a story using references to parts of the story				
(C) Uses inferences to bring meaning to text				

Additional behaviors (noted at teacher's discretion [e.g., concepts about print]):

Areas of Reading

(PA) Phonemic Awareness   (P) Phonics   (F) Fluency
(V) Vocabulary   (C) Comprehension

FLUENT READER ASSESSMENT

Student Name _____

Directions: Place a check mark and date in the indicator box that best reflects the student's behavior.

Observable Behaviors	Indicators			
	Never	Rarely	Often	Always
(P) Demonstrates complex word analysis				
(P/C) Integrates and cross-checks cueing systems				
(F) Demonstrates pacing, expression, and accuracy in oral reading				
(V) Uses contextual vocabulary with confidence				
(V) Analyzes word to determine meaning/ uses structural analysis (prefix, suffix, multiple meanings)				
(C) Summarizes and synthesizes the text				
(C) Distinguishes between significant and supporting details of text				
(C) Evaluates, interprets, and analyzes literary elements				
(C) Selects and reads a wide variety of genres independently				
(C) Contributes in complex literary discussions				

Areas of Reading
(PA) Phonemic Awareness   (P) Phonics   (F) Fluency
(V) Vocabulary   (C) Comprehension

DRAW A RHYME

When you draw your teacher, blue, green, or red,
Use whatever color you like to draw her _____.

head

To show her how much you care,
Please draw her some beautiful _____.

hair

She can see how each student tries,
When she uses both of her _____.

eyes

If you bring her a beautiful rose,
She can smell it with her _____.

nose

From her coffee cup she sips,
When you draw her a set of _____.

lips

She understands computer tech,
And wears a nametag chain around her _____.

neck

Please be careful because she does not like dirt
On her new, clean white _____.

shirt

At recess, please watch out for ants.
Make sure they don't crawl on your teacher's _____.

pants

Most of all we hope the teacher won't lose
Her really crazy pair of _____.

shoes

Written by Terry Vitiello and Jacey Jozwiakowski

PAIR-SHARE MATCH

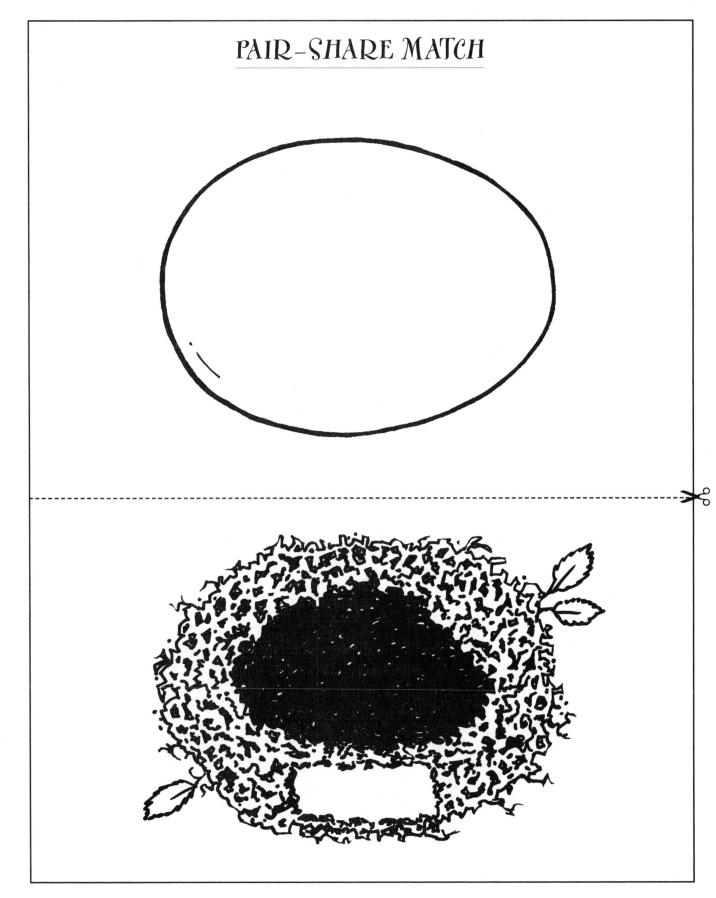

THINK SOUNDS

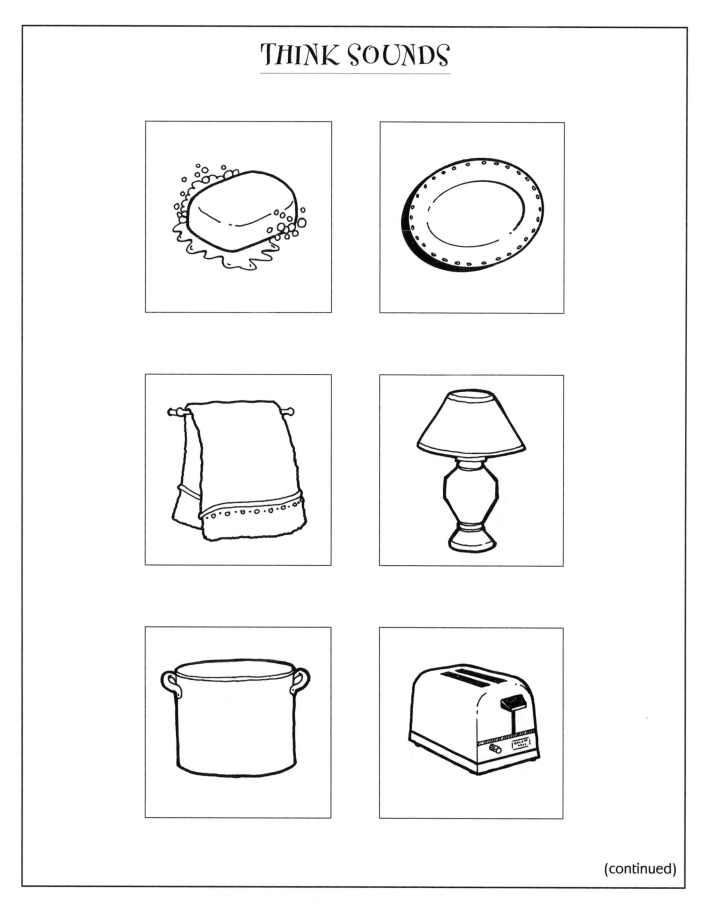

(continued)

THINK SOUNDS (cont.)

GRAPHING PHONEMES

(continued)

GRAPHING PHONEMES (cont.)

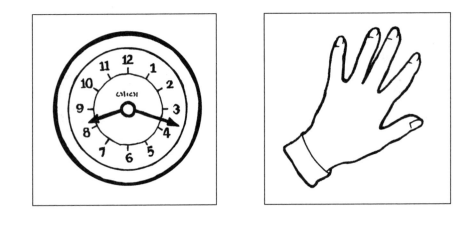

(continued)

(continued)

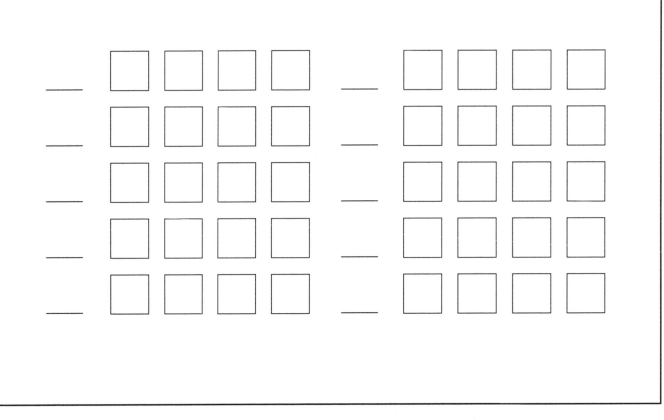

FE-FI

I have a song we can sing

I have a song we can sing

I have a song we can sing

It goes something like this:

Fe-Fi-Fiddly-i-o

Fe-Fi-Fiddly-i-o-o-o-o

Fe-Fi-Fiddly-i-ooooo

Now try it with the _____ sound!

LETTERBOXES

WORD DETECTIVES

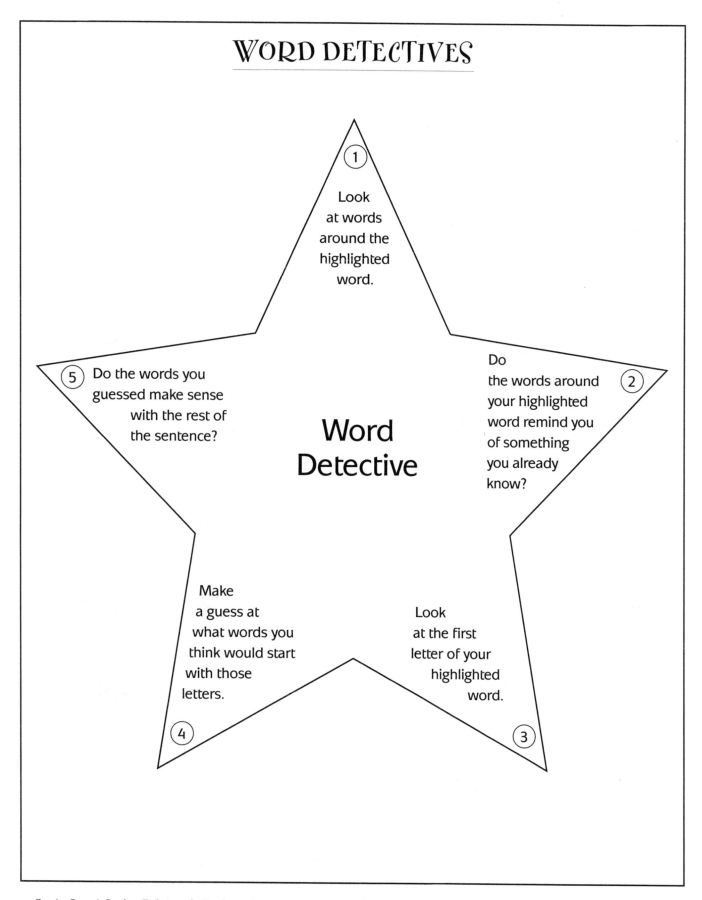

1 Look at words around the highlighted word.

2 Do the words around your highlighted word remind you of something you already know?

3 Look at the first letter of your highlighted word.

4 Make a guess at what words you think would start with those letters.

5 Do the words you guessed make sense with the rest of the sentence?

Word Detective

ONSET AND RIMES

-ack	-ail	-ain	-ake	-ale
-ame	-an	-ank	-ap	-ash
-at	-ate	-aw	-ay	-eat
-ell	-est	-ice	-ick	-ide
-ight	-ill	-in	-ine	-ing
-ink	-ip	-it	-ock	-oke
-op	-ore	-ot	-uck	-ug
-ump	-unk			

Adapted from Wylie and Durrell (1970)

VOWEL PATTERNS

Closed Vowel Pattern

One lonely vowel

squished in the middle

says its special

sound—just a little.

Open Vowel Pattern

If one vowel

at the end is

free,

it pops way up

and says its name to me.

Silent *e* Pattern

When the *e* is at the end,

the sound is gone;

it makes the other vowel in

the word

say its name long.

Two-Vowel Pattern—Digraphs

When two vowels

go walking,

the first one

does the talking

and says its name.

Adapted from Cheyney and Cohen (1998)

(continued)

VOWEL PATTERNS (cont.)

Two-Vowel Pattern—Diphthongs

Sometimes when

two vowels are together

they make a whine sound,

like when you fall down

and want to be found

(ow, aw, oy, boo-hoo).

Bossy *r* Pattern

When the vowel

is followed by

the letter *r*,

the vowel has to

let the *r*

be the star.

Consonant-*le* Pattern

The –*le* grabs the

consonant

right before it,

and makes a

clean syllable break

to form the split.

BRAIN TRICKS: MAKING CONNECTIONS

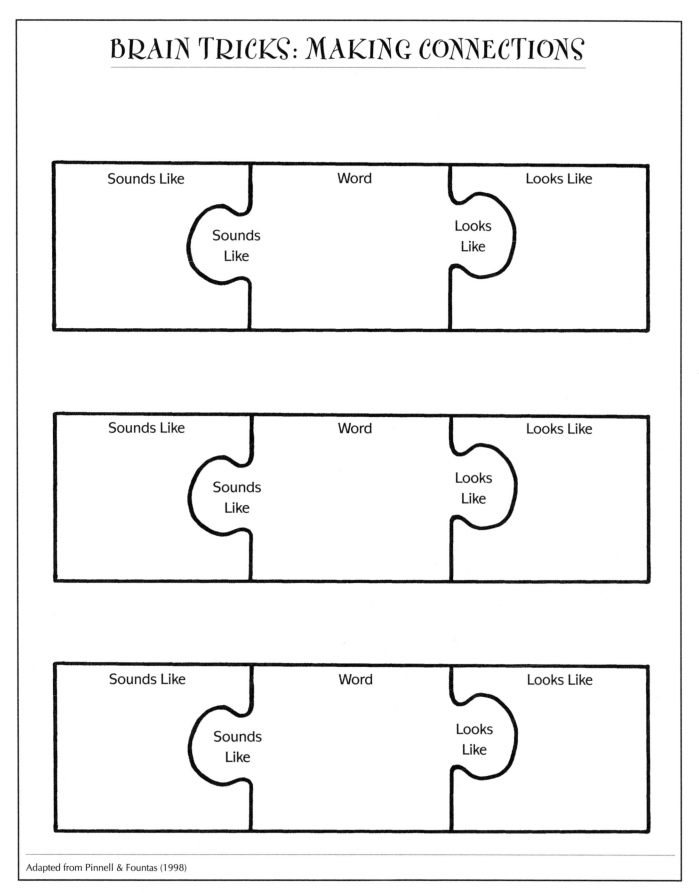

BRAIN TRICKS: VISUALIZE

In each frame, write a word you took a picture of in your mind.

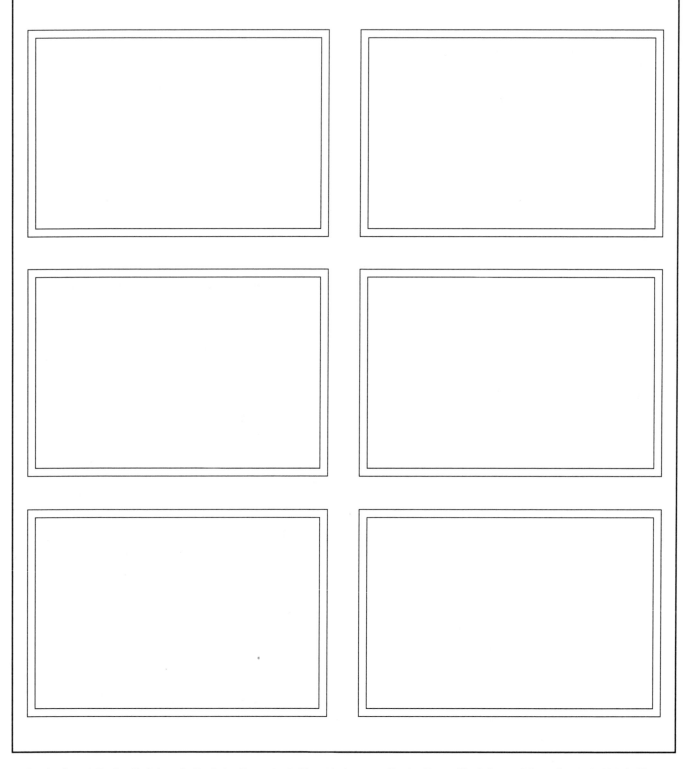

IF I CAN SPELL

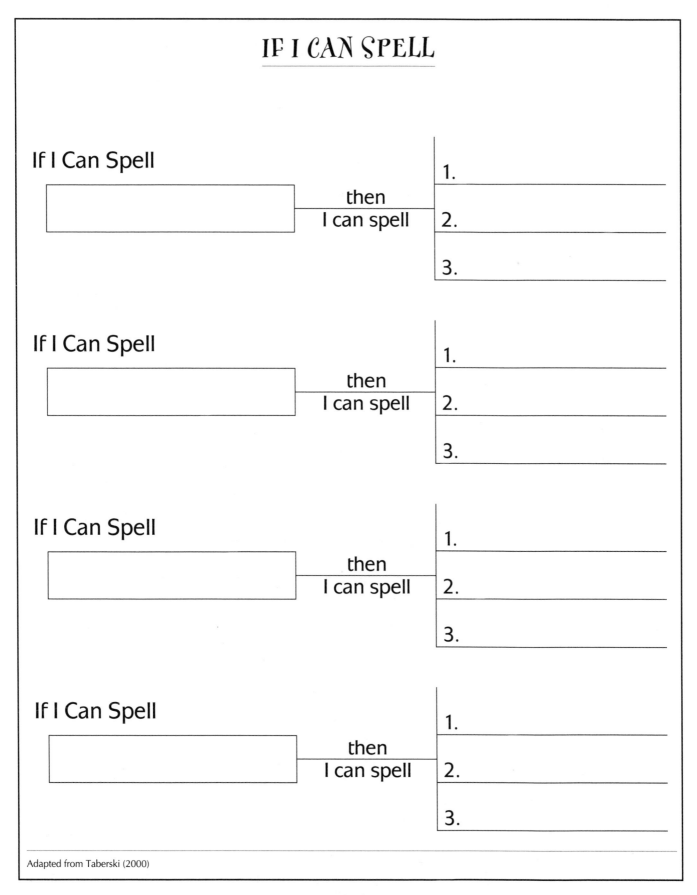

If I Can Spell

	then I can spell	1.
		2.
		3.

If I Can Spell

	then I can spell	1.
		2.
		3.

If I Can Spell

	then I can spell	1.
		2.
		3.

If I Can Spell

	then I can spell	1.
		2.
		3.

Adapted from Taberski (2000)

MAKING WORDS

Name _____

Date _____

Place cut up letters in space below to practice making words

_____

2-Letter Words	3-Letter Words	4-Letter Words	5-Letter Words
_____	_____	_____	_____
_____	_____	_____	_____
_____	_____	_____	_____
_____	_____	_____	_____
_____	_____	_____	_____
_____	_____	_____	_____

Adapted from Cunningham and Hall (1994)

LOOK/SAY/COVER/WRITE/CHECK

10 WAYS TO HELP KNOW MY WORD

1. Say the word.   (Auditory)

2. Stretch the word.   (Segmenting)

3. See the word.   (Visualizing)

4. Clap the word.   (Kinesthetic/rhythmic)

5. Compare the word.   (Analogies)

6. Draw the word.   (Visual/spatial)

7. Sing the word.   (Musical)

8. Make the word.   (Artistic)

9. Write the word.   (Kinesthetic)

10. Use the word.   (Application; Meaning)

PHRASE STRIPS CHOICES

2-Word Phrases	3-Word Phrases
I am	Yes I will
on the	I will go
in the	I will see
in my	She will see
by the	I did not
it was	it is blue
he said	we went to
she said	come over here
I had	it is just
at the	it is about
with her	we like to
with him	this is my
I can	I like to
I could	I have a
I will	that was in
I would	here it is
they went	it is about
	all day long

READING BOOKMARK

Before Reading

- [ ] Show cover
- [ ] Read title
- [ ] Tell what book is mainly about (Introduction)
- [ ] Invite predictions
- [ ] Show, read dedication page

During Reading

- [ ] Read aloud story
- [ ] Show pictures
- [ ] Pause to reflect and answer any listener questions

After Reading

- [ ] Ask listener how he or she liked story
- [ ] Talk about favorite parts
- [ ] Reread if necessary
- [ ] Respond to questions

Before Reading

- [ ] Show cover
- [ ] Read title
- [ ] Tell what book is mainly about (Introduction)
- [ ] Invite predictions
- [ ] Show, read dedication page

During Reading

- [ ] Read aloud story
- [ ] Show pictures
- [ ] Pause to reflect and answer any listener questions

After Reading

- [ ] Ask listener how he or she liked story
- [ ] Talk about favorite parts
- [ ] Reread if necessary
- [ ] Respond to questions

Before Reading

- [ ] Show cover
- [ ] Read title
- [ ] Tell what book is mainly about (Introduction)
- [ ] Invite predictions
- [ ] Show, read dedication page

During Reading

- [ ] Read aloud story
- [ ] Show pictures
- [ ] Pause to reflect and answer any listener questions

After Reading

- [ ] Ask listener how he or she liked story
- [ ] Talk about favorite parts
- [ ] Reread if necessary
- [ ] Respond to questions

Adapted from Strickland et al. (2002)

LISTEN TO ME

Classroom Form

	OK	Good	Super
1st Read	├—————————————————————┤		
2nd Read	├—————————————————————┤		
3rd Read	├—————————————————————┤		

Think about how your buddy read to you, and mark an X on the line.

☐ Remembered more words
☐ Read faster
☐ Read smoother
☐ Read with expression

Home Form

Listen to Me Read

I have been reading this book in class. Please listen to me read it to you and you can respond to my reading.

Comments

1. _____

2. _____

3. _____

PUNCTUATION POLICE

Punctuation Ticket

Issued to _____ Date _____

Infraction ☐ ? ☐ !
           ☐ . ☐ Verbal expression

Comments_____

_____

Officer _____
                   Signature

Punctuation Ticket

Issued to _____ Date _____

Infraction ☐ ? ☐ !
           ☐ . ☐ Verbal expression

Comments_____

_____

Officer _____
                   Signature

Punctuation Ticket

Issued to _____ Date _____

Infraction ☐ ? ☐ !
           ☐ . ☐ Verbal expression

Comments_____

_____

Officer _____
                   Signature

Punctuation Ticket

Issued to _____ Date _____

Infraction ☐ ? ☐ !
           ☐ . ☐ Verbal expression

Comments_____

_____

Officer _____
                   Signature

Punctuation Ticket

Issued to _____ Date _____

Infraction ☐ ? ☐ !
           ☐ . ☐ Verbal expression

Comments_____

_____

Officer _____
                   Signature

Punctuation Ticket

Issued to _____ Date _____

Infraction ☐ ? ☐ !
           ☐ . ☐ Verbal expression

Comments_____

_____

Officer _____
                   Signature

REFLECTION CONNECTION

Examples

Antonym	— opposite	off : on
Synonym	— same	little : small
Homonym	— sound alike	see : sea
Whole to part	— whole is related to its part	car : steering wheel
Part–whole	— part is related to whole	slice : pie
Function	— object is related to its use	radio : listening

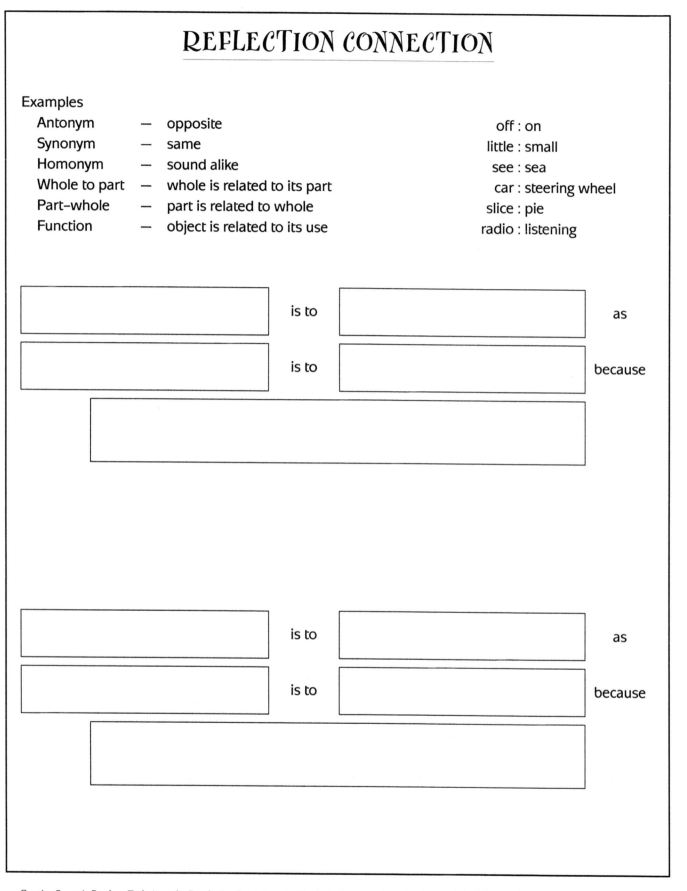

is to _____ as

is to _____ because

is to _____ as

is to _____ because

SEMANTIC FEATURE ANALYSIS

Name _____

Date _____

Text _____

	Characteristics, Properties, Features, Elements						
(Check one) ☐ Examples ☐ Categories ☐ Vocabulary words ☐ Phrases ☐ Concepts							

Adapted from Baldwin et al. (1981)

WHAT DO YOU MEAN?

Directions: Have students use each word as a noun and as a verb in sentences.

cut	plan	taste
pet	burn	hit
fish	love	help
name	color	talk
place	dress	walk
list	set	cry
map	dance	snack
swing	touch	light
play	run	trip
show	sign	watch

CONTEXT COMPLEX CLUES

Example Types of Context Clues

Definition: Defined when it appears. To <u>clutch</u> is to grasp or hold tightly to something.

Compare/Synonym/Appositive: Paired with a word(s) with the same meaning or comparisons, linked to a familiar word. The lady <u>clutched</u>, held tightly, to her purse.

Contrast/Antonym: Clarified with a word or phrase that means the opposite of the word or contrast. The lady <u>clutched</u> her purse, not wanting to let go of it.

Classification: Defined by its relationship to known words. The lady <u>clutched</u> her purse; she wanted to grasp it and hold on tight while she was on the ride.

Directions:

Word	Word in Context	Type of Clue

ALPHABOXES

Name _____

Book _____

A	B	C	D
E	F	G	H
I	J	K	L
M	N	O	P
Q	R	S	T
U	V	W	XYZ

LIST/GROUP/LABEL

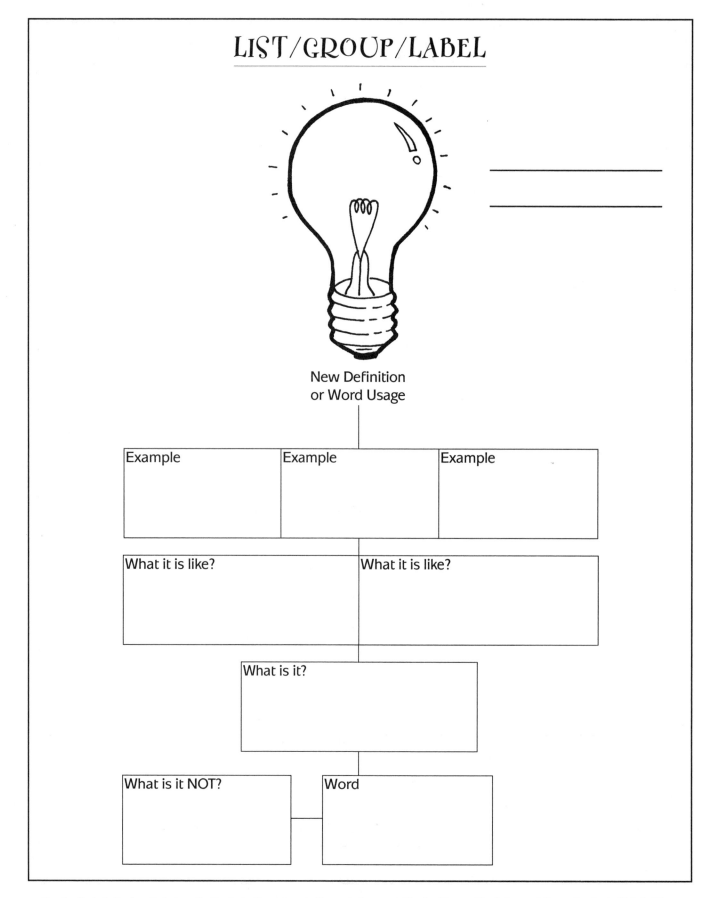

New Definition
or Word Usage

Example	Example	Example

What it is like?	What it is like?

What is it?

What is it NOT?	Word

VOCABULARY TREE

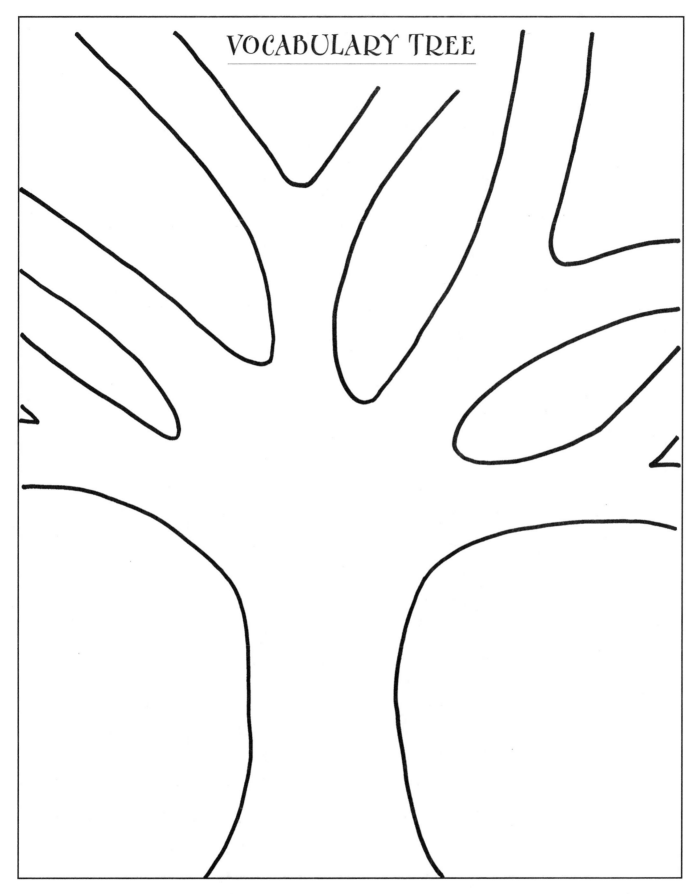

KNOWLEDGE RATING

Word		No idea of meaning	I've heard of it	I've seen it	I know it	It means
	Before Reading					
	After Reading					
	Before Reading					
	After Reading					
	Before Reading					
	After Reading					
	Before Reading					
	After Reading					

THINK SHEET

Main Topic

TWO-COLUMN NOTE PREDICTION FORM

I think . . .	Why I think that . . .

QARs

In the
Book

In My
Head

Right
There

Author
and Me

Think and
Search

On My
Own

SQ₃R

Name _____

Title of Book _____

Date _____

Survey	*when* *where* Question? *who* *what*	Read/Recite/Review
What is the title of the chapter?	1.	1.
Is there a chapter summary at the beginning or end of the chapter?	2.	2.
What are the main sub-headings in this chapter?	3.	3.
Are there any graphs, charts, or pictures?	4.	4.
Are there bold words or key vocabulary?	5.	5.
What do you think the chapter will be about?	6.	6.

Adapted from Vacca & Vacca (1989)

SENSORY IMPRESSIONS

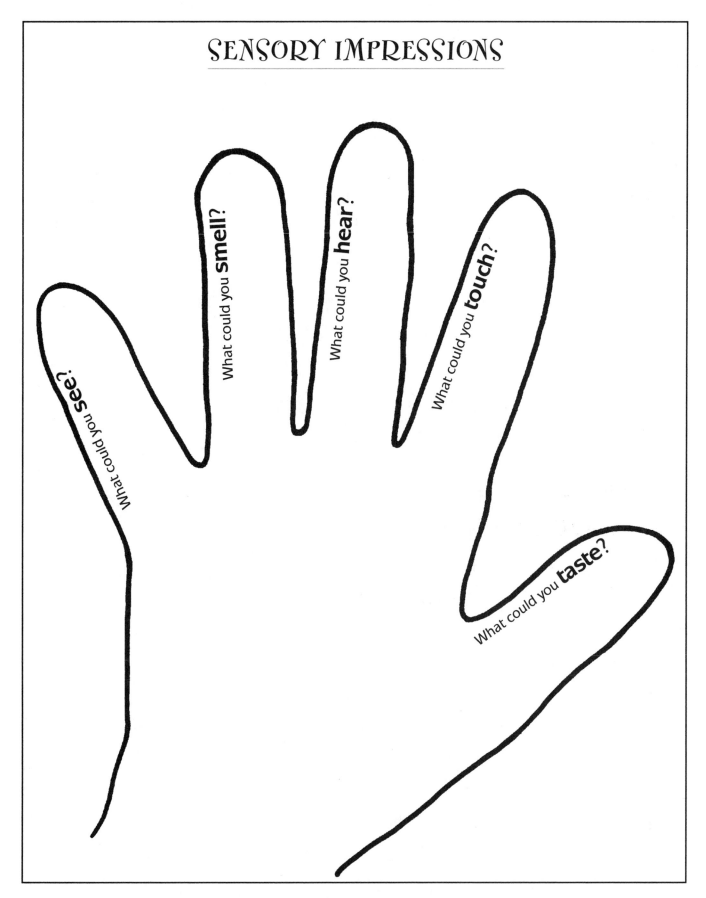

What could you **see**?

What could you **smell**?

What could you **hear**?

What could you **touch**?

What could you **taste**?

STORY MAP

Name_____

Date_____

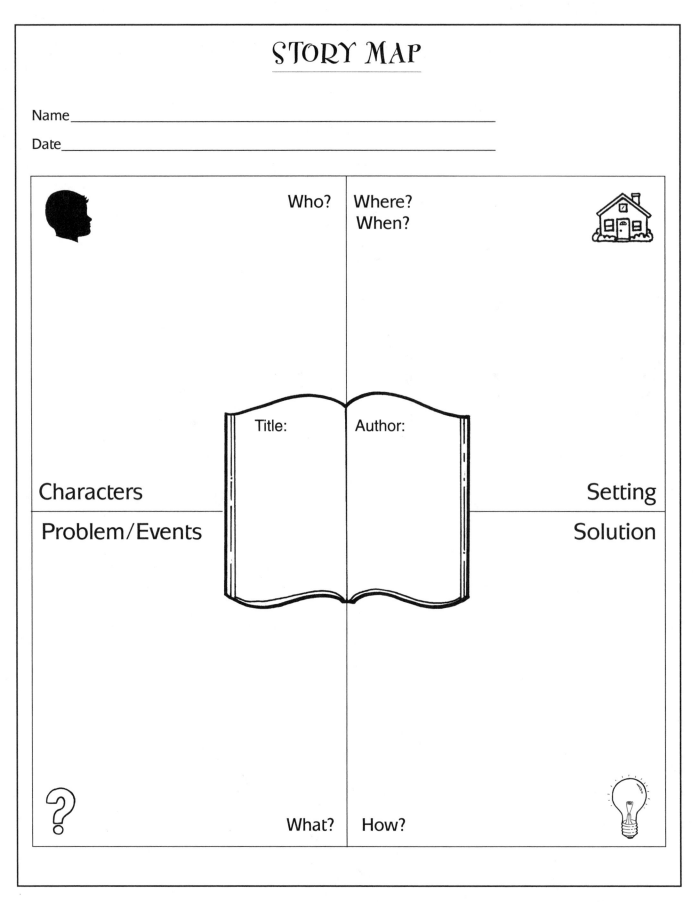

Who?

Where?
When?

Characters

Setting

Problem/Events

Solution

Title:

Author:

What?

How?

MAIN IDEA WHEEL

Name_____

Date_____

Text _____

Adapted from Irwin & Baker (1991)

TWO-COLUMN NOTES

Name _____

Date _____

Text _____

Factual Information (Book Thinking)	Practical Information (Process Thinking)
1.	
2.	
3.	
4.	

Adapted from Harvey & Goudvis (2000)

Recommended Resources

Cambourne, B. (1998). *The whole story*. New York: Ashton Scholastic.

Davidson, M., & Jenkins, J. (1994). Effects of phonemic processes on word reading and spelling. *Journal of Educational Research, 87*, 148–157.

Fredericks, A.D. (2001). *The complete phonemic awareness handbook*. Crystal Lakes, IL: Rigby.

Gardner, H. (1999). *The disciplined mind: What all students should understand*. New York: Simon & Schuster.

Irvin, J.L. (2001, May). Assisting struggling readers in building vocabulary and background knowledge. *Voices From the Middle, 8*(4), 37–43.

Lindfor, J.W. (1999). *Children's inquiry: Using language to make sense of the world*. New York: Teachers College Press.

Marzano, R., Pickering, D., & Pollock, J. (2001). *Classroom instruction that works: Research-based strategies for increasing student achievement*. Alexandria, VA: Association for Supervision and Curriculum Development.

Pressley, G.M. (1976). Mental imagery helps eight-year-olds remember what they read. *Journal of Educational Psychology, 68*, 355–359.

White, T.G., Power, M.A., & White, S. (1989). Morphological analysis: Implications for teaching and understanding vocabulary growth. *Reading Research Quarterly, 24*, 283–304.

Wiggins, G., & McTighe, J. (2001). *Understanding by design*. Upper Saddle River, NJ: Prentice Hall.

References

Adams, M.J. (1990). *Beginning to read: Thinking and learning about print.* Cambridge, MA: MIT Press.

Adams, M.J., Foorman, B.R., Lundberg, I., & Beeler, T. (1998). *Assessment test: Phonemic awareness in young children: A classroom curriculum* (pp. 108–131). Baltimore, MD: Brookes Publishing.

Adams, M.J., & Treadway, G. (2000). *Fox in a box: An adventure in literacy.* New York: McGraw-Hill.

Allen, J. (2002). *On the same page: Shared reading beyond the primary grades.* York, ME: Stenhouse.

Allington, R.L. (2001). *What really matters for struggling readers: Designing research-based programs.* New York: Longman.

Anderson, R.C., Hiebert, E.H., Scott, J.A., & Wilkinson, I.A.G. (1985). *Becoming a nation of readers: The report of the Commission on Reading.* Washington, DC: National Institute of Education.

Anglin, J.M. (1993). Vocabulary development: A morphological analysis. *Monographs of the Society for Research in Child Development, 58*(10), Serial No. 238, p. 35.

Archer, A.L., Gleason, M.M., & Vachon, V. (2000). *Rewards.* Longmont, CO: Sopris West.

Armbruster, B.B., Lehr, F., & Osborn, J. (2001). *Put reading first: The research building blocks for teaching children to read, kindergarten through grade three.* Washington, DC: U.S. Department of Education.

Baldwin, R.S., Ford, J.C., & Readence, J.E. (1981). Teaching word connotations: An alternative strategy. *Reading World, 21,* 103–108.

Ball, E., & Blachman, B. (1991). Does phoneme segmentation training in kindergarten make a difference in early word recognition and developmental spelling? *Reading Research Quarterly, 26,* 49–66.

Bear, D.R., Invernizzi, M., Templeton, S., & Johnston, F. (2000). *Words their way* (pp. 37–43). Upper Saddle River, NJ: Prentice Hall.

Beaver, J. (1997). *Reading assessment database for grades K–12.* Columbus, OH: Pearson Learning.

Beaver, J. (2001). *Developmental reading assessment.* Upper Saddle River, NJ: Pearson Education.

Beaver, J., & Carter, M. (2003). *Developmental reading assessment 4–8.* Upper Saddle River, NJ: Pearson Education.

Bishop, A., & Bishop, S. (1996). *Teaching phonics, phonemic awareness, and word recognition.* Westminster, CA: Teacher Created Materials.

Blachowicz, C. (1986). Making connections: Alternatives to the vocabulary notebook. *Journal of Reading, 29,* 643–649.

Blachowicz, C., & Fisher, P. (2000). Vocabulary instruction. In M.L. Kamil, P.B. Mosenthal, P.D. Pearson, & R. Barr (Eds.), *Handbook of reading research* (Vol. 3, pp. 503–523). Mahwah, NJ: Erlbaum.

Blair-Larsen, S., & Williams, K. (1999). *Balanced reading program: Helping all students achieve success.* Newark, DE: International Reading Association.

Blevins, W. (1999). *Phonemic awareness activities for early reading success.* New York: Scholastic.

Blevins, W. (2001). *Building fluency: Lessons and strategies for reading success.* New York: Scholastic.

Brozo, W.G., & Simpson, M.L. (2002). *Readers, teachers, and learners: Expanding literacy across the content areas* (4th ed.). Englewood Cliffs, NJ: Prentice Hall.

Buzan, T. (1993). *The mind map book.* London: BBC.

Calkins, L.M. (1994). *The art of teaching writing.* Portsmouth, NH: Heinemann.

Calkins, L.M. (2001). *The art of teaching reading.* New York: Longman.

Cambourne, B. (1995). Toward an educationally relevant theory of literacy learning: Twenty years of inquiry. *The Reading Teacher, 49,* 182–190.

Campbell, K.U., & Mercer, C.D. (1995). *Great leaps.* Gainesville, FL: Diarmuid.

Center for Academic and Reading Skills (CARS). (1998). *Texas primary reading inventory.* Austin, TX: Texas Education Agency.

Chard, D.J., & Dickson, S.V. (1999). Phonological awareness: Instructional and assessment guidelines. *Intervention in School and Clinic, 34*(5), 261–270.

Cheyney, W.J., & Cohen, E.J. (1998). *Phonics: Not if, but how and when.* Bothell, WA: Wright Group.

Clay, M.M. (2002). *An observational survey of early literacy achievement* (2nd ed., pp. 114–120). Portsmouth, NH: Heinemann.

Collins, N.D. (1993). *Teach critical reading through literature.* Bloomington, IN: Clearinghouse on Reading English and Communication.

Collins, A., Brown, J.S., & Newman, S.E. (1989). Cognitive apprenticeship: Teaching the crafts of reading, writing, and mathematics. In L.B. Resnick (Ed.), *Knowing, learning, and instruction: Essays in honor of Robert Glaser* (pp. 453–494). Hillsdale, NJ: Erlbaum.

Cunningham, P.M. (1990). The names test: A quick assessment of decoding ability. *The Reading Teacher, 44*, 124–129.

Cunningham, P.M. (2000). *Phonics they use: Words for reading and writing.* New York: Addison-Wesley Longman.

Cunningham, P.M., & Allington, R.L. (1998). *Classrooms that work: They can all read and write* (2nd ed.). Boston: Allyn & Bacon.

Cunningham, P.M., & Hall, D.P. (1994). *Making words: Multilevel, hands-on, developmentally appropriate spelling and phonics activities.* Parsippany, NJ: Good Apple.

Deshler, D., Ellis, E.S., & Lenz, B.K. (1996). *Teaching adolescents with learning disabilities: Strategies and methods* (2nd ed.). Denver, CO: Love.

Dole, J.A., & Smith, E.L. (1987, December). *When prior knowledge is wrong: Reading and learning from science text.* Paper presented at the annual meeting of the National Reading Conference, St. Petersburg, FL.

Dowhower, S. (1994). Repeated reading revisited: Research into practice. *Reading and Writing Quarterly: Overcoming Learning Difficulties, 10*, 343–358.

Duffy, G., & Roehler, L.R. (1986). *Improving classroom reading instruction: A decision-making approach.* New York: Random House.

Dunn, L., & Dunn, L. (1997). Peabody picture vocabulary test–III. Pines, MN: American Guidance Service.

Eldredge, J.L. (1990). Increasing the performance of poor readers in the third grade with a group-assisted strategy. *Journal of Educational Research, 84*, 69–77.

Eldredge, J.L., Reutzel, D.R., & Hollingsworth, P.M. (1996). Comparing the effectiveness of two oral reading practices: Round-robin reading and the shared book experience. *Journal of Literacy Research, 28*(2), 201–225.

Fisher, B., & Fisher Medvic, E. (2000). *Perspectives on shared reading: Planning and practice.* Portsmouth, NH: Heinemann.

Fitzpatrick, J. (1997). *Phonemic awareness: Playing with sounds to strengthen beginning reading skills.* Huntington Beach, CA: Creative Teaching.

Fletcher, R., & Portalupi, J. (2001). *Writing workshop: The essential guide.* Portsmouth, NH: Heinemann.

Flood, J., Jensen, J., Lapp, D., & Squire, J.R. (Eds.). (1991). *Handbook of research on teaching the English language arts.* New York: Macmillan.

Fogarty, R. (1997). *Brain-compatible classrooms* (2nd ed.). Glenview, IL: Skylight.

Foorman, B.R., & Mehta, P. (2002, November 6–7). *Definitions of fluency: Conceptual and methodological challenges*. Paper presented at the Focus on Fluency Forum, San Francisco, CA. Retrieved July 12, 2004, from www.prel.org/programs/rel/fluency.asp

Forbes, S., & Briggs, C. (Eds.). (2003). *Research in Reading Recovery, Volume II*. Portsmouth, NH: Heinemann.

Fountas, I.C., & Pinnell, G.S. (1996). *Guided reading: Good first teaching for all children*. Portsmouth, NH: Heinemann.

Fountas, I.C., & Pinnell, G.S. (1999). *Matching books to readers: Using leveled books in guided reading, K–3*. Portsmouth, NH: Heinemann.

Fountas, I.C., & Pinnell, G.S. (2001). *Guiding readers and writers grades 3–6: Teaching comprehension, genre, and content literacy*. Portsmouth, NH: Heinemann.

Frederick, A.D. (2001). *The complete phonemic awareness handbook*. Oxford, UK: Rigby Education.

Freeman, M.S. (1995). *Building a writing community: A practical guide*. Gainesville, FL: Maupin.

Fuchs, L.S., Fuchs, D., Hosp, M.K., & Jenkins, J. (2001). Oral reading fluency as an indicator of reading competence: A theoretical, empirical, and historical analysis. *Scientific Studies of Reading, 5*(3), 239–256.

Gardner, H. (1983). *Frames of mind: The theory of multiple intelligences*. New York: Basic.

Gardner, H. (1993). *Multiple intelligences: The theory in practice*. New York: Basic.

Gentry, J.R., & Gillet, J.W. (1992). *Teaching kids to spell*. Portsmouth, NH: Heinemann.

Gentry, R. (1989). *Spel is a four-letter word*. Portsmouth, NH: Heinemann.

Gillet, J., & Kita, M.J. (1979). Words, kids, and categories. *The Reading Teacher, 32*, 538–546.

Good, R.H., & Kaminski, R.A. (2002). *Dynamic indicators of basic early literacy skills* (DIBELS) (6th ed.). Eugene, OR: CBM Network, School Psychology Program, College of Education, University of Oregon.

Graves, D.H. (1982). *Writing: Teachers and children at work*. Portsmouth, NH: Heinemann.

Graves, M.F. (2000). A vocabulary program to complement and bolster a middle-grade comprehension program. In B.M. Taylor, M.F. Graves, & P. van den Broek (Eds.), *Reading for meaning: Fostering comprehension in the middle grades* (pp. 116–135). Newark, DE: International Reading Association.

Graves, M.F., Juel, C., & Graves, B.B. (1998). *Teaching reading in the twenty-first century*. Englewood Cliffs, NJ: Prentice Hall.

Hahn, M. (2002). *Reconsidering read-alouds*. York, ME: Stenhouse.

Harste, J., Short, K., & Burke, C. (1989). *Creating classrooms for authors: The reading-writing connection*. Portsmouth, NH: Heinemann.

Harvey, S., & Goudvis, A. (2000). *Strategies that work: Teaching comprehension to enhance understanding*. York, ME: Stenhouse.

Hasbrouck, J.E., Ihnot, C., & Rogers, G.H. (1999). "Read naturally": A strategy to increase oral reading fluency. *Reading Research and Instruction, 39*(1), 27–38.

Heckelman, R.G. (1969). A neurological-impress method of remedial-reading instruction. *Academic Therapy Quarterly, 4*, 277–282.

Henderson, E.H. (1985). *Teaching spelling*. Boston: Houghton Mifflin.

Henderson, E.H., Bear, D.R., & Templeton, S. (Eds.). (1992). *Development of orthographic knowledge and the foundations of literacy: A memorial Festschrift for Edmund H. Henderson*. Hillsdale, NJ: Erlbaum.

Herber, H. (1984). *Teaching reading in content areas* (2nd ed.). Englewood Cliffs, NJ: Prentice Hall.

Hiebert, E.H. (2002). *Quickreads*. Upper Saddle River, NJ: Pearson Education.

Hill, M. (1998). *Reaching struggling readers*. In K. Beers & B. Samuels (Eds.), *Into focus: Understanding and creating middle school readers* (pp. 81–104). Norwood, MA: Christopher-Gordon.

Hill, S. (1999). *Guided literacy learners*. York, ME: Stenhouse.

Holdaway, D. (1979). *The foundations of literacy*. Sydney, Australia: Ashton Scholastic.

Hoover, S., Frisbie, D., Oberley, K., Ordman, V., Naylor, G., Bray, J., et al. (2001). *Iowa tests of basic skills: Vocabulary subtest*. Itasca, IL: Riverside Publishing.

Hoyt, L. (1992). Many ways of knowing: Using drama, oral interactions, and visual arts to enhance reading comprehension. *The Reading Teacher, 45*, 580–584.

Hoyt, L. (1999). *Revisit, reflect, retell: Strategies for improving reading comprehension*. Portsmouth, NH: Heinemann.

International Reading Association. (1998). *Phonemic awareness and the teaching of reading* (A position statement of the International Reading Association). Newark, DE: Author.

Irwin, J. (1990). *Teaching reading comprehension processes* (2nd ed.). Boston: Pearson.

Irwin, J.W., & Baker, I. (1989). *Promoting active reading comprehension strategies: A resource book for teachers*. Englewood Cliffs, NJ: Prentice Hall.

Jensen, E. (1998). *Teaching with the brain in mind*. Alexandria, VA: Association for Supervision and Curriculum Development.

Jenson, E. (2000). *Different brains, different learners: How to reach the hard to reach*. San Diego, CA: The Brain Store.

Johnson, D.D., & Pearson, P.D. (1984). *Teaching reading vocabulary* (2nd ed.). New York: Holt, Rinehart and Winston.

Juel, C. (1988). Learning to read and write: A longitudinal study of fifty-four children from first through fourth grades. *Journal of Educational Psychology, 80*, 437–447.

Keene, E., & Zimmermann, S. (1997). *Mosaic of thought: Teaching comprehension in a reader's workshop*. Portsmouth, NH: Heinemann.

Knapp, M.S. (1995). *Teaching for meaning in high-poverty classrooms*. New York: Teachers College Press.

Koskinen, P.S., Wilson, R.M., & Jensema, C.J. (1985). Closed-captioned television: A new tool for reading instruction. *Reading World, 24*(4), 1–7.

Kuhn, M.R., & Stahl, S.A. (2003). Fluency: A review of developmental and remedial practices. *Journal of Educational Psychology, 95*, 3–21.

LaBerge, D., & Samuels, S.J. (1974). Toward a theory of automatic information processing in reading. *Cognitive Psychology, 6*, 293–323.

Langer, J.A. (1981, November). From theory to practice: A prereading plan. *Journal of Reading, 25*, 152–156.

Levine, M. (2002). *A mind at a time*. New York: Simon & Schuster.

Lindamood, C., & Lindamood, R. (1971). *Lindamood auditory conceptualization test*. Austin, TX: PRO-ED.

Love, E., & Reilly, S. (1996). *A sound way: Phonics activities for early literacy*. York, ME: Stenhouse.

Lyons, C.A. (2003). *Teaching struggling readers: How to use brain-based research to maximize learning*. Portsmouth, NH: Heinemann.

Manzo, A.V. (1969). The ReQuest procedure. *Journal of Reading, 13*, 123–126.

Martin, M.A. (1985). Students' application of self-questioning study techniques: An investigation of their efficiency. *Reading Psychology, 6*, 69–83.

McCarrier, A., Pinnell, G.S., & Fountas, I. (1999). *Interactive writing: How language and literacy come together*. Portsmouth, NH: Heinemann.

McEwan, E.K. (2002). *Teach them all to read: Catching the kids who fall through the cracks*. Thousand Oaks, CA: Corwin.

McGinley, W., & Denner, P. (1987). Story impressions: A prereading/writing activity. *Journal of Reading, 31*(3), 248–253.

McKeown, M. (1993). Creating definitions for young word learners. *Reading Research Quarterly, 28,* 16–33.

McMaster, J.C. (1998). "Doing" literature: Using drama to build literacy classrooms: The segue for a few struggling readers. *The Reading Teacher, 51,* 574–584.

Miller, D. (2002). *Reading with meaning: Teaching comprehension in the primary grades.* York, ME: Stenhouse.

Misulis, K. (1999). Making vocabulary development manageable in content instruction. *Contemporary Education, 70*(2), 25–30.

Moore, D.W., Moore, S.A., & Cunningham, P.M. (1998). *Developing readers and writers in the content areas, K–12* (3rd ed.). Boston: Allyn & Bacon.

Morris, D. (1992). *Case studies in teaching beginning readers: The Howard Street tutoring manual.* Boone, NC: Fieldstream.

Morrow, L.M., & Tracey, D.H. (1997). Strategies used for phonics instruction in early childhood classrooms. *The Reading Teacher, 50,* 644–651.

Moustafa, M. (1997). *Beyond traditional phonics: Research discoveries and reading instruction.* Portsmouth, NH: Heinemann.

Murray, B.A., & Lesniak, T. (1999). The letter box lesson: A hands-on approach for teaching decoding. *The Reading Teacher, 52,* 644–650.

Nagy, W.E. (2003). *Teaching vocabulary to improve reading comprehension.* Newark, DE: International Reading Association.

Nagy, W.E., Anderson, R.C., & Herman, P.A. (1987). Learning word meanings from context during normal reading. *American Educational Research Journal, 24,* 237–270.

Nagy, W.E., Diakidoy, I.N., & Anderson, R.C. (1991). *The development of knowledge of derivational suffixes* (Tech. Rep. No. 536). Champaign, IL: Center for the Study of Reading.

Nathan, R.G., & Stanovich, K.E. (1991). The causes and consequences of differences in reading fluency. *Theory Into Practice, 30*(3), 176–184.

National Institute of Child Health and Human Development. (2000). *Report of the National Reading Panel. Teaching children to read: An evidence-based assessment of the scientific research literature on reading and its implications for reading instruction* (NIH Publication No. 00-4769). Washington, DC: U.S. Government Printing Office.

Nilsen, A.P., & Nilsen, D.L.F. (2003). Vocabulary development: Teaching vs. testing. *English Journal, 92*(3), 31–37.

Nist, S.L., & Olejnik, S. (1995). The role of context and dictionary definitions on varying levels of word knowledge. *Reading Research Quarterly, 30,* 172–193.

No Child Left Behind Act of 2001, Pub. L. No. 107-110, 115 Stat. 1425 (2002).

Ogle, D.M. (2000). Make it visual: A picture is worth a thousand words. In M. McLaughlin & M. Vogt (Eds.), *Creativity and innovation in content area teaching* (pp. 55–71). Norwood, MA: Christopher Gordon.

Olson, M.W., & Gee, T.C. (1991). Content reading instruction in the primary grades: Perceptions and strategies. *The Reading Teacher, 45,* 298–307.

Opitz, M. (1998). *Flexible grouping in reading: Practical ways to help all students become better readers.* New York: Scholastic.

Paris, S.G., Cross, D.R., & Lipson, M.Y. (1984, December). Informed strategies for learning: A program to improve children's reading awareness and comprehension. *Journal of Educational Psychology, 76*(6), 1239–1252.

Paris, S.G., Wasik, B.A., & Turner, J.C. (1991). The development of strategic readers. In R. Barr, M.L. Kamil, P.B. Mosenthal, & P.D. Pearson, (Eds.), *Handbook of reading research* (Vol. 2, pp. 609–640). White Plains, NY: Longman.

Parkes, B. (2000). *Read it again! Revisiting shared reading.* York, ME: Stenhouse.

Payne, C.D., & Schulman, M.B. (1999). *Getting the most out of morning message and other shared writing lessons.* New York: Scholastic.

Pearson, P.D., & Duke, N.K. (2002). Comprehension instruction in the primary grades. In C.C. Block & M. Pressley (Eds.), *Comprehension instruction: Research-based best practices* (pp. 247–258). New York: Guilford.

Pearson, P.D., & Gallagher, M. (1983). The instruction of reading comprehension. *Contemporary Educational Psychology, 8,* 317–344.

Perfetti, C.A., Beck, I., Bell, L., & Hughes, C. (1987). Phonemic knowledge and learning to read are reciprocal: A longitudinal study of first grade. *Merrill-Palmer Quarterly, 33,* 283–319.

Pinnell, G.S., & Fountas, I.C. (1998). *Word matters: Teaching phonics and spelling in the reading/writing classroom.* Portsmouth, NH: Heinemann.

Pinnell, G.S., Pikulski, J.J., Wixson, K.K., Campbell, J.R., Gough, P.B., & Beatty, A.S. (1995). *Listening to children read aloud data from NAEP's integral reading performance record CIRPR at grade 4* (Report No. 23-FR-04 prepared by the Educational Testing Service). Washington DC: Office of Educational Research and Improvement, U.S. Department of Education.

Pittelmann, S.D., Heimlich, J.E., Berglund, R.L., & French, M.P. (1991). *Semantic feature analysis: Classroom applications.* Newark, DE: International Reading Association.

Pressley, M., El-Dinary, P.B., Gaskins, T., Schuder, T., Bergman, J.L., Almasi, J., et al. (1992). Beyond direct explanation: Transactional instruction of reading comprehension strategies. *The Elementary School Journal, 92*(5), 513–555.

Pressley, M., Goodchild, F., Fleet, J., Zajchowski, E., & Evan, E. (1989). The challenges of classroom strategy instruction. *The Elementary School Journal, 89*(3), 301–342.

Rafoth, M.A. (1999). *Inspiring independent learning: Successful classroom strategies.* Washington, DC: National Education Association of the United States.

Raphael, T.E. (1986). Teaching question-answer relationships, revisited. *The Reading Teacher, 39,* 516–522.

Rashotte, C.A., & Torgesen, J.K. (1985). Repeated reading and reading fluency in learning disabled children. *Reading Research Quarterly, 20,* 180–188.

Rasinski, T.V. (1989). Fluency for everyone: Incorporating fluency instruction in the classroom. *The Reading Teacher, 42,* 690–693.

Rasinski, T.V. (2000). Speed does matter in reading. *The Reading Teacher, 54,* 146–150.

Rasinski, T.V. (2003). *The fluent reader: Oral reading strategies for building word recognition, fluency, and comprehension.* New York: Scholastic.

Rayner, K. (1998). Eye movement in reading and informational processing: Twenty years of research. *Psychological Bulletin, 124,* 372–422.

Readence, J.E., Bean, T.W., & Balwin, R.S. (1998). *Content area literacy: An integrated approach* (6th ed.). Dubuque, IA: Kendall/Hunt.

Redfield, D.L., & Rousseau, E.W. (1981). Meta-analysis of experimental research on teacher questioning behavior. *Review of Educational Research, 51,* 237–245.

Robb, L. (1997). Stretch your students' reading vocabulary. *Instructor, 106*(8), 34.

Robbie, S., Ruggierello, T., & Warren, B. (2001). Using drama to bring language to life: Ideas, games, and activities for teachers of languages and language arts. Concord, ON: Captus Press.

Robinson, F. (1961). Study skills for superior students in secondary schools. *The Reading Teacher, 25,* 29–33.

Rosner, J. (1975). *Helping children overcome learning difficulties: A step-by-step guide for parents and teachers.* New York: Walker & Company.

Roswell, G., & Chall, J. (1992). *Diagnostic assessment of reading.* Itasca, IL: Riverside.

Routman, R. (2000). *Conversations: Strategies for teaching, learning, and evaluating.* Portsmouth, NH. Heinemann.

Routman, R. (2003). *Reading essentials: The specifics you need to teach reading well.* Portsmouth, NH: Heinemann.

Rupley, W., Logan, J.W., & Nichols, W.D. (1999). Vocabulary instruction in a balanced reading program. *The Reading Teacher, 52,* 336–346.

Samuels, S.J. (1979). The method of repeated readings. *The Reading Teacher, 32,* 403–408.

Samuels, S.J. (2002). Reading fluency: Its development and assessment. In A.E. Farstrup & S.J. Samuels (Eds.), *What research has to say about reading instruction* (3rd ed., pp. 166–183). Newark, DE: International Reading Association.

Samuels, S.J., & Farstrup, A.E. (Eds.). (1992). *What research has to say about reading instruction* (2nd ed.) Newark, DE: International Reading Association.

Saunders-Smith, G. (2003). *The ultimate guided reading how-to book: Building literacy through small-group instruction.* Tucson, AZ: Zephyr.

Schmidt, B., & Buckley, M. (1990). Plot relationships chart. In J.M. Bacon, D. Bewell, & M. Vogt (Eds.), *Responses to literature: Grades K–8* (p. 7). Newark, DE: International Reading Association.

Schulman, M.B., & Payne, C.D. (2000). *Guided reading: Making it work.* New York: Scholastic.

Schwartz, R.M. (1988). Learning to learn vocabulary in content area textbooks. *Journal of Reading, 32,* 108–118.

Schwartz, R.M., & Raphael, T.E. (1985). Concept of definition: A key to improving students' vocabulary. *The Reading Teacher, 39,* 198–205.

Shanahan, T. (2002, November 6–7). *A sin of the second kind: The status of reading fluency in America.* Paper presented at the Focus on Fluency Forum, San Francisco, CA. Retrieved July 12, 2004, from www.prel.org/programs/rel/fluency.asp

Shepard, A. (1994). From script to stage: Tips for Readers Theatre. *The Reading Teacher, 48,* 184–185.

Silver, H., Strong, R., & Perini, M. (1998). *Tools for promoting active, in-depth learning* (2nd ed.). Woodbridge, NJ: Thoughtful Education.

Sippola, A.E. (1995). K-W-L-S. *The Reading Teacher, 48,* 542–543.

Sloyer, S. (1982). *Readers Theatre: Story dramatization in the classroom.* Urbana, IL: National Council of Teachers of English.

Smith, D.R. (2000). *Early reading diagnostic assessment.* San Antonio, TX: Harcourt Assessment Company.

Snow, C.E., Burns, S., & Griffin, P. (Eds.). (1998). *Preventing reading difficulties in young children.* Washington, DC: National Academy Press.

Stahl, S.A., Duffy-Hester, A.M., & Stahl, K.A. (1998). Everything you wanted to know about phonics (but were afraid to ask). *Reading Research Quarterly, 33,* 338–355.

Stanovich, K.E. (1986). Matthew effects in reading: Some consequences of individual differences in the acquisition of literacy. *Reading Research Quarterly, 21*(4), 360–407.

Stanovich, K.E. (1992). Are we overselling literacy? In C. Temple & P. Collins (Eds.), *Stories and readers: New perspectives on literature in the elementary classroom* (p. 226). Norwood, MA: Christopher Gordon.

Stayter, F., & Allington, R.L. (1991). Fluency and comprehension. *Theory Into Practice, 30,* 143–148.

Strickland, D.S. (1998). *Teaching phonics today: A primer for educators.* Newark, DE: International Reading Association.

Strickland, D.S., Ganske, K., & Monroe, J.K. (2002). *Supporting struggling readers and writers: Strategies for classroom intervention, 3–6.* Newark, DE: International Reading Association.

Taberski, S. (2000). *On solid ground: Strategies for teaching reading K–3.* Portsmouth, NH: Heinemann.

Tate, M.L. (2003). *Worksheets don't grow dendrites: Twenty instructional strategies that engage the brain.* Thousand Oaks, CA. Corwin.

Taylor, B.M., Frye, B., & Maruyama, G.M. (1990). Time spent reading and reading growth. *American Educational Research Journal, 27,* 351–362.

Taylor, B.M., Pressley, M.P., & Pearson, P.D. (2000). Research-supported characteristics of teachers and schools that promote reading achievement. Washington, DC: National Education Association, Reading Matters Research Report.

Tierney, R.J., & Readence, J.E. (1999). *Reading strategies and practices: A compendium* (5th ed.). Boston: Pearson.

Tompkins, G.E. (2000a). *Literacy for the twenty-first century: A balanced approach* (2nd ed.). Englewood Cliffs, NJ: Prentice Hall.

Tompkins, G.E. (2000b). *Teaching writing: Balancing process and product.* Upper Saddle River, NJ: Prentice Hall.

Topping, K.J., & Ehly, S. (1998). *Peer assisted learning.* Mahwah, NJ: Erlbaum.

Torgeson, J.K., Rashotte, C.A., & Alexander, A.W. (2001). Principles of fluency instruction in reading: Relationships with established empirical outcomes. In M. Wolfe (Ed.), *Dyslexia, fluency, and the brain* (pp. 333–355). Timonium, MD: York.

Traill, L. (1995). *Highlight my strengths: Assessment and evaluation of literacy learning.* Crystal Lake, IL: Rigby.

Trelease, J. (2001). *The read-aloud handbook* (5th ed.). New York: Penguin.

Tyner, B. (2004). *Small-group reading instruction: A differentiated teaching model for beginning and struggling readers.* Newark, DE: International Reading Association.

U.S. Department of Education. (1998). *Every child a reader: Applying reading research to the classroom.* Ann Arbor: Center for the Improvement of Early Reading Achievement, University of Michigan School of Education.

Vacca, J.L., Vacca, R.T., & Gove, M.K. (1995). *Reading and learning to read.* Reading, MA: Addison-Wesley.

Vacca, R.T., & Vacca, J.L. (1989). *Content area reading* (3rd ed.). Glenview, IL: Scott Foresman.

Vacca, R.T., & Vacca, J.L. (1996). *Content area reading* (5th ed.). Glenview, IL: Scott Foresman.

Vygotsky, L.S. (1978). *Mind in society: The development of higher psychological processes* (M. Cole, V. John-Steiner, S. Scribner, & E. Souberman, Eds. & Trans.). Cambridge, MA: Harvard University Press. (Original work published 1934)

Wagner, R., Torgesen, J.K., & Rashotte, C.A. (1994). Development of reading-related phonological processing abilities: New evidence of bi-directional causality from a latent variable longitudinal study. *Developmental Psychology, 30,* 78–87.

Waldo, B. (1991). Story pyramid. In J.M. Macon, D. Bewell, & M.E. Vogt (Eds.), *Responses to literature: Grades K–8* (pp. 23–24). Newark, DE: International Reading Association.

Wiederholt, J.L., & Bryant, B.R. (2001). *Gray oral reading test-IV*. Austin, TX: PRO-ED.

Wood, K., Lapp, D., & Flood, J. (1992). *Guiding readers through text: A review of study guides*. Newark: DE: International Reading Association.

Woodcock, R. (1987). *Woodcock reading master test-revised*. Circle Pines, MN: American Guidance Service.

Wylie, R.E., & Durell, D.D. (1970). Teaching vowels through phonograms. *Elementary English, 47*, 787–791.

Yopp, H.K. (1992). Developing phonemic awareness in young children. *The Reading Teacher, 45*, 696–703.

Yopp, H.K. (1995). A test for assessing phonemic awareness in young children. *The Reading Teacher, 49*, 20–29.

Yopp, H.K, & Yopp, R.H. (1996). *Oo-pples and boo-noo-noos: Songs and activities for phonemic awareness*. Orlando, FL: Harcourt Brace.

Young, T.A., & Vardell, S. (1993). Weaving reader's theatre and nonfiction into the curriculum. *The Reading Teacher, 46*, 396–406.

Zgonc, Y. (1999). *Phonological awareness: The missing piece to help crack the reading code*. Eau Claire, WI: Otter Creek Institute.

Zgonc, Y. (2000). *Sounds in action: Phonological awareness activities and assessment*. Peterborough, NH: Crystal Springs.

Zutell, J. (1998). Word sorting: A developmental spelling approach to word study for delayed readers. *Reading and Writing Quarterly, 14*, 219–238.

Children's Literature and Music Cited

Abercrombie, B. (1990). *Charlie Anderson*. New York: M.K. McElderry.

Adams, P. (1990). *This is the house that Jack built*. New York: Child's Play.

Benjamin, A. (1987). *Rat-a-tat, pitter pat*. New York: HarperCollins.

Bennett, R. (1988). The gingerbread man. In B. Schenk de Regniers, E. Moore, M. White, & J. Carr (Eds.), *Sing a song of popcorn: Every child's book of poems* (p. 50). New York: Scholastic.

Biel, T. (2003). *Zoobooks: Tigers*. Poway, CA: Wildlife Education.

Braun, W., & Braun, C. (2000). *A Readers Theatre treasury of stories*. Winnipeg, Canada: Portage and Main.

Brinckloe, J. (1986). *Flireflies*. New York: Aladdin.

Brown, M. (1998). *Buster's dino dilemma* (Arthur Chapter Book #7). New York: Little, Brown.

Bunting, E. (1988). *How many days to America? A Thanksgiving story*. New York: Clarion.

Bunting, E. (1991). *Fly away home*. New York: Clarion.

Cannon, J. (1993). *Stellaluna*. New York: Scholastic.

Carle, E. (1983). *The very hungry caterpillar*. New York: Philomel.

Carle, E. (2002). *"Slowly, slowly, slowly," said the sloth*. New York: Penguin Putnam.

Cherry, L. (1990). *The great kapot tree: A tale of the Amazon rain forest*. San Diego, CA: Gulliver Green/Harcourt.

Cleary, B. (1981). *Ramona Quimby, age 8*. New York: Morrow.

Cowley, J. (1996). *Annabel*. Bothell, WA: Wright Group.

dePaola, T. (1973). *Andy: That's my name*. New York: Prentice Hall.

DiCamillo, K. (2000). *Because of Winn-Dixie*. Cambridge, MA: Candlewick.

Donnelly, J. (1988). *The Titanic: Lost—And found*. New York: Random House.

Dr. Seuss. (1963). *Hop on pop*. New York: Random House.

Freeman, M. (2002). *Go facts: Insects*. Littleton, MA: Newbridge/Sundance.

Guarino, D. (1991). *Is your mama a llama?* New York: Scholastic.

Hartmann, J. (1996). Humpty Dumpty. On *Rhymin' to the beat, Volume I* [CD]. St. Petersburg, FL: Planet Visions. Available: www.jackhartman.com

Hartmann, J. (2002). Rock around and rhyme. On *Shake, Rattle 'n Read* [CD]. St. Petersburg, FL: Planet Visions. Available: www.jackhartman.com

Henkes, K. (1988). *Chester's way*. New York: Greenwillow.

Henkes, K. (1991). *Chrysanthemum*. New York: Greenwillow.

Henkes, K. (1993). *Owen*. New York: Greenwillow.

Hoose, P., & Hoose, A. (1998). *Hey Little Ant*. Berkeley, CA: Tricycle.

Hutchins, P. (1986). *The doorbell rang*. New York: Greenwillow.

Keats, E.J. (1992). *Over in the meadow*. New York: Scholastic.

Kellogg, S. (1978). *Much bigger than Martin*. New York: Puffin.

Kesselman, W. (1993). *Emma*. New York: Bantam Doubleday Dell.

Konigsburg, E.L. (1997). *The view from Saturday*. New York: Scholastic.

Langstaff, J. (1989). *Oh, a-hunting we will go*. Boston: D.C. Heath.

Lasky, K. (1994). *The librarian who measured the Earth*. New York: Little, Brown.

Lionni, L. (1970). *Fish is fish*. New York: Knopf.

Lionni, L. (1976). *A color of his own*. New York: Knopf.

Martin, B., Jr (1974). *Sounds of a powwow*. New York: Holt, Rinehart, and Winston.

Martin, B., Jr, & Archambault, J. (1987). *Knots on a counting rope*. New York: Henry Holt.

Martin, B., Jr, & Archambault, J. (1988). *Barn dance*. New York: Holt.

Martin, B., Jr, & Archambault, J. (1989). *Chicka, chicka boom boom*. New York: Scholastic.

Miranda, A. (1997). *To market, to market*. Orlando, FL: Harcourt.

Most, B. (1996). *Cock-a-doodle-moo*. San Diego, CA: Harcourt Brace.

Naylor, P.R. (1992). *Shiloh*. New York: Bantam Doubleday Dell.

Noble, T. (1980). *The day Jimmy's boa ate the wash*. New York: Dial.

Numeroff, L. (2002). *If you take a mouse to school*. New York: Laura Geringer.

O'Neill, A. (1999). *Dogs*. New York: Kingfisher.

Pallotta, J. (1990). *The frog alphabet book*. Watertown, MA: Charlesbridge.

Parish, H. (1995). *Good driving, Amelia Bedelia*. New York: Greenwillow.

Penn, A. (1993). *The kissing hand*. Washington DC: Child Welfare League of America.

Plater, I. (1998). *Jolly olly*. Crystal Lakes, IL: Rigby.

Polacco, P. (1988). *The keeping quilt*. New York: Simon & Schuster.

Prelutsky, J. (1982). *The baby uggs are hatching*. New York: Greenwillow.

Prelutsky, J. (1983). *The Random House book of poetry for children*. New York: Random House.

Priddy, R. (2001). *My big book of everything*. New York: Dorling Kindersley.

Raffi. (1990). *Down by the bay*. New York: Crown.

Rovetch, L. (2001). *Ook the book*. San Francisco: Chronicle.

Rylant, C. (1985). *The relatives came*. New York: Atheneum.

Rylant, C. (1996). *Henry and Mudge*. New York: Simon & Schuster.

Schlein, M. (1990). *The year of the panda*. New York: Crowell.

Showers, P. (1991). *The listening walk*. New York: HarperCollins.

Silverstein, S. (1996). Furniture bash. In *Falling up* (p. 32). New York: HarperCollins.

Stevenson, J. (1998). *Popcorn: Poems*. New York: Greenwillow.

Taback, S. (1997). *There was an old lady who swallowed a fly*. New York: Viking.

White, E.B. (1974). *Charlotte's web*. New York: HarperTrophy.

Wood, A. (1984). *The napping house*. New York: Harcourt Brace.

Yolen, J. (1991). *Greyling*. New York: Philomel.

Young, E. (1992). *Seven blind mice*. New York: Philomel.

Zolotow, C. (1994). *The seashore book*. New York: HarperTrophy.

Index

Note: Page numbers followed by *t* and *r* indicate tables and reproducibles, respectively.

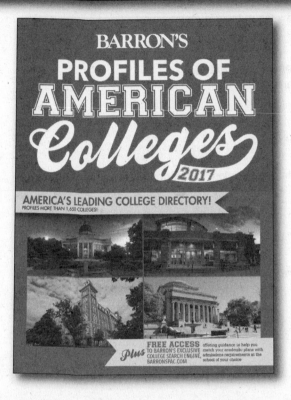
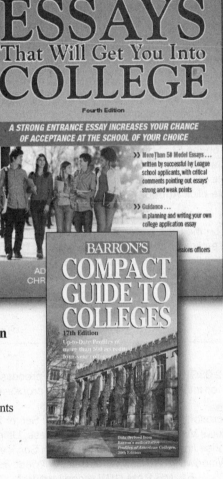

How to Use the CD-ROM

The software is not installed on your software; it runs directly from the CD ROM. Barron's CD-ROM includes an "autorun" feature that automatically launches the application when the CD is inserted into the CD-ROM drive. In the unlikely event that the autorun feature is disabled, follow the manual launching instructions below.

Windows®
1. Click on the Start button and choose "My Computer."
2. Double-click on the CD-ROM drive, which will be named **PSAT_18th_Edition**.
3. Double-click **PSAT_18th_Edition.exe** to launch the program.

MAC®
1. Double-click the CD-ROM icon.
2. Double-click the **PSAT_18th_Edition** icon to start the program.

Adobe AIR software is necessary to open the PSAT/NMSQT test application. If your computer does not have Adobe Air software already installed, follow the instructions given below.

Windows®
1. Click on the Start button and choose "My Computer."
2. Double-click on the CD-ROM drive, which is named **PSAT_18th_Edition**.
3. Double-click on the folder **Windows Adobe Air Installer**.
4. Double-click **AdobeAIRInstaller.exe** to install this software.

MAC®
1. Click on the Start button and choose "My Computer."
2. Double-click on the CD-ROM drive, which is named **PSAT_18th_Edition**.
3. Double-click on the folder **Macintosh Adobe Air Installer**.
4. Double-click **AdobeAIR.dmg** to install this software.

SYSTEM REQUIREMENTS

Microsoft® Windows®
2.33GHz or faster x86-compatible processor,
or Intel Atom™ (2.2GHz or faster processor
for netbook class devices)
Microsoft® Windows® XP, Windows® Server 2008,
Windows Vista® Home Premium, Business, Ultimate, or
Enterprise (including 64-bit editions) with Service Pack 2,
Windows 7, Windows 8 Classic, or Windows 10
512MB RAM (1GB recommended)

MAC® OS X
Intel® Core™ Duo 1.83GHz or faster processor
Mac OS X v10.6, v10.7, v10.8, or v10.9
512MB RAM (1GB recommended)